MW01137901

BY BARBARA DEMICK

Nothing to Envy

Logavina Street

Eat the Buddha

Daughters of the Bamboo Grove

Daughters of the Bamboo Grove

DAUGHTERS

of the

BAMBOO

GROVE

FROM CHINA TO AMERICA,

A TRUE STORY OF ABDUCTION, ADOPTION,

AND SEPARATED TWINS

Barbara Demick

Random House
New York

Published in the United States by Random House,
an imprint and division of Penguin Random House LLC, New York.

RANDOM HOUSE and the HOUSE colophon are registered trademarks of Penguin Random House LLC.

Some of the information in this work originates from the article "Stolen Chinese Babies Supply Adoption Demand" by Barbara Demick (*Los Angeles Times,* September 20, 2009).

Library of Congress Cataloging-in-Publication Data
Names: Demick, Barbara, author.
Title: Daughters of the bamboo grove / Barbara Demick.
Description: First edition. | New York, NY: Random House, [2025] |
Includes bibliographical references and index.
Identifiers: LCCN 2024046759 (print) | LCCN 2024046760 (ebook) |
ISBN 9780593132746 (hardcover) | ISBN 9780593132753 (ebook)
Subjects: LCSH: Intercountry adoption—China. | Intercountry adoption—United
States. | Adopted children—United States. | Twins—China—Social conditions. |
Family reunification—China.
Classification: LCC HV875.58.C6 D46 2025 (print) | LCC HV875.58.C6 (ebook) |
DDC 362.734092 [B]—dc23/eng/20241123
LC record available at https://lccn.loc.gov/2024046759
LC ebook record available at https://lccn.loc.gov/2024046760

Printed in the United States of America on acid-free paper

randomhousebooks.com

2 4 6 8 9 7 5 3 1

First Edition

BOOK TEAM: Production editor: Mark Birkey • Managing editor: Rebecca Berlant • Production manager: Richard Elman • Copy editor: Hilary Roberts • Proofreaders: Diana Drew, Judy Kiviat, Barbara Jatkola • Indexer: Stephen Callahan

Book design by Fritz Metsch

The authorized representative in the EU for product safety and compliance is Penguin Random House Ireland, Morrison Chambers, 32 Nassau Street, Dublin D02 YH68, Ireland. https://eu-contact.penguin.ie

Contents

PART FIVE

Prologue

New York

On a cold January afternoon in 2017, I was prone on the couch in my apartment and home office in New York, fighting off the urge to take a nap, when a message popped up on Facebook from a name I didn't recognize.

> Ms. Demick. You contacted me a long time ago? Are you still interested in talking with me? If so, my family and I are interested.

I wasn't in a receptive mood. I was a journalist covering New York for the *Los Angeles Times*. And like many of us, I'd been working without a day off for months, covering the aftermath of Donald Trump's election and inauguration. I was slumped on the sofa, dejected by the animus emanating from my television set. I tapped out a curt reply, telling this man, in essence, that I didn't know who he was or what he wanted from me. He wrote back immediately.

> My mom adopted a little Chinese girl years ago . . . and it appears like she has a twin sister still in China.

I bolted upright. Before New York, I'd spent seven years as a China correspondent for the *Los Angeles Times*. I was based in Beijing but often worked in the countryside, writing about life in the left-behind backwaters of modern China. Reporting on this little girl was one of my most memorable experiences. This was a story that took me to places few foreigners had seen, geographically and psychically. Not only into remote mountain villages but also deep into the intimate realm of Chinese families. Of course, I hadn't forgotten.

This is the story as it unfolded for me. It is dedicated to the 160,000 Chinese adoptees around the world, with the hope it might in some small way help them understand where they came from and how they got to where they are today.

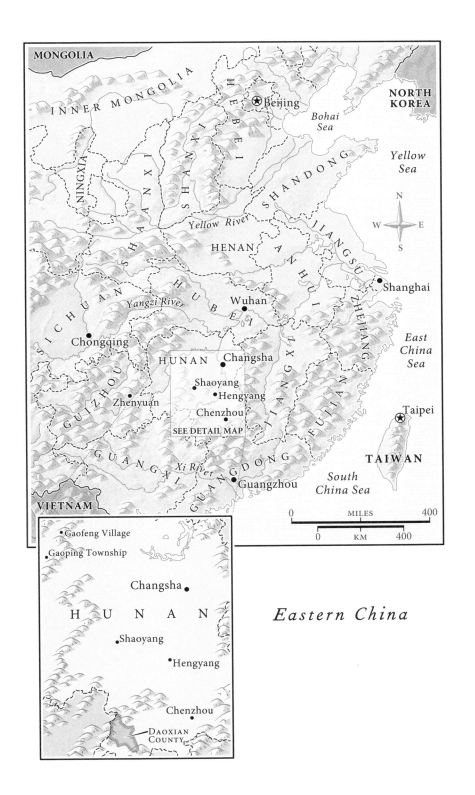

MONGOLIA

NORTH KOREA

INNER MONGOLIA

HEBEI

★ Beijing

Bohai Sea

Yellow Sea

NINGXIA

SHAANXI

SHANXI

SHANDONG

N
W   E
S

Yellow River

HENAN

ANHUI

JIANGSU

SICHUAN

Yangzi River

HUBEI

Wuhan

ZHEJIANG

Shanghai

East China Sea

Chongqing

HUNAN

Changsha

GUIZHOU

Shaoyang
Hengyang

JIANGXI

FUJIAN

Taipei

Zhenyuan

Chenzhou

SEE DETAIL MAP

★

TAIWAN

GUANGXI

Xi River

GUANGDONG

Guangzhou

South China Sea

VIETNAM

0   MILES   400

0   KM   400

• Gaofeng Village

• Gaoping Township

Changsha •

Eastern China

H U N A N

• Shaoyang

• Hengyang

• Chenzhou

DAOXIAN COUNTY

Part One

GAOFENG

VILLAGE

CHAPTER ONE

BORN IN THE BAMBOO

Yuan Zanhua.

SEPTEMBER 9, 2000. FROM ABOVE, THE LANDSCAPE WAS A PATCH-
work of florid greens and yellows climbing up and down a dizzying
staircase. Chinese farmers hacked these terraced fields out of the mountains more than two thousand years ago with the ingenuity and persistence to shape the earth to their will. A single rutted road wound around
the terraces, now flooded for growing rice, vanishing into the low-
hanging mist before emerging at the entrance of a small village.

In a house at the edge of the rice paddies, a twenty-eight-year-old
woman was trimming vegetables for lunch when she was interrupted by
a familiar sensation. It was like a belt cinching around her middle. Zanhua wasn't alarmed. Although she wasn't sure exactly how far along she
was, the ballooning size of her belly told her the baby was coming any
day now. She was eager to give birth sooner rather than later, because

the hundred-degree temperatures of an unusually hot summer left her overripe body drenched in sweat. Even as another contraction gripped her body, she smiled through the grimace. It was about noon, time for lunch, but she had other priorities. She carefully set down her kitchen utensils and covered the bowl of rice with a plate to protect it from the circling flies. The first flush of autumn had yet to settle upon the rice paddies of Hunan. She wiped her brow and washed her hands, even tidied up a bit. Then she called out to her mother in the next room that they should get ready.

Zanhua moved quickly but deliberately. She wasn't agitated. This would be her third time around. She was hardly bigger than a child herself, standing well under five feet, narrow in the hips, at least when she wasn't pregnant, but she was confident in her physical prowess. Since early childhood, she'd helped out in the family fields, which left her arms and back taut with muscle. She had a broad, flat nose and a ruddy complexion from working outside, although this summer she was paler than usual, since she'd mostly stayed indoors, not wanting to advertise her condition. She'd taken care to buy extra-large clothing to conceal her swollen body. She was anxious, not about childbirth itself—she wasn't the type to complain about pain—but about the need for secrecy.

Since 1979, China had limited most families to only one child. Under the law, you were supposed to apply for a permit even before you got pregnant. It was the signature policy of the ruling Communist Party, which had developed an almost mystical belief that population control was the secret to jump-starting the economy. The law was enforced by an agency euphemistically known as the *jisheng ban*, literally "planned birth" or "family-planning agency." It didn't actually plan or advise so much as punish. Violators could be fined more than a year's wages, their homes demolished and property confiscated. If you were visibly pregnant without a permit, you could be hog-tied and hauled away for a forced abortion. Then they'd send you a bill for the favor. No matter that the village where Zanhua grew up in Hunan Province was deep in the mountains, almost an hour's drive from the nearest government offices or a two-hour walk when mountain roads were washed out; the law was never far away. The village was full of spies and Communist Party loyalists who might rat you out.

The Communist Party ruled here with impunity. Hunan Province is in more ways than one the heartland of modern China. With a population as large as that of France, Hunan is a landlocked province smack in the middle of the country, just below the Yangtze River. The founder of modern China, Mao Zedong, was a Hunan man, born about one hundred miles away from Zanhua's village, in Shaoshan—roughly the same neighborhood, although not nearly as mountainous nor as poor. Mao was the son of what the Chinese called a "prosperous peasant." He was educated in the Hunan provincial capital of Changsha, where he read the classics and organized one of the first branches of the Socialist Youth League. In 1927, he led a few hundred peasants to become guerrilla fighters in the Jinggang Mountains, which, bordering Hunan and Jiangxi provinces, would become known as the cradle of the revolution.

Mao was inspired by the plight of Hunan's peasantry and the need for land reform. Hunan is the largest rice-producing province in China, its semitropical climate just warm enough, the rainfall generous, and the soil red and fertile. It should have been a place of abundance. But rice farming was a precarious existence. Rice farmers survived at the mercy of floods, droughts, and unscrupulous landowners, who often demanded most of the crop in rent. When he founded the People's Republic of China in 1949, Mao vowed to redistribute the land and liberate the underclasses from the tyranny of the ruling class.

Instead, it got worse. Farmers were forced into inefficient communes that were required to sell most of their grain at below-market prices for export abroad. Farm equipment and kitchen utensils were melted down in backyard furnaces to create steel. This was all part of an ill-conceived vision to turn China into an industrial powerhouse that would rival the United States and the Soviet Union. But the furnaces produced pig iron of such poor quality that it was of little use. Meanwhile, fueling the furnaces led to widespread deforestation. The diversion of the workforce away from agriculture resulted in a famine. An estimated forty-five million people died during what was known as the Great Leap Forward. It was followed by another man-made disaster—the decade-long Cultural Revolution, in which the intelligentsia or anybody perceived as elite were eradicated in the name of class justice. Neighbors were goaded into persecuting one another. The madness endured until Mao died in 1976. His successors wasted little time in rolling back the worst of his excesses.

At the time of Zanhua's birth in 1973, China already was on the cusp of reinventing itself. Although Mao's portrait remained on everybody's walls, the country had started to wriggle free of the strictures of doctrinaire communism. In Zanhua's village, farmers took it upon themselves to dismantle the communes even before the land was legally distributed to households. Although they didn't own the land outright, they earned the right to farm their plots individually. Productivity soared. Zanhua was told she should be grateful for the food of the land—the rice, sweet potatoes, and cabbages grown on her family's fields. Unlike her parents, she didn't have to survive on wild grass, roots, and bark. Her father had a job at a state-owned factory that made dishware. It was an hour's walk away and paid a tiny salary, but there were perks, like an occasional bundle of pork or a chicken. She wasn't starving, but she was still hungry.

The village, then called Shanghuang, literally "on the yellow," was poor even by the standards of one of the poorest countries in the world. It was so wild that until the 1960s tigers were still seen in the nearby mountains. The steep terrain dictated that the terraced fields be small and irregularly shaped, with little of the postcard-perfect symmetry that attracted photographers to the undulating green terraces elsewhere in China. The houses were built mostly of wood, weathered and flimsy, brick still outside the reach of many villagers. The roads were poor to nonexistent.

Zanhua occupied an unfortunate position in her family's birth order. As the fourth of six children and the third daughter, she wore her older siblings' hand-me-down clothing, so threadbare it was beyond patching. When her parents went to the township for the market, held every five days, she begged her mother to buy her clothing of her own.

"Only if you work harder" was the retort.

That was impossible because she already worked all the time. As a small child, her work began at dawn, when she tended to the oxen. She weeded the fields and washed laundry, an ordeal without running water or soap. It required multiple trips to the well, since she was too small to carry more than one bucket of water at a time. She cared for her younger siblings, hand-washing diapers made of old clothing. From the time she was seven, she prepared her own meals, since her parents and older siblings were busy with their own work.

Her village had an elementary school housed in four ramshackle wooden buildings, one for each grade. An empty lot served as the playground. The school offered basic instruction in math, Chinese, physical education, and, most important, music. The kids couldn't read well, but they were indoctrinated through song.

> *Without the Communist Party, there will be no new China.*
> *The Communist Party toiled for the nation.*
> *The Communist Party of one mind saved China.*
> *It pointed to the road of liberation for the people.*
> *It led China toward the light.*

Zanhua attended the school but rarely finished her chores quickly enough to get there by the start of the school day. She also had in tow one of her baby brothers. There was nobody else to take care of him. The teachers were sympathetic. Most people in the village were relatives, so they understood her predicament. Nonetheless, the toddler fussed so much that the school eventually asked Zanhua to leave. As a result, she dropped out after three years and barely learned to read.

Later in life, when asked what were her happiest memories from childhood, she said that she had none.

IT WAS DENG XIAOPING, a two-time survivor of Mao's repeated purges, who would give Zanhua a chance to escape. In 1978, Deng became China's paramount leader and launched what he called reform and opening—prying open the economy and repairing relations with the

West. In 1979, Deng visited the United States, once the sworn enemy. Americans were charmed to see the pint-size leader don a ten-gallon cowboy hat. Although the Chinese Communist Party continued to rule and does so to this day, long outlasting the Soviet Union and the rest of the Communist Bloc, after Deng's rise, it was not the same party. Deng embraced what he called "socialism with Chinese characteristics." (Wags called it "capitalism with Chinese characteristics.") Now the party was all about making money. To rebuild legitimacy in the eyes of the people, the Chinese needed to get rich. And it would be acceptable to "let some people get rich first." (Contrary to popular belief, Deng did not say it was glorious to get rich.)

Zanhua's family would not be among those getting rich, but they did get a little less poor. In 1985, Deng lifted controls on domestic travel. Until then, it had been a crime to live or work outside the place you were registered, leaving villagers tethered to their impoverished villages. Zanhua was turning thirteen, just old enough that she could be sent out with her older brother, a sister, and a brother-in-law. They had a simple trading business: They bought schoolbags and suitcases wholesale from a factory in Shaoyang, the nearest big city, and sold them retail on the streets. It was an opportune time to sell bags, as millions of Chinese like them were on the move, needing to transport their possessions as they left their villages. The siblings took their merchandise to sell in neighboring Jiangxi Province, which was closer to the east coast and slightly more prosperous.

Joining the lowest rung of peddlers, they didn't have a stall at one of the markets. Instead, they fanned out during the day to well-trafficked locations and spread their wares on a tarpaulin on the street. Zanhua was usually working alone, which was intimidating for a shy, still very small teenager. But she was a quick study. Despite almost no formal education in math, she was good at bargaining with customers. After being fleeced once, she figured out how to spot counterfeit bills. Even after sending money home, she had enough left over to buy her own clothing. She bought trousers for her little brothers. She didn't begrudge the better opportunities afforded the boys, and she helped support their education. She was proud to be one of the first girls from her little village to *chuqu*, literally to "go out." It was a term that defined the lifestyle of millions of Chinese similarly escaping their village to work.

Chinese migrants are expected to come home for the Lunar New Year, a holiday so baked into the calendar that businesses close down for weeks. No matter where you live or your professional status, people return to what they call the *laojia*, the "old home." So much of the country is on the move that it is the largest human migration in the world, albeit only for a few weeks.

The year Zanhua was turning twenty, she decided to buck tradition and work through the holiday. She figured she could sell off her remaining inventory, since people needed bags to transport the gifts they were buying and receiving, and those who'd received cash or bonuses would be relatively flush.

Her father, though, was insistent.

"Forget about the bags. Come home."

When she arrived, she found out why. Modernity had nibbled away at only so much of tradition. Her parents had hired a matchmaker for her. Even though girls were allowed to go out to work, even encouraged because families wanted their earnings, they weren't supposed to have a social life. It was frowned upon for them to meet somebody on their own, worse still somebody from another province. Since the custom was for daughters to live with their husband's family after marriage, parents wanted them nearby. But not in the same village. People in villages were usually related to one another and aware of the genetic risks. They needed matchmakers to find the right person.

The young man selected for Zanhua was invited to her home for an introduction. At first, she was disappointed. Zeng Youdong came from a village called Gaofeng (literally "high phoenix") at the top of a four-hundred-meter mountain of the same name. It had no shops, no little businesses, nothing but a few hundred households, often hidden in the low-hanging clouds. Her own village, Shanghuang, was barely a mile away, but it was down the hill, in the direction of the main town. Zanhua hoped to advance her situation in life by moving to a more urban area. In China, you always wanted to go down the hill, not uphill.

Youdong* was barely taller than she was. In China, height is a proxy for social status, and it was evident from his stature that he had been poorly nourished as a child. The Zengs were rice farmers, and they raised pigs, but they didn't have the perks that Zanhua's father enjoyed from the factory. Chinese use the expression "family doors of equal size," matching young people of similar economic standing. The Zeng family didn't quite live up to that standard.

Zanhua thought about saying no—this was the 1990s, after all, and a young woman had the right to reject her match. But the quiet young man felt right when he stood up next to her. He had a slim, limber physique, a narrow face, and a long sloped nose, a feature prized by many Chinese, who associate the look with the Manchurian rulers of the north. Side by side, they looked like a pair of gymnasts. Unlike her brothers, who could be loud and boastful, he was soft-spoken and gentle. He didn't show his teeth when he smiled but pressed his lips together as though enjoying a private joke. He had been educated through junior high school and was comfortably literate, much better at reading and writing than most in his social class. He didn't smoke cigarettes, which made him an outlier among Chinese men. He rarely drank. A few months after their introduction, she agreed to get married. They had a large engagement party, setting up ten tables in front of her house and serving bottles of *baijiu,* a cheap white liquor, to neighbors and family.

Zanhua and her fiancé were not so much a romance as a partnership, in life and in business. Youdong was as hardworking as Zanhua. He accompanied her to Jiangxi Province to sell bags. With a partner, business improved. They began to save money so that they could build their own house.

Engagements were more important in the village than weddings, so it was no scandal for them to live together. By the time they were formally married ten months later, Zanhua was already pregnant.

---

*In China, the family takes precedence over the individual. Accordingly, the family name comes first and the given name after it.

* * *

THEIR FIRST CHILD was born in 1995, a healthy baby girl. They named her Ping, a popular name meaning "even" or "calm." They were happy to have a daughter. Under a loophole in the family-planning laws, rural families were entitled to have a second baby if their first was a girl. Zanhua and Youdong were born before the implementation of the one-child policy—her family had six children, his had seven—and having only one child felt unnatural. As much as Zanhua resented her lowly position in the birth order, wearing hand-me-downs and caring for little brothers, she took comfort in the size of her family. She was close to all her siblings and was relieved that her daughter wouldn't be an only child.

Under the law, Zanhua and her husband were supposed to wait for five years before the second birth. But they were impatient. When Zanhua got pregnant again the following year, family members advised her to get an abortion. Abortions were a common and inexpensive method of birth control in China, but Zanhua resisted. Their second daughter was born in 1997. They named her Yan, which means "splendid." She was an adorable baby and they were immediately smitten. But for the first time in their lives, they understood they had done something illegal.

The fines for having a second baby without the required waiting period amounted to the equivalent of several hundred dollars, which they didn't have. All their cash had been poured into a house they were building. They would have to leave the village to raise the money for the fines, since there were no jobs nearby. They left their two small daughters in the care of grandparents and skipped town, figuring they'd earn enough to pay up.

When the young couple came home to the village, they had an unpleasant surprise. The officials from the family-planning agency were furious that they'd fled town. As punishment, they'd punched a hole in the tile roof of their still-under-construction house and walked off with a table and chairs, the only furniture in the place. Vandalizing houses, confiscating livestock, repossessing appliances and furniture, and administering beatings were usual tactics to coerce people to pay their fines. The law didn't prescribe this kind of penalty, but it was common nonetheless. Zanhua and her husband were outraged.

"Monsters," "Common thieves."

They ranted. They swore. But there was little they could do to avoid paying entirely. They talked to the officials and negotiated the fine down to eight hundred yuan, about one hundred dollars, and paid up.

They had just enough to repair the damage and keep building. And to think about having another baby.

Youdong's father urged them to try again. He wanted a boy. Despite all the changes sweeping China, women still occupied a tenuous place in the social hierarchy. They left their village when they married, moved to their husband's home, and were expected to serve their in-laws. And yet they did not become full-fledged members of their husband's family. They retained their father's surname for life. Zanhua would never be known as a Zeng—she would always be Yuan, the name with which she was born, although her children would carry the family name Zeng. She could be buried next to her husband in the Zengs' family cemetery only if she gave birth to a boy. And only a boy, grown into a man, would be able to conduct the ritual displays of filial piety at the cemetery, burning incense, bowing to the ancestors. Women might care for the elderly, cook, and clean, unpaid servants to their in-laws, but in the afterlife, it was men who were supposed to propitiate the ancestors.

Zanhua and her husband fancied themselves modern Chinese, free of what the Communist Party dismissed as feudal superstition. In this progressive new era, girls were supposed to be as valuable as boys.

But Youdong's father persisted, making it clear that Zanhua was a disappointment as a daughter-in-law.

"You have to have a boy."

"It doesn't matter anymore. Males and females are equal," Zanhua retorted. She echoed the Communist Party's slogans about ending gender discrimination. The one-child policy was accompanied by a propaganda campaign touting the value of girls. Perhaps it was less about genuine concern for gender equality than about keeping down the birth rate.

"But when you get old. Who will take care of you in your old age?" he shot back.

"My daughters will take care of me."

"But for the cemetery. You need to have a boy at least for the cemetery."

Zanhua took this criticism to heart. She didn't agree with her father-in-law, but she also understood that her status in the family, indeed in the village as a whole, suffered by her failure to produce a son. Families without sons were often bullied, believed to have no future beyond the current generation. It wasn't uncommon for women to commit suicide if they didn't bear a son. Zanhua had accomplished too little to be proud of in her life. She wanted to be a good wife and a good mother. Even if her husband didn't seem to care, she felt she needed to produce a son for her own self-esteem.

Within two years of the birth of her second daughter, she was pregnant again.

This time, she felt confident. She had gone for an ultrasound in her fourth month. Although the hospital was not supposed to inform her of the gender, the technician winked at her in a way that made her think that the baby was a boy. And this pregnancy felt different from the others. She was more tired, her complexion sallow and splotchy. Her belly was so much bigger. It protruded like an overinflated basketball. Zanhua and her husband rejected the folk wisdom of the elders—to eat sour food for a male offspring. Unlike other villagers, they didn't pray to Guanyin, the Buddhist deity of compassion. But Zanhua felt the odds were in their favor. It was 2000, the start of the millennium in the Western calendar and the Year of the Dragon in the twelve-year Chinese zodiac. People born under the sign of the dragon are supposed to be strong and independent, the boys in particular destined for success and wealth. Chinese communities often experience a bumper crop of births during dragon years. Although Zanhua and her husband abhorred superstition, they couldn't help thinking it was an auspicious time.

That's why they were taking no chances. To avoid the eyes of the law, they decided Zanhua would spend the final months of her pregnancy with her oldest brother in her own village. Local tradition had it that it would be bad fortune for a woman to give birth in her mother's home, but another relative's house would be fine, especially if it was a place where local authorities didn't expect to find you.

Her brother's place was a two-story house of red brick with double doors that swung open to the road like a storefront. During the summer months, those doors were often left open to let in the air, and it was common in the village for people to pop in unannounced, especially since few had telephones.

More secure, there was a hideaway behind the house where the land sloped downward into a thicket of bamboo and a swampy pond. The bamboo was used for every conceivable purpose—for carrying poles, baskets, furniture—but it also provided the necessary privacy.

Next to the bamboo, Zanhua's father had planted two hundred young pomelo saplings, which had matured into nearly full-grown trees. Citrus grows well in Hunan's warm, moist climate, and the fat pomelos were sold at the market, an extra source of cash for the family.

Nearby, the family had built a small shed out of bamboo and leftover roof tiles so that somebody could keep watch over the ripening fruit. Even in a small village where everybody knew one another, thieves sometimes plucked fruit from the orchards. The shed was the perfect retreat, cradled deep in the bamboo grove, secret and safe.

There was no running water or electricity, but it was big enough for a small bed, a table, and a chair. Zanhua spent much of the summer resting there during the day to avoid nosy visitors. She also figured it would be a discreet place for her to give birth. In preparation, the family outfitted the shed with quilts and towels and a basin. They were ready.

Zanhua's mother came to the house as Zanhua was tidying up. She fussed about her daughter.

"You should eat a little something first. Keep up your strength," Zanhua's mother advised. She pointed to a freshly cut watermelon.

Zanhua felt another contraction. Her previous childbirths had been slow, but this baby felt like it was in a hurry to get out.

She waved aside her mother's suggestion.

"No time. This one's going to be quick."

The women headed down the path to the bamboo grove, Zanhua clutching her oversize belly with both hands so she wouldn't stumble on the slope. A relative ran to summon Li Guihua, a midwife who lived a few doors down. Her house was three stories high with Juliet balconies out front, befitting one of the wealthiest people in the village. She had studied at a nursing school, so she was also the best educated.

Heavy in the hips and already in her later years, she moved slowly, so by the time she navigated the uneven path to the shed in the bamboo grove, Zanhua's water had broken.

The contractions were coming quickly now. Zanhua arranged herself on the small bed and clenched her mouth to avoid any moans or screams that could alert somebody lurking nearby. She felt like an old pro at childbirth, a contraction, a grimace, a push. This seemed like an uncomplicated birth, easier than the previous two. A few more pushes and the baby's head was crowning. The midwife barely needed to pull.

The midwife was quiet, uncharacteristically so. She was a talkative woman who usually kept up a cheerful patter to distract her patients from the pains of labor. From her silence, Zanhua understood. Zanhua turned her head to the side rather than look the midwife directly in the eye. They didn't need to voice their disappointment.

But the girl seemed healthy enough. Perhaps not as big as Zanhua had expected given the size of her belly—maybe about five pounds.

Her color was good and she let out a reassuring wail to announce her presence to the world. Zanhua tried to roll onto her side to get up off of the bed to take a better look at her newest daughter, but something seemed off. Her cramps hadn't subsided. She felt her innards were alive with something wriggling inside her. She tried to arrange herself more comfortably on the small cot as the midwife peered between her legs at a protruding foot.

"Wait. There's another one," yelled the midwife.

CHAPTER TWO

COMEUPPANCE

Zeng Youdong.

YOUDONG JUST LAUGHED. HE COULDN'T STOP HIMSELF. HE KNEW
he was supposed to be cursing and stomping his feet in frustration that
he still didn't have a son, but he couldn't help himself.

Under Confucian ideals, a man's chief duty in life was to sire a son.
He'd been harangued for years about perpetuating the family line and
paying homage to the ancestors. But Youdong was a practical man who
concerned himself more with the here and now.

Even as he worked the rice paddies, Youdong knew little about the
ancestors who had transformed the mountains into terraced fields. His
uncle kept a genealogy book known as a *jiapu*, but he had never bothered to study it. He knew that the Zengs had lived in Gaofeng village for
about two centuries, maybe even three, and that they'd come from another county, the name of which nobody seemed quite sure of. The

Zeng name belonged to about one hundred of eight hundred residents of the village, enough that the family had its own cemetery. It was tucked into the mountains and badly overgrown. Youdong visited at most once a year during the Qingming festival, also known as the "tomb sweeping" holiday. He and his relatives would clear away the underbrush and conduct a small ceremony. They knelt in tribute and left offerings of food and burnt joss paper, scented like incense. Some other families would buy elaborate offerings—cars, houses, boats, made out of this scented paper—to be burned for the ancestors to enjoy in the afterlife. But the Zengs kept things simple. They'd leave an offering of rice, fruit, and a chicken. Youdong was dutiful enough to go through the motions, but nothing more.

The superstitions of the patriarchy simply didn't hold much appeal.

The truth, which Youdong was loath to voice aloud, was that he preferred girls to boys. He didn't hang out with the other men. He'd never enjoyed the alcohol-fueled swagger and clouds of cigarette smoke that hung over gatherings of men. He resented the expectations of Chinese manhood. His daughters had given him more joy than anything else in his challenging three decades of life. He'd been delighted to see that his oldest girl, Ping, now five, resembled him, with the same long face and high-bridged nose, which looked more fitting on a girl than on a man. She was on her way to being the village beauty.

When his wife gave birth to a second daughter, Yan, he was admittedly a little disappointed. But only until the girl started to show her personality. As a toddler, Yan was the spitting image of her mother: a little turned-up nose, a mischievous personality—*taoqi*, or "naughty," as the Chinese liked to say, though usually with affection. She was a spirited child. No matter what else happened on a given day, no matter how bad a mood he might have, Yan could always make him smile.

Now two more girls! He was in Jiangxi Province selling bags when his brother-in-law, one of the first people he knew to own a cellphone, got a call informing him that Zanhua had given birth to the twins. He came rushing back in excitement. He couldn't believe his luck. Twins! Where did they come from? He wondered what twist of fate had given him four daughters. Nobody else in his family had twins. It was a novelty in the village, something special to distinguish the Zeng family. He knew that the birth of the twins might be regarded as tragedy by his father, but Youdong could only view it as comedy.

Perhaps Youdong was secretly pleased at his father's distress. This would be his father's comeuppance. His entire life, Youdong had been a most obedient son, acceding to the wishes of his father and sacrificing his own ambitions for the good of the family. This felt like a quiet act of subversion. He was the second-youngest of seven children and the third son. He worked from a young age in the fields and at home. Even with minimal time to study, he had managed to get excellent grades in school, better than his older brothers. He was academic enough to finish middle school—that in itself an achievement for a village boy—and would have earned a place in a high school that prepared him for a university education. But his second brother was already in college and the family couldn't afford to educate another son.

Youdong dropped out of school and started hiring himself out for construction jobs. These were the boom years. China experts like to recite the statistics: China was building the square-foot equivalent of Rome every two weeks. For all the cement that the United States used in the entire twentieth century, China went through that much every three years.

It was easy for him to find work. Youdong's skills were highly valued in the construction industry. He was light, fast, and sure-footed. He could scramble quickly up and down the scaffolding. With his abstemious habits, eschewing alcohol and cigarettes, he was energetic enough to do a second shift after sunset while other workers would slink off to drink beer. He sent his wages home to support the brother in college.

Marriage hardly relieved Youdong's obligations to his family. His oldest brother died young from liver cancer. The next-eldest brother, with his college degree, remained in Changsha in a management job, rarely able to return to the village. The sisters had, according to tradition, married out of the village and were living with their in-laws. That left Youdong to shoulder the responsibilities of an eldest son, caring for the aging parents and maintaining the rice terraces. But at least his two older brothers had sons, so Youdong didn't feel the urgency. He was proud to have four daughters, secretly pleased that he'd thumbed his nose at tradition.

That's why he laughed so hard.

THE NEWBORN TWINS had moon-shaped faces, plump cheeks, and button noses like their mother. He wasn't aware of the distinction between identical twins—born from a single fertilized egg that divides in the womb—and fraternal twins, who are no more genetically alike than ordinary siblings. These twins looked almost the same, but not exactly. The family didn't own a scale, but they could tell the firstborn was a little bigger and stronger.

As is common with twins, the second was a breech birth. She was a little sallow in complexion and fussier. But in the weeks after their birth, thriving on breast milk, the twins put on weight and grew more alike. When in doubt as to who was who, they would examine the babies' ears. The firstborn had a little extra tag on her left earlobe, not a birth defect exactly, just a little bump that served almost like a label that would distinguish her from her twin.

Chinese men usually left the raising of babies to mothers and grandmothers, but not Zeng. In another time and culture, he might have chosen to be a stay-at-home dad. He was a good cook, better than his wife, his daughters would later boast. Zanhua would breastfeed during the day and then prepare bottles with a combination of rice milk they made at home and baby formula, something of a luxury item bought in the township. Zeng held the babies close to his chest when he fed them. They didn't have a crib, but he bought a big family-size bed so that the babies could sleep with their parents. When he was snuggled up with the babies on either side, he was the happiest he'd ever been. But he knew it couldn't last. The one-child policy overshadowed everything.

At least in theory, Zeng respected the law. He couldn't help but absorb the endless propaganda extolling the one-child policy. Chinese people had been easily convinced by the 1980s that their country's problems were due to overpopulation: Whenever they squeezed onto a crowded bus or tried to book an oversold train or get their children into a school, they would nod their heads in agreement. Too many people.

"The economy rises as the population falls" was painted on brick walls and hung on banners over intersections.

"Fewer births, better births, to develop China vigorously."

Everywhere you could find cheerful posters showing pink-cheeked babies and stylishly dressed mothers.

There is a popular view among political scientists both inside and outside the country that the Chinese people acquiesce to restrictions on their freedom in an implicit bargain in exchange for prosperity. It was true that the Communist Party had lifted millions out of poverty. Even in a backwater like Gaofeng village, people had seen living standards rise exponentially over the course of their lifetime, making them loath to complain. "I can't blame the officials for carrying out the law. It was our fault. I have to blame myself for violating the law," Zeng would later say.

But respecting the law didn't mean complying with the law. It was hard to follow rules that were subject to the whims of their mercurial leaders. "The Communist Party is as changeable as the weather," people liked to say. Ideas went quickly in and out of fashion. So did people. Heroes of the revolution, celebrated in the 1950s, would be purged in the 1960s, rehabilitated in the 1970s. China's laws were fleeting, but a child could bring the family a lifetime of happiness. In fact, the one-child policy would be lifted in 2015, after a decade of gradual erosion.

Perhaps the villagers, despite their lack of formal education, were more prescient than their leaders. They sensed all along that this one-child policy couldn't last. It simply was not in the Chinese tradition.

FOR THOUSANDS OF YEARS, Chinese rulers had encouraged their people to procreate. Power and population size were seen as inextricably intertwined during the time of the emperors. Bigger was simply better.

"A state of vast territory, abundant output, big population, and strong military forces had the conditions to attain supremacy" is how Guan Zhong, an ancient Chinese philosopher (720–645 B.C.E.), boasted of his nation. Besides, until the midtwentieth century, as many as one out of five children died before they reached their first birthday. Multiple births were required to sustain the population.

Even after the founding of the People's Republic of China in 1949, the government pushed for more children. As in the Soviet Union, women who gave birth to large broods were celebrated as "heroic mothers." The ever-quotable Mao frequently extolled the wonder of China's large population. "As long as we have people, any human miracle can be created," he said. On another occasion, he denigrated suggestions that the country rein in births. "It is a very good thing that China has a big population. Even if China's population multiplies many times, she is fully capable of finding a solution; the solution is production." In 1953, China briefly banned the import of contraceptives.

After the mass starvation of the Great Leap Forward, the Communist Party had a hard rethink. But they couldn't quite admit the obvious—that it was the failed policy of their hallowed leader that had led to famine. The party's elders couldn't simply toss out the founding father, who imparted legitimacy to the party's continued rule. Deng Xiaoping would go only as far as to assess Mao as 70 percent right and 30 percent wrong. It was more convenient for the party to blame the Chinese people for having too many babies. There were simply too many mouths to feed. Mao's successors viewed China's ballooning population not as a miracle but as a demographic nightmare.

The Chinese were not alone in fixating on population control. In the late 1960s, there was a revival of interest in the works of British economist Thomas Robert Malthus, whose 1798 "Essay on the Principle of Population" posited that humanity was trapped in a perpetual cycle of poverty because the population always outpaced the food supply. The United Nations launched the Fund for Population Activities (later the UN Population Fund) in 1969 with the goal of curbing population growth in developing countries—as it happens, countries populated by people of color. These ideas have been discredited in recent decades, with scholars instead embracing Indian economist Amartya Sen's assertion that famines result from political dysfunction and rarely occur in democratic countries with a free press. But in the 1960s, it was taken as a matter of faith that overpopulation and starvation went hand in hand. ("It was an idea du jour . . . , like bell-bottoms and est therapy," wrote Mei Fong in her book *One Child: The Story of China's Most Radical Experiment.*)

Conservationists and ecologists joined in a chorus of doom. "Population control or race to oblivion," screamed the cover of *The Population Bomb,* by Stanford professor Paul Ehrlich and Anne Howland Ehrlich. Published in 1968, this bestselling manifesto predicted that hundreds of millions of people would die of starvation and contemplated extreme solutions like spiking the water supplies with contraceptives. The Ehrlichs' Chinese counterpart was a rocket scientist named Song Jian who, in an erudite tome, *Population System Control,* published in 1988, explored the unlikelihood of colonizing other planets for China's burgeoning population. "Even with an unlimited future, man has only a very limited space to live in," wrote Song and co-author Yu Jingyuan. Song would eventually devise the mathematical formulas used by the Chinese government to design the one-child policy.

Elsewhere in the world, population-control policies could be political suicide. A 1976 campaign in India resulting in the sterilization of millions of men was so unpopular that Indira Gandhi and her Congress Party were booted out of office the following year in a landslide. China had an easier time implementing its policy. Without elections or political accountability, China was the perfect laboratory for an epic experiment in manipulating human population growth. The Han Chinese (the majority ethnicity in China) did not have strong religious prohibitions against contraception or abortion, and the country's authoritarian infrastructure made it possible to enforce a policy that would have been unthinkable elsewhere.

Still, China started with a campaign of gentle persuasion. "Later, longer, fewer" was one of the slogans rolled out in the 1970s. The government wanted people to get married later and space their children further apart to achieve population limits. It promoted equal regard for girls and boys and encouraged families to invest more in the upbringing of each child. Quality rather than quantity. During the 1970s, the average number of children born to each woman dropped from six to three, in part because more women were working outside the home.

But for the leadership, propaganda wouldn't be enough. Deng Xiaoping was a man in a hurry to establish his legitimacy. A technocrat by disposition, Deng laced his speeches with statistics, and what the numbers revealed about China was mortifying. China was one of the poorest countries in the world, poorer than much of Africa: Its per-capita income in the 1970s and 1980s lagged behind that of North Korea. Most embarrassing, China's 1979 per-capita annual income of $164 was dwarfed by the $1,957 in archrival Taiwan—not to speak of the $11,674 annual income in the United States. Deng promised he would boost income to $1,000 by the new millennium, which would require not only robust economic growth but also a mathematical sleight of hand. Reducing the number of people—the capita of the equation—looked to be easier than boosting output.

"Economic development is like a cake. . . . We need to slow down the growth of the number of people eating the cake" is how Li Bin, the head of the State Family Planning Commission, would later explain it.

IN 1979, as China's population was about to cross the one-billion threshold, the law was passed limiting most Chinese couples to one child. It took effect the following year and quickly became the defining policy of the Chinese Communist Party. "China is a populous country. Family planning is a fundamental state policy. The State shall adopt a comprehensive approach to controlling population size and improving socio-economical and public health characteristics of the population," read the introduction to the new law.

The State Family Planning Commission was set up in 1981 with ministry-level powers, an elevated status within the government hierarchy. Family-planning offices were installed in every province, township, and even village. The following year, birth limits were enshrined in a revision of the Chinese constitution.

The era of gentle persuasion was over. Family Planning morphed into a monstrous organization that dwarfed the police and military in manpower. It swallowed most other aspects of the Chinese bureaucracy. By the 1990s, it was estimated that eighty-three million Chinese worked at least part-time for Family Planning. (At the same time, China's combined armed forces were estimated to have roughly three million personnel.) Family Planning recruited retired military as enforcers, physically fit men trained to keep order. Everybody had to play a part: Communist Party secretaries in workplaces and universities, village chiefs, heads of neighborhood committees, doctors and midwives. If more muscle was needed, for a violator to be roughed up or a property seized, they could always hire common thugs.

Family Planning was intrusive in the extreme. Female factory workers had to report when they had their menstrual periods. Inspectors would sometimes ask to see their blood-stained sanitary napkins. ("The period police" is what writer Lijia Zhang called them in her memoir *"Socialism Is Great!,"* about working in a rocket factory.) After giving birth to their first child, women were required to have an IUD inserted— a specially modified IUD that couldn't be easily removed without a medical professional. Regular ultrasounds and X-rays were scheduled to make sure the IUD remained in place. In some workplaces, women had to regularly submit urine samples to prove that they weren't pregnant.

People who violated the law were subject to fines of two to six times their annual earnings, with the amounts ballooning for each child beyond their quota. The fines were euphemistically known as "social maintenance fees" based on the reasoning that "those who bear excess births in violation of law add more burden to society and they ought to make appropriate compensations." If the violators were civil servants or worked for a state-owned company (much of the working population in a still largely communist country), they could lose their job and often the housing that was assigned to go with it. An extra baby could spell ruin for middle- and working-class families.

In the countryside, poor people had less to lose—no jobs, no state housing. Since persuasion didn't work so well with these people, the policy was implemented with brute force. What happened to the Zengs when their roof was smashed after the birth of their second daughter was a slap on the wrist, relatively speaking. At least one man from a nearby village was beaten to death in a confrontation with the Family Planning office in Gaoping, the township that administered the Zengs' village.

More often, houses were entirely demolished or set on fire. Pigs, oxen, and chickens were confiscated. A tractor that might represent the life savings of the family could be taken away.

"If you violate the policy, your family will be destroyed," read a sign painted onto a brick wall in Shaoyang, not far from the Zengs' village. It was a threat villagers knew to take seriously.

People living on impassable roads in remote villages might have expected to be left alone ("The mountains are high and the emperor is far away" is a deservedly popular Chinese proverb). But on the contrary, the government was most merciless in enforcing the law in the countryside. The long arm of the Chinese Communist Party reached into every mountaintop village. Family Planning officers from the township liked to show up unannounced. If the roads were washed away, they would hike into the village. They looked for baby clothing hanging out to dry. They would cock their ears listening for the cry of a new baby.

They also kept their eyes out for women with protruding bellies and forced pregnant women to undergo abortions. The methods were crude, often barbaric. Doctors would sometimes induce labor and then kill the baby with an injection of formaldehyde into the cranium before the feet emerged. "If you kill the baby while it's still partly in the womb, it's considered an abortion. If you do it after birth, it's murder," a doctor from Inner Mongolia was quoted telling a journalist. One critic of the one-child policy, John Aird, described the forced abortions as "the most

Draconian campaign against babies since King Herod's slaughter of the innocents."

Just as dreaded were the periodic mobilizations to force people to get sterilized. During these campaigns, Family Planning officers had quotas to meet and rounded up women by the hundreds. They sometimes targeted men, although less frequently. During one campaign around 2001 in Longhui County, which included the Zengs' village, officials forced a recently married and still-childless man to have a vasectomy. Five years later the operation was reversed, but the man remained sterile.

How did people become so cruel? This is something that the Chinese will be reckoning with for decades to come. It had to do with a system of collective punishment that made the entire population culpable for excess births. Family Planning administrators set a quota for how many births were allowed in a county or township in a given year. All civil servants in a jurisdiction, not just those involved with family planning, could be penalized. The regulations in Longhui County laid out the parameters: If a village was designated "a quality family planning village," employees were entitled to a 20 percent pay increase at year-end. Conversely, "if there is one over quota birth . . . , all unit leaders, team leaders, and staff based in the village" would not be eligible for promotion.

Ordinary residents could be punished as well. If too many births took place in a given area, the family-planning regulations called for a sterilization campaign in which all women who had given birth were forced to undergo tubal ligations. The men could also be required to undergo vasectomies. The collective punishments gave everybody an incentive to squeal on their pregnant neighbors.

"One person gives birth, the whole village must ligate," read one slogan seen on brick walls in the countryside.

"Better blood flowing like streams than children born outside the state plan."

"It's better to add ten tombs than one child."

"After the first child: insert an IUD; after the second: sterilize; after the third: kill, kill kill!" read a slogan seen by a Chinese writer in southern Guangxi Province.

This wasn't the first time that the Chinese Communist Party used incendiary rhetoric to lead otherwise sensible people into madness. Three decades earlier, during the Cultural Revolution, the placid rice-farming countryside descended into unfathomable violence. People were exhorted to exterminate "class enemies," a designation that could mean anybody marginally less poor than the others or better educated. One of the most infamous massacres took place nearby in 1967 in Hunan's Daoxian County, where nine thousand people and their children were barbarically tortured and murdered. So many bodies were dumped into the nearby Xiang River that they clogged the dams and turned the waters red with blood. The well-documented killings later spread to Shaoyang.

All of this happened less than a day's drive from Gaofeng village, where the Zeng family lived. If their village had been swept up in the violence, they either didn't know or didn't tell. In any case, Youdong and his wife were young enough, their families sufficiently impoverished and inconsequential, that most likely they were spared the worst of the Cultural Revolution, which ended in 1976. For this generation, for this class of rural, powerless Chinese, the one-child policy was the terror.

Of all the tentacles of the Chinese Communist Party, this was the one that most impacted the lives of the people in Gaofeng village. Nothing else impinged so intimately on personal freedom. They weren't concerned about censorship. They didn't have a television or radio. They didn't read newspapers. They weren't looking for freedom to travel abroad, which they couldn't have afforded anyway. They had too little money to worry about taxes. They were not among the Chinese who were clamoring for democracy in 1989, the year that demonstrations at Tiananmen Square led to a brutal crackdown. They wanted the government to stay away and let them live their lives without interference. Family planning was the intrusion that they most loathed.

This was the new face of repression in rural China.

THE NEAREST FAMILY PLANNING office to the Zengs was in the township of Gaoping, around the corner from the main market and down a semipaved, often-muddy side street. It was housed within a four-story concrete office building with urine-yellow tiles on the façade and barred windows on the ground floor. In the entranceway was a large billboard with drawings of mothers and babies, with big red letters across the top reading "Your happiness is our pursuit."

In smaller print below was a menu of the penalties imposed for various violations. An unauthorized extra birth would cost two to six times the previous year's income, the fine to be tripled for each out-of-plan birth. Anybody pregnant without a marriage certificate would have to terminate the pregnancy at a fee of 2,000 yuan, about $240.

Villagers dreaded the building itself, not merely a symbol of oppression but a place like a prison where you might not emerge unscathed. If there was occasion to go, it meant trouble. They needed to control their tempers. If they raised their voices or lost their cool in any way, they were likely to come out with a black eye or a broken bone. They swapped stories about who had gotten beaten up when they went in to complain. The Family Planning office had a room on the second floor used as a makeshift jail. An eighty-year-old grandfather who went to complain about a fine was held for two days and emerged with a concussion and a burst eardrum. One pregnant woman who had strenuously resisted a forced abortion was held there for days with limited food and water until she miscarried.

Behind this repressive apparatus lay a financial incentive. From the 1980s onward, Chinese authorities collected upward of $314 billion in penalty fees, according to calculations by He Yafu, a Chinese demographer and critic of the one-child policy. Many rural jurisdictions were almost entirely dependent on those fines for their budgets. (It was not unlike the small American towns that set up speed traps to raise revenues from traffic fines; the little Chinese communities had no other way to fund their operations.) A nationwide overhaul of the tax system in 1994 had redirected revenues to Beijing—which would more than double its share of taxes from 22 to 56 percent. Local governments were left scrambling for alternative sources of revenue, some of them rather dodgy—selling junk bonds and confiscating land for fly-by-night real estate developments. Rural jurisdictions with no land worth developing instead extorted money from the poorest people—the farmers.

Their budgets were so reliant on these fines that the higher-ups didn't question Family Planning officers too closely about what methods they used to obtain the money. Don't ask, don't tell. Just collect the money.

THE TERM "ONE-CHILD POLICY" is shorthand for a system that was much more complicated. It wasn't only about excess births. Some people couldn't have even one. A raft of regulations detailed who could give birth and under what circumstances. To limit births, the government had also raised the legal age of marriage in 1980: If the wife was under twenty and the husband under twenty-two, the marriage couldn't be registered and any child born would be illegal.

You were supposed to have a birth certificate *before* getting pregnant, and you couldn't do that until you had a marriage certificate issued by the Ministry of Civil Affairs. If you were rushing to tie the knot because you were already pregnant—as it so often happens everywhere in the world—you still wouldn't get permission to give birth. Forget about single mothers or gay couples. In rural China, couples often celebrated their weddings but didn't get around to filling out all the forms to legally register their marriages, for which they needed to provide their original birth certificate and the *hukou,* a document required for all Chinese showing where they were registered to live. If the husband and wife weren't from the same province, as was increasingly the case in an age of migration, meeting each other at their factories or workplaces, they would have to travel back and forth to their respective hometowns collecting the documents.

In 1984, the government amended the law to give each province more power to adapt the law to circumstances. There were exceptions for ethnic minorities, disabled soldiers, and only children of only children.

For example, in Hunan Province, the law stated that people could have a second child if both parents were farmers and they met the following criteria:

1. Husband or wife is from a family of two generations of only children.
2. Husband or wife is the only child of a martyr for the nation or disabled soldier of the second rank, second class or above.
3. Husband from another county marries an only daughter of a family, registered in this county and gives birth to one child only.
4. Husband and his brother or two or more brothers are farmers with only one who is potent, and has only one child and other brothers have no adopted child.

The rules were so intricate and confusing that one might need to consult a lawyer before conceiving a child.

It was bewildering to people who wanted to believe they were living in a golden age of liberalism. They were able to travel, eat their own crops, open shops, and choose their occupations, but now the government was prying into their sex lives, practically peering into their bedrooms.

Enforcement varied from place to place, waxed and waned over the years. In Longhui County, officials sympathetic to rural families warned pregnant women to hide when an outside inspection team was coming. An envelope of cash or an occasional gift helped. But overlooking pregnancies was risky for officials. They could receive what they called a "yellow card," a term borrowed from soccer, a warning that they were in violation of the law. That happened in 2004 in Gaoping, after which officials swung to the other extreme, becoming merciless in implementing the law.

One of Zanhua's most vivid memories was of a neighbor who was forced to have an abortion. It happened in the mid-1980s when Zanhua was about thirteen years old. The woman, who was far enough along to be visibly pregnant, was living alone with her two young daughters. Her husband was a migrant worker. A group of men and women from Family Planning came and carried her out of her house and down the street. It was the middle of winter, and a freezing rain drenched the woman as she was dragged through the muddy road. Zanhua could recall the scene with almost photographic memory. The woman's chin-length hair plastered to her face in the rain. The way she kicked with all the force she could muster. The young daughter shrieking as her mother was captured like an animal.

Hearing the commotion, everybody in the village came out in the rain, watching in horror.

"You're not human." "How could you?" people yelled at the Family Planning staff.

What Zanhua would remember most clearly was that, despite all the fist-waving and screaming, nobody budged to help the stricken woman. They cursed, but they didn't move.

"Nobody dared to stop them," Zanhua would say later.

The message was clear, even to a child: You couldn't fight Family Planning.

Chapter Three

SUBTERFUGE

Aunt Xiuhua with her grandchildren; Zanhua on left.

THE ZENGS WERE TERRIFIED. THEY HAD WITNESSED ENOUGH brutality in their lives to know that some awful punishment awaited them.

Houses demolished. Crippling fines. The penalty for excess births increased exponentially with multiple violations. They had been flagged already for failing to comply. After working on their house and repairing the roof, they had no spare cash lying around. What was left of the house could be completely demolished. Zanhua could be arrested and forced to undergo tubal ligation, a painful sterilization procedure that could also be dangerous, given the less-than-hygienic conditions at local clinics. And it would mean giving up on their quest for a son.

But unlike some other families in the same predicament, they never contemplated abandoning the twins.

They could try to hide the babies, keeping them inside so they wouldn't be ogled by curious neighbors who might be tempted to tip off authorities. Twins were a rarity in a village always in need of fresh fodder for gossip. People would talk. Soon enough, the girls would start to toddle out the door and into the street. Eventually, they would need to go to school, and for that they'd need a *hukou*. *Hukou*s were the obsession of most rural Chinese. An urban *hukou*—especially for a big city—would let you live in a place with better education and employment opportunities. But even a *hukou* in the most miserable village was better than no *hukou* at all. Without a *hukou*, you couldn't get an ID card, receive medical insurance, work in an official job, open a bank account, or even buy a railroad ticket. There were millions of these "black children" whose parents hadn't dared to register their births. (It was not until December 2015, after the one-child policy was lifted, that the Chinese government announced that it would belatedly grant *hukou*s to thirteen million people, most of whom had been born in violation of the one-child policy.)

Youdong and Zanhua discussed it between themselves and agreed it would be unfair to inflict this kind of nonpersonhood on their babies.

Money was the only solution. They would both need to work, while finding somebody to take care of their four daughters, all under the age of six.

Like other exhausted grandparents, Zanhua's mother already did more than her share. By the time the twins were born, most of the able-bodied adults had migrated to the cities, needing cash to build their homes, support their children's education, and, of course, pay their fines. UNICEF estimated that one-quarter of China's children—some sixty-one million—had been left behind in their villages. Zanhua's mother, who had worked multiple jobs while raising her own six children, was prematurely aged by her late fifties, her back arched toward the ground. Zanhua worried she couldn't handle twins.

The harried parents went round and round, hashing through their options. They floated various ideas and shot them down. Each option seemed worse than the last, but finally, they hit upon the least undesirable. They would leave the babies with Zanhua's oldest brother, Guoxiong.

In his late thirties, Guoxiong was the consummate big brother. He'd always been Zanhua's mentor in the family. He'd taught her how to bargain and how to spot counterfeit bills. It was his house near the bamboo grove where she'd taken refuge while she was pregnant. Guoxiong (his name meant "manly") was a stocky man with a boxy haircut that matched his physique. He kept a cigarette tucked behind his ear, at the ready. His wife, Xiuhua, was a lanky, angular woman, half a head taller than her husband. Both husband and wife could fill a room with their booming voices. In disposition, they were nothing at all like Zanhua and her introverted husband. But the couples got along so well that boundaries between the households dissolved. Even after cellphones came along, they didn't bother to call. They'd just drop in. Guoxiong and his wife had taken over the pomelo orchard and had also started raising chickens, ducks, and pigeons to sell to restaurants. He was slightly less poor than the rest of the family. He already had his sons, a thirteen-year-old and a ten-year-old, but his wife desperately wanted the companionship of a daughter.

"A boy and a girl make a family complete," she used to say.

So, what if the family pretended the twins belonged to Guoxiong and Xiuhua? The babies would still be "out of plan"—the term for illegal children—but the penalties less because the uncle had already paid the fines for his second son. He wouldn't have to pay as much to get them legally registered with *hukou*s. The aunt, though, was reluctant to take in twins. She could continue working with one baby strapped to her back, but not two. Twins would attract too much attention. Maybe, she thought, it would be better to temporarily separate them. Zanhua was initially resistant: She thought the twins should stay together. Although she'd never met anybody else with twins, she had the idea that they were an inseparable unit. But boarding one baby with the aunt and uncle was still the best option. As is common with twins, the second-born—the breech birth—was less healthy than the first. She was smaller and paler and was often fussy after she ate, likely suffering from colic. Zanhua thought she was too difficult to leave with the relatives and needed more time breastfeeding.

They came up with the ruse: Just one twin would stay with the aunt and uncle, and the other would accompany the parents to Chongqing.

Before they left, the families settled on the names for the girls. Although infant mortality had lessened, Chinese families thought it safer to wait a few months, until it was clear a child would survive, lest evil spirits snatch away the newborn. Old superstitions lingered on.

For the larger twin, the firstborn, they decided on Fang, a popular girl's name meaning "fragrant" or "virtuous." They would call her Fangfang, as names are often doubled in Chinese. For a family name, she would take the uncle's, *Yuan*, rather than the *Zeng* of her father, to disguise her origins. Nobody was supposed to know exactly whose baby she was, or that she was a twin. The only hint that there had been twin girls was in the name of the second baby. She was named Shuangjie, literally meaning "double purity."

JUST AFTER THE Lunar New Year in 2001, they put their plan in place. After six months together, sharing a bed, sharing their mother's breasts, and nine months together in their mother's womb, the twins were separated. Shuangjie left the village with her parents. Fangfang was moved into the home of her aunt and uncle.

At least for a while, it was an excellent solution. Although Fangfang had joined the ranks of the millions of other "left-behind" children, her situation was about as good as it gets. Her uncle doted on her. His wife was thrilled to finally have a girl in the house. Their boys loved having a baby sister and rushed home from school to play with her. They became expert babysitters as well. The grandmother and the older sisters lived across the street, in a cozy house nestled in bamboo. The two older sisters, Ping and Yan, would soon be enrolled in the same village school that their mother had attended, which was also close by. They would stop by to play after school. Fangfang was surrounded by people who loved her.

She grew plump and pink. She had a voracious appetite. She guzzled down homemade rice milk in the first months, then took quickly to solid foods. Raising poultry, the family had a reliable supply of fresh eggs to satisfy a hungry child. She would eat two for breakfast. She loved sticky rice, and what she didn't eat she smeared on her hands and cheeks. Even when she was naughty, she seemed conscious of what she was doing. She'd take one look at Xiuhua with mournful eyes and turn down the sides of her mouth in a frown, as though to apologize for her mistake. Then she'd laugh. There was no need to scold her.

Xiuhua marveled at the girl's intelligence. "She always knew if I was angry. It was like she could read people's faces and expressions," she'd later say.

Over time, Xiuhua began to think Fangfang might be a child prodigy. Fangfang seemed to comprehend what people were saying and even thinking. She talked early. She was walking by her first birthday and expertly explored her surroundings. When she wasn't yet two, she would toddle to her grandmother's house to visit family and then navigate her way back. Xiuhua couldn't help comparing the little girl to her own sons, who, although healthy, normal kids, exhibited nothing out of the ordinary.

"Look at that. You boys couldn't walk until two, and this little girl already knows her way around," Xiuhua would say to her sons.

XIUHUA WOULDN'T HAVE called herself a feminist and had probably never heard of the concept. But like many of her generation, she was reappraising the traditional preference for sons.

At the dawn of the twenty-first century, the value of girls was on the upswing. As China transitioned away from an agrarian economy, young women from the villages were in demand as workers. No matter that they weren't as strong as the menfolk; their nimble fingers, relative obedience, and sobriety gave them an edge in the modern workplace. After China joined the World Trade Organization in 2001, gaining access to its exports, demand for female workers soared. In the factories of Guangdong Province, the real-life Santa's workshop, producing many of the world's toys, young migrant women made up close to 60 percent of the workforce. Since they weren't as useful as men on the farm, they could be sent out to earn cash for the family. Zanhua had been a maverick of sorts when she left the village at the age of thirteen, but now everybody did it. Thousands of years of patriarchy were eroding, like an ancient stone being eaten away by drops of water.

The persistence of the preference for boys was in part tied to the lack of a safety net in the countryside. China doesn't have a comprehensive social security system. Outside of the cities, people relied on their offspring. And that meant their sons and daughters-in-law, since their own daughters moved to the husband's family—a pattern that social anthropologists call patrilocal. That was one of the villagers' main arguments against the one-child policy. ("Those in Beijing who made these policies all have their pensions," complained one village leader to a researcher. "Have any offered to give them up? They ask that we give up our sons.") It wasn't all about love; money and security were part of the equation. They needed sons to support them in their old age.

Girls were "like spilled water," went an old derogatory expression. Sexism was baked into the language and literature of old China. A grandmother from the mother's side of the family is known in some parts of China as the *waipo*, literally "outside grandmother," signifying that the maternal relatives are not as important as the father's. Poetry going back thousands of years relegates females to a lowly place. An oft-quoted ode from the Book of Songs, a collection of folk poetry dating from the eighth century B.C.E., states flatly that a girl's only purpose is to "give no trouble."

Other ancient texts refer to female newborns drowned or strangled or left out in the elements to die. It was considered a form of birth control, with boys also the victims, although in lesser numbers. Historian D. E. Mungello, in his book *Drowning Girls in China: Female Infanticide Since 1650*, wrote that infanticide was more common during famines, but sometimes families simply didn't want to pay for a dowry or the cost of foot-binding, which, though mandatory to ensure a girl's marriageability, rendered her useless to help out at home. Since Chinese families often didn't recognize a baby's existence for three days, parents could excuse themselves for thinking that the newborn wasn't so much killed as sent back: If they were Buddhists, they could salve their consciences with the belief that the child would be reborn under better circumstances. Then again, it sometimes backfired, Mungello wrote, citing folktales in which the angry ghosts returned to kill sons.

Sensational accounts of infanticide were later relayed by Christian missionaries, like Baptist Adele Fielde, who wrote in an 1884 memoir, "That the drowning of a three-month's-old [sic] girl should excite no more comment than the drowning of a kitten . . . is marvelous to anyone who does not know how lightly the lives of Chinese girls are esteemed." Among researchers, Mungello writes, there is debate about whether infanticide was exaggerated to depict the Chinese as heathens in need of salvation. (Lest Western readers disdain the Chinese, scholars point out that in eighteenth- and nineteenth-century Europe up to 40 percent of babies were abandoned. The philosopher Jean-Jacques Rousseau disclosed in his *Confessions* that he had dumped three children in a foundling home, where they most likely died.)

Infanticide persisted into the twentieth century. The British Chinese writer Xinran wrote in *Message from an Unknown Chinese Mother: Stories of Loss and Love* about the common custom of "doing a girl": "They had different terms for it, depending on where you were, and the ways of disposing of the babies was different, but there was no avoiding the fact that it was a normal part of a woman's life." But the practice became less common under the disapproving rule of the Communist Party. The marriage law enacted in 1950 explicitly banned killing newborns along with other now-out-of-fashion feudal customs: polygamy, concubinage, and the forced marriage of minor children. Even if he didn't practice what he preached, Mao (who maintained a harem of concubines) opined frequently that equality between the sexes was essential for his socialist vision. "Women hold up half the sky" is one of his often-quoted slogans, plastered today on T-shirts and mugs sold in souvenir shops in Beijing.

The killing of newborns resumed after the implementation of the one-child policy, an aberration in the historical trend line. Boys were killed and abandoned as well as girls, although at a lesser rate. Gruesome stories of murdered babies emerged throughout the 1980s. In 1985, *The Washington Post* published a three-part series under the headline "China's Birth Control Policy Drives Some to Kill Baby Girls." People spoke of finding dead babies in cardboard boxes or fishermen of pulling from the water dead female babies with stones tied to their feet. Among the chilling examples, Liu Chunsan, a farmer in Shandong Province, threw his four-year-old daughter down a well in 1983 while she screamed *Baba!*, begging him to stop. In an interview from prison, where he was serving a fifteen-year sentence, Liu told Chinese journalists that he loved his daughter but needed a son.

Environmentally minded Western governments that had applauded China's population controls turned away in disgust. Horror stories about murdered and discarded baby girls filled the news pages. They were endlessly repeated and sometimes amplified. After 1991, when China opened up for international adoption, the adoption agencies pointed to the killings of baby girls in their appeals for potential clients. In fact, many Westerners decided to adopt out of pity for the unwanted girls.

No accurate statistics have ever emerged of the girls whose births didn't take place—or at least weren't recorded. Researchers can only consult statistics to compare anticipated births with actual births. In some provinces, births of as many as 140 boys were recorded for each 100 girls. Extrapolating from those figures, demographers calculated that up to 60 million girls are missing. The initial assumption was that they were aborted, killed, or abandoned. But researchers who have examined more recent census data believe they have actually "found" some of those lost girls. In a 2019 book, *Lost and Found: The "Missing Girls" in Rural China*, University of Kansas professor John James Kennedy and Chinese scholar Yaojiang Shi surmised that large numbers of girls were hidden away, their births unreported, until a change in the law in 2015 made it easier for them to get legally registered. The late Kay Ann Johnson, one of the leading scholars of Chinese adoptees and an adoptive mother herself, posited in her groundbreaking book *China's Hidden Children* that Chinese parents were not as heartless toward their daughters as reports suggested. With Chinese colleagues, Johnson surveyed 350 sets of Chinese parents who had abandoned daughters. All but a handful were second, third, or fourth daughters who were given up under duress. In a larger survey, she found that "most parents, caught in the squeeze between the state's harsh demands and their own needs and desires, found ways to hold on to both the girls and the boys they gave birth to, . . . often with great difficulty and sometimes great cost."

In Fangfang's case, the family claimed they hadn't had twins, to make hiding their babies easier. Others did just the opposite. They would claim that two babies close in age were twins. It wasn't illegal per se to have twins, as long as the parents had permission to give birth (which, of course, the Zengs did not), so both babies could be registered. Sometimes wealthy women underwent fertility treatments in hopes of having multiple births as a loophole to get out of the family size limitations.

The Zengs' various schemes to circumvent the rules were not terribly original. Many Chinese mothers, like Zanhua, gave birth secretly— if not in a bamboo grove then in some other secluded location where their labors would not draw the attention of Family Planning. One hid away on a houseboat. People often disguised their out-of-plan children by leaving them with friends or relatives, most commonly aunts and uncles, who might be in a better position to register them, perhaps by paying a bribe in exchange for the *hukou*.

Like Fangfang, countless children lived under false names with fabricated ages. If you ask a young person in China their birth date, you sometimes get a complicated answer—there might be the day they were really born and another date that was more convenient for the purpose of registration. Kids were instructed to lie about their ages and the identities of their birth parents and siblings. They pretended they were twins when they were not. Mothers were aunts. Aunts were mothers. Siblings were cousins and cousins were siblings. So many children had more than one birthday. They had more than one name. Sometimes they didn't have to lie, because they hadn't been told the truth about their parentage. Family relations were complicated.

Living for generations under callous rulers, rural Chinese had become adept at circumventing rules that often made no sense. They wanted to keep their families intact and children close to their hearts. They devised various strategies to do so, creative and often brilliant. Except that there was so much that could go wrong.

Chapter Four

THE BABY SNATCHERS

Family-planning poster.

In early 2001, just after the Lunar New Year, the Zengs left the village again to work. This time their destination was farther afield. More than five hundred miles to the west, Chongqing was one of the fastest-growing cities in China, and therefore in the world. Straddling a tributary of the Yangtze River, Chongqing was a beneficiary of a government initiative to develop China's inland, which lagged behind the Pacific coast. New office towers and condominiums rose as fast as magic beanstalks, jutting out from the hills that lined both sides of the river. The city's population, twenty million and growing by several million more each year, was swelling with an influx of migrants. It was a city in a hurry that drew people in a hurry to earn money. In Chongqing, migrants could earn the equivalent of ten to twenty dollars per day—four times the wages at home. Payment was in cash, no residency papers required, no questions asked.

The quickest way to earn money was to work as a porter, hauling goods up and down Chongqing's notoriously unnavigable streets rising steeply from the banks of the river. The porters balanced loads as heavy as one hundred pounds on their shoulders with long bamboo sticks called *bangzi*, earning themselves the comical nickname *bang-bang men*. The bang-bang men became the symbol of Chongqing, scrambling up and down the stone steps, carrying goods from the barges, and supplying delicacies to the Yangtze River cruises. Zeng liked being his own boss, not worrying if he'd get paid at the end of the month by some fly-by-night contractor.

Most migrants settled for airless basement rooms, sleeping on bunk beds, but the Zengs needed more space, since they had brought Shuangjie, a fast-growing toddler like her twin. They were lucky to meet an elderly widow who rented them a decent-size private room with a kitchen at one end. Their accommodations were relatively comfortable. And safely out of reach of the Family Planning authorities in Longhui County, since enforcement took place in the jurisdiction where a family was registered. But it was a strictly temporary arrangement. Migrants like the Zengs were tolerated in Chongqing—their labor was needed—but they had no right to establish themselves as permanent residents. They would not be able to own a home or send their children to school, because they didn't have *hukou*s for Chongqing. It was a precarious existence. All they wanted was to earn enough money to return home, to repair their house, and for the family to be together again. That couldn't happen until they paid off the fines for the twins. Family Planning kept families like theirs ripped asunder in a perpetual cycle of poverty.

BACK IN THE VILLAGE, Fangfang was beginning to attract notice. She could toddle her way down the street to visit her sisters and grandmother and then navigate her way home. People laughed when they saw her walking down the street. Fangfang was small for her age but so advanced that she looked like an ambulatory doll. The large double doors of her aunt and uncle's redbrick house opened directly onto the main road of the village, set back by only a small stoop. Unlike in other parts of China, most houses in the village didn't have walled courtyards or gates. Doors weren't always locked, and in the warm months, they were often left open in hopes of a cooling breeze. Chickens and ducks sauntered in and out of the houses—people would just shoo away unwelcome animals; in this free-range society, small children wandered about just as casually. Parents weren't too mindful about their children crossing the street, because the few motor vehicles that passed by on the rutted road out front could barely go faster than a crawl. Neighbors were friendly enough, too, but many of them held positions with the local government. It was only a matter of time before somebody noticed an unregistered toddler and reported her to Family Planning.

The first time the authorities came to the house was early in the spring of 2002, when the adults were all at work. The older boy, Zan, was left in charge. At thirteen, tall and lanky like his mother, he was a capable teenager, experienced in the care and feeding of a toddler. But he wasn't as mindful about unfamiliar visitors approaching the house. By the time he and his brother realized what was happening, there were men at the doorstep pushing their way through the front door. The boys could tell they weren't from the village by the button-down shirts they wore and the leather shoes. These were the *ganbu,* or "cadres," the civil service bureaucrats carrying out the will of the Communist Party. Even at a young age, the boys knew that the intrusion had to do with the unregistered toddler.

"Get the baby!" Zan yelled at his younger brother. The ten-year-old, Dong, quickly scooped up the startled Fangfang under his arm.

The double doors of the house swung open into a large main room, where the family spent most of their time. It was sparsely furnished with a square wooden table and backless stools—typical of the Chinese countryside. Behind the main room on one side was a narrow kitchen leading to a garden and an outdoor toilet that was attached to the rear of the house. On the other side was a staircase leading up to the bedrooms.

The boys realized that they couldn't reach the kitchen, so they opted for the staircase. The uninvited visitors stormed across the room, trying to catch them. The wooden table and stools toppled, clattering on the tile floor. The boys made it to the top of the stairs and looked frantically for an escape. The only exit would be a window from the second floor that led to the roof of the outhouse. They climbed outside.

Still holding the baby, the ten-year-old quickly assessed the drop—not quite an entire floor from the roof to the sloping yard. He held on tight and jumped, somehow managing not to drop the girl. The Family Planning cadres had made it up the staircase, but they were too slow. Well-fed, chain-smoking bureaucrats, they were no match for limber young boys. The boys jumped again over a ditch out back and ran through the bamboo grove, then navigated their way around the rice paddies and into the thick forest at the foot of the mountains. The boys knew every crook and crevice. This was their territory. They hid in the mountains until after dark.

When their mother came home and heard of their narrow escape, she panicked. She knew Family Planning would try again. Although the weather was already warm, she made sure to keep the front doors locked and the baby indoors. Xiuhua was on edge, waiting, ears cocked like a watchdog. Few cars passed by out front, and each time, she'd peek out to make sure she recognized them. When the Family Planning officers came back a few weeks later, as she knew they would, she was able to slip out the back door with a small bag she'd packed in advance. She trekked through the mountains with the baby until she reached another village, where she took refuge with some relatives. But she couldn't stay there forever. She had responsibilities at home. She tried to contact her brother-in-law and sister-in-law. She knew they'd gone to Chongqing but couldn't find a phone number. They didn't yet have their own mobile phones.

"This little girl is so much more *mafan* than my sons," she'd grumble, using a frequently uttered Chinese word for "big trouble." Xiuhua had had her share of grief when she'd given birth to her second son—and she'd paid a year's worth of income in fines to Family Planning to prevent them from vandalizing her house.

Xiuhua knew how much rougher they could be—she'd seen the houses demolished, the farm animals taken, the people beaten up when they violated the policy. This time, she sensed that the family's predicament was more serious. She grilled her sons about what had happened. Family Planning had sent so many people to the home, and yet they'd left without confiscating any property or punching a hole in the roof as had happened to the Zengs. They weren't just after money. What they wanted was the baby, the brilliant, beautiful girl who everybody in the family knew was so special.

CHILD TRAFFICKING WAS a long-standing plague in China. The U.S. State Department estimated in 2015 that twenty thousand children in China were kidnapped each year, with some researchers believing the number to be much higher. The Chinese government acknowledged a figure of ten thousand. Especially in the countryside, small children tended to be free-range, wandering through markets or playing in the streets with little supervision. Few people hired babysitters or put their children in daycare. Small children were cared for by grandparents or barely older siblings, who weren't always attentive. In small towns, even the city, you might see them playing alone in the street in front of stores or shops where their parents were working. Chinese criminologist Pi Yijun once observed, not entirely in jest, that it was far easier in China to steal a child than a car or computer.

Even older children were at risk. Mentally impaired boys and teenagers were kidnapped as forced laborers, often in brick factories. Preteen girls were taken as domestic servants, sexual partners, or brides. By 2001, more than two decades into the one-child policy, the enduring preference for sons had led to a shortage of marriageable young women.

When it came to babies, though, it was usually the boys who were snatched. Families who needed sons would buy them to raise as their own. In some rural areas, buying a child was considered an informal adoption, acceptable for the childless or infertile.

At least in the past, baby girls hadn't been so desirable, and so it seemed that something strange was going on. Xiuhua had heard rumors that Family Planning was taking children, but what was this all about? Did the Family Planning officers intend to traffic the baby? Or—she shuddered—were they just selling her organs? This was a persistent rumor in the Chinese countryside, urban legend perhaps, and it speaks to people's distrust of local government that many believed it.

Whatever their motive, Xiuhua was certain that Family Planning would try again. After she came back from her hideout in the mountains, an official from the village committee—the most local level of governance—stopped by the house and warned her again. "You're not entitled to keep this baby." They seemed to know everything—that this was neither her own baby nor a child she'd picked up abandoned. That this was the over-quota daughter of her husband's sister. At that point, she had nowhere to go. She waited for the inevitable.

It happened on May 30, 2002, already like summer, steamy with the evaporation rising from the rice paddies. The door was propped open to let air into the house.

Xiuhua was home with Fangfang, just the two of them alone. Her husband was out working. Her sons were at school. The first sign that something was amiss was that a man walked past the doorstep with a towel over his head. She didn't recognize him but could tell from his cheap plastic sandals that he was one of the villagers. (You could always tell who worked for the government and who worked as a laborer by their footwear.)

Only later did she realize that the towel was a disguise; he was probably somebody she knew who had been paid off to alert Family Planning that Xiuhua was home alone.

Before she could articulate her fears, a bunch of men burst into the house—definitely officials. It seemed like there were more and more pouring through the door. There were some she recognized from Gaoping. She knew what they wanted. She rushed to hold Fangfang, but she wasn't fast enough. Instead of going for the baby first, they grabbed her. The men were all over her. Two held her arms behind her back, pulling her so roughly she feared dislocating a shoulder. Two others knelt on the floor to secure her legs.

Although she was a strong woman, taller than some of the men holding her, Xiuhua couldn't wriggle free.

Fangfang was then three months shy of her second birthday. She could talk and walk. She knew enough to be afraid. She ran to her aunt and held on tightly. She reached for the hem of Xiuhua's shirt, clutching it in her little fist as though it were a life rope. For a moment, they were all still, immobilized together—the men holding Xiuhua, the toddler holding on, nobody able to budge, until one of the stronger men managed to pry loose Fangfang's grip and swept her into his arms.

There was no paperwork, no arrest warrant, just force.

"You're not allowed to keep this child," one of the men told her, echoing what she had been warned earlier. She yelled back; exactly what she said she couldn't later remember, but it wasn't polite.

Everybody was screaming, especially Fangfang, struggling to escape from the man.

The commotion began to draw a crowd. Neighbors poured out of their houses, rushing to intervene. Even five-year-old Yan heard the screaming from her grandmother's nearby house and ran outside. People yelled that she should go inside, for fear the posse would take her as well, but she squirmed out of their grasp and ran as fast as her little legs could carry her. She was determined to protect her baby sister.

It wasn't the same as the 1980s, when onlookers watched helplessly, without daring to move. This time, they had the courage and determination; they just lacked the brute strength and speed.

Quick as they had come, the Family Planning officers emerged from the house, carrying Fangfang like a captured trophy. Anticipating resistance, they had parked their car down the hill, facing away from the house so they could make a quick escape. Some in the crowd tried to pursue them.

Xiuhua led the pack. She burst out of the house and sprinted down the road. She was an athletic woman but no match for a car. Especially as she hadn't had time to put on her shoes.

CHAPTER FIVE

A PETITION
SIGNED IN BLOOD

Petitioner Yang Libing (second from right).

BACK IN CHONGQING, ZENG YOUDONG COULD BARELY CATCH
his breath. He was working around the clock, carrying unbearable loads
on his bamboo poles up and down the steep slopes of the riverbank and
taking as many extra shifts as he could squeeze into a day. He needed to
pay those escalating fines to Family Planning. He had just acquired his
first mobile phone, a major rite of passage for a migrant worker, but he
didn't always turn it on. Several days elapsed before he got the call.
Guoxiong, his brother-in-law, had a loud voice to begin with, but now
he was practically shouting into the phone.

"They took the baby away."

Guoxiong was almost hyperventilating. The story came out between
great gulps of breath. He told of the dramatic home invasion in which

Fangfang was stolen. How their efforts to retrieve her had so far failed. He wanted his brother-in-law to know everything they'd done so far and to appreciate the trauma the family had suffered on behalf of his little girl.

Xiuhua was in a state of shock. She had been assaulted, incapacitated, and robbed in a way she never could have imagined. She couldn't go to the police, since her assailants worked for the government. Failing to catch the car, she had traipsed through the mountains to the home of the same relative who had hidden them before. Panting and disheveled, teary-eyed and still shoeless, she begged the relatives to ask the people they knew to find out where the girl had been taken.

This was the way you did things in the village—indirectly, asking a better-connected friend or relative to ask somebody who knew somebody for help. You needed to have *guanxi,* connections.

As it happened, Xiuhua's uncle did know somebody on the village committee connected with Family Planning. This was no coincidence, since nearly half of the village staff had a role in enforcing the birth limits. The message he sent back was not encouraging. Their ruse hadn't worked. Family Planning hadn't swallowed any of the excuses they'd tried, hoping to win sympathy from the officials and get the fines reduced. The baby, they knew, belonged to Zeng Youdong and Yuan Zanhua, repeat offenders and scofflaws, long in trouble with the law. As far as Family Planning was concerned, they were on the equivalent of the most-wanted list. The family couldn't get the girl back unless they paid fifteen thousand Chinese yuan—two thousand dollars, the equivalent of five years of earnings for a rural Chinese family.

Through the intermediaries, a series of negotiations ensued. The price went up and down and finally settled at about ten thousand yuan as a down payment. Guoxiong kept Zeng Youdong abreast of the negotiations in a flurry of subsequent calls.

"You need to come home with some money to get back the baby," he begged his brother-in-law.

Youdong would send money, he promised. But he didn't have the entire amount right away. And he couldn't come home either, because he'd have no chance of earning the money unless he stayed in Chong-qing. And he needed money more than ever before.

IN EARLY 2002, three months before Fangfang was taken, Zanhua had given birth in Chongqing to a baby boy. They named him Jialiang, meaning "good and bright." At long last, they had fulfilled their respon-sibility to the family. They would no longer have to endure complaints from Zeng's father or the scorn of the old-fashioned scolds in the vil-lage. For the moment, they were safely out of reach of the officials back home. But the birth of the long-awaited son put them even deeper into legal jeopardy. In a country that still enforced a strict one-child policy, they now had five. Only two of those five were legally registered. They couldn't stay in Chongqing indefinitely and they couldn't afford to go home. They were trapped, fugitives, in debt and unable to see a way to climb out of their hole.

To outsiders, it would seem that Zeng Youdong should have done more to get Fangfang back. Or that he sacrificed the girl for the boy. But the truth is, once the girl was taken it was a lost cause. Youdong and his brother-in-law were what is called *laobaixing*, a ubiquitous ex-pression that translates to "old hundred names" but means "the com-mon people." They had no power, no voice, and little *guanxi*. They didn't know where they could complain or how to get a lawyer or find a journalist. They felt utterly helpless to fight back. It was illegal for Family Planning officials to confiscate a child, but they weren't versed in the law.

Although Zeng now lived in Chongqing, the big city, he still had the mindset of a villager. And villagers were not highly literate or well-versed in the latest dicta of the Chinese Communist Party. Current events swirled around and above their heads, leaving them swept away by events with little awareness of the reasons and without recourse to resist. If they happened to catch the television news, they consumed only the relentlessly cheerful. While the United States was reeling from the aftermath of the September 11 terrorist attacks and already mired in Afghanistan, China was boasting of double-digit economic growth. China Central Television (CCTV) extolled the country's economic miracle, the upcoming 2008 Summer Olympics in Beijing, and two successful launches of the unmanned *Shenzhou* space shuttle. The Chinese people knew of the world what the party told them.

The communications revolution that would radically transform China was still a few years in the future. In a decade, there would be more than one billion mobile phones in China—as many as the entire adult population—and people would be reading uncurated news on the internet (at least before the censors got around to scrubbing it) and texting one another. But in 2002, rural people mostly knew what was conveyed by word of mouth, first- or secondhand, or in rumors as diffuse as the dust on the unpaved roads. The mountainous topography also challenged communications. If you lived on one mountain, you wouldn't know what was happening on the next unless you came into the township to hear the gossip.

For the Zengs, that township was Gaoping, which lay in a valley among four mountains. Just a small town by Chinese standards, it was the nerve center for some seventy thousand people scattered around the surrounding mountains, among those the people living in Gaofeng. At the main crossroads was the bus station, the bank, and a cluster of government offices, including the dreaded headquarters of Family Planning. The main attraction was the wet market, so named since the ground underfoot was always slippery with the effluence of freshly slaughtered animals. Back in the eighties and nineties, the market had been held only every five days for farmers from the mountain villages to sell whatever they were raising—be it pomelos or pigeons—but now it was a permanent fixture of China's market economy. There were counterfeit Adidas and Nike athletic shoes, sweatshirts stenciled with incomprehensible English slogans, mobile telephones and SIM cards. A *wangba*, literally "net bar," an internet café, would open soon for the kids to play games and exchange messages with their friends. Until then, older people congregated near the market, sitting on plastic stools to drink tea and gossip. Going to town was an occasion not just to shop but also to acquire information.

In the summer of 2002, the talk was all about Family Planning. It was a perennial topic. People who wouldn't otherwise dare raise a voice against the government cursed about the beatings, the confiscations of property, the extortionate fines. This time, it was more serious. Family Planning had been taking pigs or tractors. Now it was children. When people compared notes, they realized that Fangfang wasn't the only child snatched.

A few months after Fangfang was taken, there was another case: A woman in her sixties who was bringing her granddaughter to a doctor's appointment in Gaoping was intercepted by Family Planning officers who had her under surveillance. They told the grandmother that the child's parents hadn't registered their marriage, and therefore the birth was illegal. There on the street, they took the girl away. She had just celebrated her first birthday.

Then in early September, a three-year-old girl napping inside her home was taken as her parents worked in the fields outside their house. The girl, abandoned as a newborn, had been raised by a couple who already had two sons. They had gone through what they thought were the correct legal procedures and paid the "social maintenance fee" to register the child, but the Family Planning officials told them their payment was inadequate and that they owed an additional five thousand dollars.

As far as the family was concerned, these children had been kidnapped and the perpetrators were criminals demanding ransom for their release. They used the verb *qiang*, an informal term for stealing, like "snatched." Family Planning referred to its actions as confiscations, implying that it was acting within the confines of the law. But whatever term, it continued through the next two years. More newborns were taken, more adopted children. Officials were strategic in picking their victims. The families targeted all had a vulnerability that could be exploited. The parents were often migrants who had left their children with illiterate grandparents; they were exceptionally poor. They lived deep in the mountains, out of touch with others and less likely to make a fuss.

The identity of the culprits was no mystery. In a small community, everybody recognized the *ganbu,* a term for Communist Party members who serve in government. "Cadres" they are usually called in English. There was Liu Tangshan, who lived nearby and was so disliked that he kept fierce watchdogs outside his house to dissuade people from confronting him in the off-hours. Zhou Xiaofang, the head of the township Family Planning office, was said to have powerful relatives in the Hunan provincial government. She couldn't be touched. Liu Shude replaced her as the head of the office in 2005. Some of the lower-level people were decommissioned soldiers. They were capable of inflicting a beating if challenged.

When people tried to complain, they were roughed up. An illiterate woman in her sixties who refused to hand over her three-month-old granddaughter was dragged to the Family Planning office inside the yellow building near the Gaoping market. She was locked up overnight in a room with just a bare wooden bench, cradling the baby. The next day, a man came from behind, grabbed her hand, pressed her thumb onto an ink pad, and had her stamp a raft of documents she couldn't read. They then sent her home without the baby.

Other parents were dismissed with contempt. They were told simply that they weren't allowed to keep these children. The children were being transferred to an orphanage, but Family Planning wouldn't reveal which of the more than forty orphanages in Hunan Province. The parents wouldn't be allowed to see them. They weren't entitled to more information. There seemed to be no recourse. The message was the same one they had heard their whole lives: You can't fight Family Planning.

PERHAPS THE FIRST miscalculation of Family Planning was in 2005 when they dared to take a boy. Not only a boy but a five-year-old who was already attending school. His name was Wei Hailong (meaning "sea dragon") and he had been adopted by a young couple from a village on the outskirts of Gaoping. The family was just slightly better connected than others, living close to town, where they had a carpentry shop. They made coffins and supplied lumber for many construction projects, making them well known around town. The boy's grandfather used to watch the boy while he worked, but one afternoon, two cadres from Family Planning strolled into the house and instructed the boy, "Little kid, follow us."

The boy was an only child who had been adopted by the grandfather's son and daughter-in-law. She had a uterine abnormality that left her infertile. Family Planning officials cited various technicalities: The parents had started the adoption procedure in another province, Guizhou, where they'd been migrants, and had not completed the paperwork in Hunan Province. And they were in violation of a recently tightened domestic adoption law that required both parents to be at least thirty years old. Wei Taixi, the boy's father, was still two months short of his thirtieth birthday. (The boy's mother was three years older.)

The family had suffered a series of costly setbacks—their house had been gutted in a fire, and the grandmother had died, necessitating an expensive funeral. The family's hardship engendered sympathy in the neighborhood. And the boy, with an infectious grin, was a good student, popular with classmates and teachers. His elementary school lodged a complaint.

> Our student, Wei Hailong, has been absent since Monday. After a home visit, we learned that the Family Planning Office has taken him away. May the Family Planning Office please prioritize his academic studies and allow him to come back to school so that he will not fall behind on his schoolwork?

Family Planning had overplayed its hand. A local politician who served in the National People's Congress, a legislative body, echoed the complaint. After twenty-nine days, the boy was returned to his family. He was in poor shape, traumatized, malnourished, and covered with rashes. But he was home.

Word quickly spread from village to village that this one family had scored a victory against Family Planning. It opened the floodgates. More people were emboldened to fight back. The families started to talk to one another and organize.

The next miscalculation by Family Planning was confiscating the daughter of a middle-aged farmer named Yang Libing. Yang lived in a ramshackle house with a pigsty in back and drying meats and cornstalks hanging from the rafters. The family was as poor as everybody else, but they had a few advantages. Yang was charismatic, articulate, and most of all obsessive. He would quickly emerge as a leader of the pack of aggrieved parents.

Yang had worked in hotels for several years, which allowed him to enjoy a bachelor's lifestyle. He was tall and gangly, with a brush of raven hair swept across a high forehead that gave him a touch of the debonair. Shortly before his fortieth birthday, he befriended a teenage hotel attendant named Cao Zhimei. Pleasingly plump, with a heart-shaped face, Cao was pretty enough that friends thought her to be out of Yang's league, but she was in trouble. She was pregnant, perhaps by another man, and was in need of a husband. Yang liked her and felt some urgency to settle down and start a family before his upcoming birthday. They moved back to his parents' place in the village, set out some banquet tables for friends and relatives, and pronounced themselves married. That was the way things had always been done in the village. In any case, Cao was not yet twenty, the legal age for a marriage certificate, and was from another province, which made it burdensome to collect the documents needed to register the marriage.

The baby was delivered at the family home in 2004 with the help of Yang's mother and a local midwife. Whether or not she was his biological child, Yang doted on the little girl with her big, round eyes. Over Lunar New Year, they went to a photo studio in Gaoping to take a portrait in front of a backdrop of plum blossoms. The parents dressed casually in jeans and parkas, but the baby wore an elaborate outfit—a fuzzy jacket with a matching hat, flowered booties, and pink leggings. She was their little princess, their proudest achievement.

Like many new parents in need of money to provide for their child's future, Yang and his wife took jobs outside the village after the New Year holiday. The baby was left with the grandparents. That was the moment for Family Planning to swoop in. The grandmother took refuge with the baby in the pigsty behind the house, but the cadres forced them out. The seventy-year-old grandfather, Yang Qinzheng, argued with them. He was a veteran of the People's Liberation Army and a member of the Chinese Communist Party. It's one of the largest political parties in the world, with nearly one hundred million members, roughly 7 percent of China's population, hardly an exclusive club. But membership still confers heightened status. Their house had a poster of Mao plastered to the wall. Peeling around the edges, it looked like it had been there since the 1970s, when the chairman's portrait was obligatory, but the fact that it hadn't been removed attested to the family's continued devotion to the party. The older Yang was a man not to be trifled with, he insisted. The Family Planning officials seemed to treat him with deference. They explained that the usual fine for having a baby from an unregistered marriage would run 20,000 yuan—about $2,400. But out of respect for the veteran's service to the motherland, the cadres could do a work-around to lower the fine. If he signed papers saying the baby was found abandoned (obviously untrue, since she'd been born at home), the family could adopt her for a fraction of the amount of the fine. The encounter was cordial enough. It was not until after they left that the grandfather realized he had been tricked.

The older Yang wore black heavy-rimmed eyeglasses with thick lenses. He was literate but could barely see. Trusting the official, he had effectively signed away the family's rights to the child. This was a favorite tactic of Family Planning. They convinced parents to falsely claim that these were not birth children but adopted. Once the paperwork was signed, the families were told they didn't meet the qualifications to adopt. His granddaughter was lost.

Yang Libing rushed back from Guangdong Province and stormed into the Family Planning office in Gaoping. He screamed for the return of his daughter. He ended up badly beaten and, by his own account, came crawling out on all fours like a dog. But he kept going back. Again and again. Although he and his wife had another child—a boy—the following year, it did not diminish his resolve to recover his daughter. He got into repeated scrapes with law enforcement. At one point, he was arrested on trumped-up charges of soliciting prostitution. (This happened after an undercover official, pretending to be an aggrieved parent, invited him to a bathhouse.)

Yang just wouldn't give up. In frustration, Liu Shude, one of the top officials of the agency, tried to buy him off. He invited Yang to the office and promised to give him a special permit that would allow him to have two children without paying fines.

"But you must give me back my daughter," Yang persisted.

It was impossible, Liu told him. The girl had already been transferred to an orphanage and could not be retrieved.

"Stop asking me about her," Liu told him. "You could pay one hundred thousand yuan for her, but you are not going to get her back. Don't make trouble."

Sweetening the deal, he offered to procure a veteran's pension for Yang's father.

"Isn't your father a veteran? He is entitled to a basic living allowance. I will take care of it."

No way would he be bought off, Yang told Liu with a few choice expletives, before storming out of the office. He then started prodding the other parents to get organized.

People from the isolated villages now found common cause. They organized the Child Search Association. The Wei family, although they had recovered their son, volunteered the use of the carpentry house, which had living quarters above. It was a dilapidated two-story brick building located on the outskirts of Gaoping, close enough to town for convenience but far enough away not to attract too much attention.

The first formal meeting was held in March 2006, just after the Chinese New Year holiday. Dozens of people squeezed into the main sitting room of the house—the grieving and the infuriated, mothers, fathers, aunts and uncles, grandparents, who had most often served as the caretakers of the confiscated babies. People smoked and swore, cried, and vowed revenge. They clutched plastic bags stuffed with dog-eared documents, account books, crumpled receipts for fines already paid, and paperwork showing they'd obtained household registration for their children.

If they had had the wherewithal to consult a lawyer, they would have realized that the law definitely did not allow the government to confiscate children. The law only spelled out the monetary fines for violations. But to sue the government was unthinkable, and lawyers were understandably reluctant to take such cases for fear they would end up in prison themselves. Instead, Yang advised the families that they could draft a petition to officials laying out their case and demanding the return of their children.

Petitioning is a Chinese system of addressing grievances that substitutes for an independent judicial system. People who believe themselves wronged write out their grievances to appeal to higher-ups. The practice, known as *shangfang*, or "visit up," dates back to imperial times. In the old days, commoners would bang a drum outside the court to get attention or throw themselves in front of a sedan chair. Now, instead of petitioning the emperor, they go to the Communist Party complaining about everything from land confiscation to job termination. Elsewhere similar complaints might be handled with a civil lawsuit. Petitioners hope that the national or provincial leaders will rectify the wrongs inflicted on them at the lower level. Mostly petitioning is an opportunity for people to vent. "The petition system in China is like a drug, a hallucinogenic, intended to give people the mere illusion of change" is how Pang Jiaoming, a Chinese investigative journalist, put it. Petitioners are often intercepted and detained on their way to Beijing by local officials who fear reprisals if their complaints are heard. Still, for lack of any better mechanism, tens of thousands of Chinese submit petitions each year. In Beijing, there is an office for accepting petitions. Often rural people too poor to afford hotels, petitioners set up encampments near the office. Scribes set up shop on the sidewalks offering to write up the complaints for a small fee.

The parents in Gaoping also needed a scribe. They found Yuan Chao-ren, a former teacher. Though still in his forties, he was addressed by the nickname of *Lao Yuan,* literally "Old Yuan," out of respect for his education. Old Yuan was a *laobaixing,* a common person, like the rest of them, a stocky man with a brush cut who used to keep a cigarette tucked behind his ear. But he'd completed high school, making him the village intellectual. He taught Chinese literature and math at a primary school. His cousin also had a child who had been taken away, so Old Yuan was eager to help.

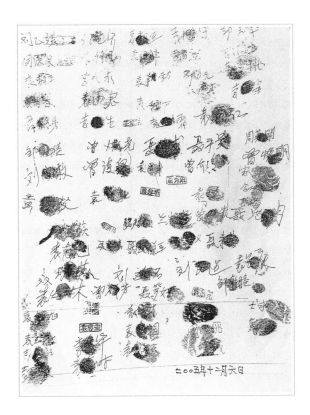

THE PARENTS AND their relatives signed the petition with their thumbprints stamped in red ink, a symbolic gesture so that they could name it "The Petition Signed in Blood." In nine pages, it detailed sixteen cases of children who had been seized by Gaoping's Family Planning officers. (Later many more cases would emerge.) Most of the writing was very matter-of-fact, listing birth dates of the parents, birth dates of the confiscated children, and identity card numbers. The petition briefly described the efforts the families had made to recover the children.

Perhaps surprisingly, the petition didn't challenge the fundamental right of the Communist Party to control the population. This was common among people living in repressive regimes, who found it easier to rage against local officials than to challenge the system that enabled them. They wanted to present themselves as loyal citizens of the People's Republic of China.

"Now, many people, including the farmers, support the state policy and consciously follow the home planning policy. It is a kind of social progress and an important signal of the country's prosperity," the petition stated.

"The Family Planning office didn't care about the welfare of children or even of society at large. They disregarded the state law and trampled human rights, abducted and robbed the babies and children . . . and extorted the farmers to pay thousands of yuan or tens of thousands of yuan to redeem their children."

The petitioners demanded that the Family Planning cadres be punished for their abuses. But above all, what they wanted was to locate the missing children.

"Where are the dozens of children who were taken from the birth parents and loving adoptive parents?" the petition queried.

The parents themselves had no idea. They traded theories. Zeng was convinced that Fangfang was still nearby, living somewhere in Hunan. Others thought they'd been sent to other provinces to prevent their families from tracking them down. Some people said the girls were sold to childless families or were being raised as sex slaves. Then there was the lingering suspicion that children were trafficked for their organs. All rumors seemed plausible.

In retrospect, it seems impossible that the parents hadn't figured out where their children had gone. It should have been so obvious that one would slap their thigh, saying, *Well, yes, of course.*

Zeng Youdong was neither unintelligent nor illiterate. He was better educated than most rural villagers. He had been living in Chongqing, one of China's largest cities, where luxury cruises carrying international tourists sailed in from the Yangtze River. He should have been more sophisticated. And yet he knew little of the economic forces that were transforming China and how it was interacting with the world beyond.

And for a long, long time he would have no idea what happened to Fangfang. It wasn't his fault. By design, people like him were kept clueless about what was happening in their own country.

Later that year, though, a scandal would erupt elsewhere in Hunan Province that would begin to lift the blinders.

CHAPTER SIX

THE SCANDAL

Duan Yueneng and his mother, Chen Zhijin.

ON THE AFTERNOON OF NOVEMBER 15, 2005, POLICE ACTING ON a tip flagged down a minibus coming off the expressway in Hengyang, Hunan's second-largest city. They followed their noses to a cardboard box stashed in a luggage area in the back of the bus and smelling of urine and feces. Inside were four very young babies, just a few months old. Listening for cries, they found other boxes containing a total of twelve infants. The babies were sent to a nearby hospital and the suspects were taken into custody on charges of human trafficking.

Over the next few weeks, the police set up dragnets around the highways and train station. They nabbed three more suspects on a train from southern China arriving at the Hengyang station. Another van was intercepted on the road. In all, twenty-seven people were arrested, many of them related and going by the family name *Duan*. There were three siblings, Duan Yueneng, thirty-seven, and his younger sisters, Meilin and Zhilin; their parents; and various in-laws and cousins.

Upon questioning, police learned that the Duans came from the lowest rung of Chinese society—they'd been chicken farmers, garbage pickers, nannies, and porters. Then by the early 2000s, they'd become entrepreneurs, owners of a thriving business that trafficked babies. The suspects freely admitted what they were doing; in fact, they were proud of it. They insisted that it was a legitimate enterprise because they were selling babies to social welfare institutions, which in turn ran orphanages. These institutions were run by the government. It had to be legal.

IN 1991, CHINA had quietly enacted a comprehensive adoption law that allowed foreigners to adopt Chinese children. Until then, adoption was available for only a handful of foreigners with family ties to China. But something needed to be done with the children who were piling up in the orphanages, sometimes three to a crib. In the 1980s and 1990s, various Chinese reports put the number of abandoned children at 100,000 to 160,000 per year. Meanwhile, domestic adoption had become practically impossible. Authorities had cracked down on the traditional practice of sending extra babies to be fostered by family or neighbors and instituted huge fees for legal adoptions, which were limited to married, childless couples both aged at least thirty-five. (It was later lowered to thirty.) For the purpose of population control, Chinese policymakers had reasoned that it was pointless for these unregistered over-quota children to remain in China, especially in orphanages, where they would be costly wards of the state.

For a country obsessed with losing face, it was an embarrassing concession. By opening up the country for international adoption, China was in effect acknowledging that the Communist Party had erred. Most babies were heading to the United States. In Chinese, the United States is called Meiguo, a rough transliteration of the sound of *America* plus *guo,* the word for "country." The name was bestowed in the nineteenth century, a time when Americans were preferred to the British and Europeans, the colonial powers who'd tried to carve up China. But the Cold War had transformed the United States into the principal adversary, and hostility lingered long after the normalization of diplomatic relations. Many of the adoption agencies were run by missionaries, the very people who had been booted out of the country after the communists took power in 1949.

Melody Zhang, a Chinese-born official with the Saint Louis–based Children's Hope International, one of the first agencies to handle Chinese adoptions, says the Chinese government's decision was motivated by rising concern about conditions in the overcrowded orphanages.

"In the early nineties, people in the government in China were open-minded enough," said Zhang, who worked closely in those years with China's Ministry of Civil Affairs in setting up the program. She believes the official who advocated for international adoption was Peng Peiyun, minister of family planning, as it happens the only female member of the State Council, a powerful body that is the equivalent of the American cabinet. Although she was not privy to the deliberations inside Zhongnanhai, the secretive leadership compound in Beijing, Zhang says she was "told the top leadership wanted to give these children a chance. And that these adoptions will build bridges of friendship with the United States."

Like the panda diplomacy, in which China supplied foreign zoos with its most photogenic export, adoptions were a way to extend the country's soft power.

The adoptees would become the "people-to-people envoys between China and foreign countries in the twenty-first century," Guo Sijin, then director of the China Center of Adoption Affairs, said at a 1999 reception for Scandinavian adoption officials.

Inside China, foreign adoption wasn't exactly a secret, but it wasn't publicized either. Orphanages were housed within larger social welfare institutions, which were discreetly tucked away in city outskirts and sometimes misleadingly labeled as kindergartens. When adoptive parents—usually Caucasian—came to China to pick up their babies, they did so at hotels in nearby cities. They were discouraged from visiting the orphanages, since the presence of *laowai*, or "foreigners," would attract stares and raise obvious questions.

On the other hand, Americans knew all about adopting from China. The program quickly exceeded expectations. In 1992, the first full year of the policy, 206 babies were adopted to the United States, according to State Department statistics; by 2005, the number had exploded to 7,906, making China the largest source of children adopted internationally, topping South Korea, which had dominated through the 1980s. Interest in Chinese adoption spread beyond the United States. Soon Spaniards, Canadians, British, Dutch, French, and Australians—among others—were enthusiastically lining up for Chinese girls.

China's approach was perfectly tailored to meet the preferences of Western families. Adopting families usually wanted girls, not boys, believing that they would assimilate more easily in new environments, and some 95 percent of Chinese children offered for adoption were female, at least through the early 2000s. White families, anxious about adopting children of another race, were often comfortable with Asians. Chinese regulations favored older adoptive parents—at least thirty-five years old—which happened to fit the demographics of Western couples, who married later and often didn't consider adoption until after failed attempts to conceive naturally or through in vitro fertilization. There were other prospective parents who'd given up on finding a mate. At least initially, the Chinese law allowed adoptive single parents, which opened a pathway for gay couples to adopt, although they couldn't openly declare their sexual orientation.

The babies from China were less likely to have birth defects than other international adoptees. Chinese birth mothers sometimes had better prenatal health than their Western counterparts, since they came from the countryside, where women tended not to drink or smoke. Fetal alcohol syndrome was rare. Rates of malnutrition had dropped dramatically in China, so birth mothers were reasonably well nourished but unlikely to suffer from obesity.

Chinese adoption looked systematic, predictable, and relatively corruption-free. The Chinese government would eventually sign a convention reached at The Hague in 1993 designed to prevent the alarmingly common problem of children from poorer countries in effect being sold to the rich. Although more than four hundred social welfare institutions were participating in the adoption program, arrangements and money were handled in Beijing through the China Center of Adoption Affairs (later renamed the China Center for Children's Welfare and Adoption). The centralized bureaucracy appealed to parents navigating the bewildering process of adoption. "China has a model adoption program which has been specifically praised by the U.S. Congress. In addition to having a large source of healthy infants, adoptions from China are often less expensive than from other countries, and the process is much more predictable and stable," advertised one adoption agency. And nobody with a heart could resist the satisfaction that came from rescuing a discarded child.

Word of mouth quickly circulated among prospective parents about how well these Chinese girls adapted to life in the United States. Unlike the earlier generation of adoptees from Korea, who were often the only Asians in white Christian communities, the Chinese adoptees usually had company. A critical mass of Chinese adoptees ensured that the girls did not feel like outliers, especially in larger cities with ethnic Chinese communities. By the mid-1990s, Chinese babies had become the international adoptees of choice. New Yorkers joked about seeing so many Chinese girls in the strollers of New York City that people did a double take if the mother also appeared to be Chinese. The phenomenon was trumpeted by a 1993 cover story in *The New York Times Magazine,* "How Li Sha, Abandoned in Wuhan, Became Hannah Porter, Embraced in Greenwich Village."

The girls, with their shiny black pigtails, were media darlings in the United States—photographed taking ballet lessons, wearing pretty velvet dresses as they attended performances of *The Nutcracker,* riding ponies, visiting Disneyland. Stories abounded about how Chinese adoptees excelled socially and academically. Celebrities boasted of their adoptee kin. "We have embraced her with a loyalty that is all the more tenacious for having not been preordained by biology," columnist Ellen Goodman wrote movingly of her adopted granddaughter. "Together, we have all learned about the globalization of love." Thoughtful adoptive parents set up Chinese-heritage camps and support groups so that their daughters wouldn't feel alienated from their culture—a complaint often voiced by the earlier generation of Korean adoptees. Pediatricians and psychologists developed specialties treating Chinese adoptees. It was a feel-good story with excellent visuals: adorable little girls who had been rescued from the garbage heaps of China now living the good life in America or Europe.

Everybody wanted a Chinese daughter. Demand was soaring. But just when it seemed the supply of abandoned baby girls was inexhaustible, it wasn't.

BY THE TURN of the new millennium, economic and social changes sweeping rural China made families more reluctant to give up their daughters. Young women who left the countryside to work in factories were making nearly as much money as men and often sending it home to their parents. They didn't always quit work when they married. From 1980 to 2010, the rural share of China's population dropped from 80 percent to under 50 percent, according to World Bank data. Urbanization meant that people were living in smaller homes. They didn't need coercion to stop having babies; they simply preferred smaller families. Chinese policymakers also were slowly beginning to grasp that a demographic catastrophe was in the making. The disproportionate number of boys born in the 1980s and 1990s was about to produce a glut of bachelors unable to find wives. Labor shortages loomed just over the horizon. Although China wouldn't get around to changing the law until 2015, the enforcement was easing in many (though not all) parts of the country. It became easier for families to keep their daughters. In any case, rural income had risen enough that farmers could pay the fines. And if somebody really didn't want a girl, they might have an (illegal) ultrasound and then abort. Fewer babies were being abandoned. China was running out of adoptable baby girls, just when demand was highest. "Supply chain problems" we would call it in today's terminology.

This was heartbreaking for the families overseas who were waiting to adopt. For the orphanages, it was a catastrophe. There was big money in adoption, and the orphanages had become dependent on it. Besides the basic adoption fees, which were handled in Beijing, adopting parents were required to make an additional off-the-books "donation" to the orphanage that had fostered their daughter. The fee was set at three thousand dollars, although in some places it later rose to five thousand. The idea, fair enough, was to compensate the orphanage for the feeding and care of the baby. But the money couldn't be tacked onto other fees paid by wire or check. It had to be delivered in person in crisp new hundred-dollar bills. If it was an uncomfortably large sum for the mostly middle-class Western parents to carry with them in cash, stashed away in fanny packs or tightly gripped briefcases, it was a veritable fortune in rural China.

All that cash injected a volatile new element of corruption into the system. Orphanage directors barely made three thousand dollars in an entire year, and it was no surprise that some got in trouble for misappropriating the money. One was charged with buying himself a Mercedes-Benz, which he claimed was necessary for escorting adoptive parents from abroad.

But in fairness, the orphanages *really* did need the money. In the Chinese administrative system, orphanages are part of larger organizations known as Social Welfare Institutes. These institutes have a range of responsibilities that include caring for the disabled and elderly. They receive government funding but are expected to supplement their budgets with various schemes. In a society governed by Confucian concepts of filial loyalty, the elderly are supposed to be cared for by their offspring (the law makes neglect of one's parents a crime), but people who'd been restricted to one child often didn't have a functional surviving adult able or willing to fill that role. Increasing numbers of disabled children, boys more than girls, were being abandoned by families who couldn't afford medical treatment. The social welfare institutions were in a bind; their obligations were growing and their funding from national and local government was minimal.

Those three-thousand-dollar "donations" were what kept the system afloat. They needed more babies.

*   *   *

THAT'S WHERE THE child traffickers came in. The Duans' story followed a familiar trajectory—rags to riches, riches to prison. At the start of the 1990s, the Duans were down on their luck. While the Chinese economy was roaring, lifting millions out of poverty, they remained in a ground-floor apartment with chipping paint in Changning, a township outside of Hunan's second-largest city, Hengyang. Duan Yueneng, the oldest son, had cycled through various low-paying jobs at factories that hadn't lasted long, in hard times falling back on scavenging scrap metal to recycle. "The only thing I hadn't done was beg," he said when I interviewed him in 2010.

Their woes mounted. His wife killed herself after failing to give birth to a son. His two younger sisters had only primary school educations and couldn't find work at all.

The Duans' mother, Chen Zhijin, rescued her hapless adult children from penury. Chen, a tiny pixie of a woman with close-cropped hair that hugged her face like a tulip, was illiterate to the point that she couldn't even write her name. In 1993, she got a job as an *ayi,* or "aunty," a Chinese term for a female domestic worker, at an orphanage in her hometown. It was the lowest level of job, paying only one dollar a day, but she didn't mind. Chen loved babies.

Enforcement of the one-child policy was at its most unforgiving at the time. By many accounts, it was not uncommon to find abandoned babies in the 1980s and early 1990s. "When it was dark, people would leave babies. Sometimes at the side of the road or in front of an orphanage," Chen would later recall. They were sometimes left with a bag of sugar, thought by rural people to give a baby strength. By the time Chen found them, the babies were often crawling with ants, attracted to the sweet smell. It broke her heart. She couldn't help but bring the babies to her home.

One girl she kept for six months, crying her eyes out when she finally decided it would be best to give up the girl to the orphanage.

"You're crying so much. You'd think that girl was your granddaughter," her boss teased her.

At first, Chen had to plead with the orphanage to take in the babies, especially if they were weak, disabled, or in need of medical attention.

"We don't have enough food or people to care for the babies. We can't take any more," the orphanage director chided her.

That attitude changed in the mid-1990s when orphanages around Hunan began participating in the international-adoption program. The director, who had once been so dismissive, now welcomed her to his office and greeted her with an ingratiating smile.

"Aunty. You're such a good person. Bring me all the babies you can find," the director told her.

Chen soon became known around town as the kindly old lady who could safely deliver unwanted babies to the orphanage. She'd be contacted by an aunt or a grandmother, sometimes a man who claimed he was just "helping a friend." There was still a social stigma to abandoning a baby, and it was against the law. Chen was a useful intermediary.

The orphanage reimbursed her expenses with a small tip, tucked discreetly into an envelope like a thank-you note. At first it was a fifty-yuan bill (roughly five dollars), then one hundred yuan. As abandoned babies became scarcer, the sums grew larger.

These were good deeds of the best kind: the kind that made money. What had been largely a charitable undertaking quickly evolved into a very profitable business. In 1999, Chen's son-in-law (the husband of daughter Duan Meilin) got a job working on a chicken farm in Wuchuan, in the southeasternmost corner of Guangdong Province. Guangdong is the manufacturing hub of southern China, which produces many of the world's toys, electronics, and Christmas ornaments, and just about any export imaginable. Babies among them, it turns out. Perhaps because of the patriarchal culture of southern China and the large population of young, unmarried migrant workers, Guangdong seemed to produce more unwanted girl babies than other parts of China.

Living near the chicken farm was an older woman, Liang Guihong, like Chen, illiterate and fond of babies. She had been a garbage collector, and in this line of work, she often came across babies. She kept up to twenty at a time lined up on a queen-size bed with blankets or plastic sheeting underneath them. She didn't have money for cribs or diapers.

For the Duan family, Liang's baby nursery was a gold mine. At the time, Hunan had many orphanages that had been cleared by the government to handle international adoptions, but they didn't have the goods. That is to say, the babies. And it was illegal to traffic the babies between provinces.

As one Hunan orphanage director, Wang Huachun, later told the police, according to court records: "Under our policies, we weren't allowed to accept babies from other provinces. But in 2001, we started a service to allow foreigners to adopt babies. The fee we would receive was three thousand dollars. Because there were not enough babies in the orphanage, I talked to my supervisor and was told yes, we can accept from other provinces."

The orphanages were competing with one another to procure babies. The envelopes of cash handed to the Duans were getting ever thicker. If a baby was especially pretty and healthy, the traffickers might get as much as six hundred dollars. Even after giving the old woman near the chicken farm her cut, they were making more money than they'd ever dreamed of.

The Duans rented a house of their own near the farm and set themselves up for a long-term business. They hired new staff and sought new sources of supply. They enlisted a midwife. They paid the elderly proprietor of a tea stall—a place where people often exchanged gossip—to tip them off about unwanted and abandoned babies. Various Duan siblings, cousins, in-laws, and neighbors signed up. Many hands were needed to transport babies on the five-hundred-mile train trip from Wuchuan up to Hunan Province, where the orphanages needed more babies. One or two couriers would work together, usually women, who attracted less attention. A pair of traffickers could carry up to four babies, often putting them in cardboard boxes stashed under the train seats. Some couriers were later accused of sedating the babies to keep them quiet.

It wasn't risk-free. On at least three occasions, the traffickers attracted the attention of railroad police and were arrested. Once, in 2003, the three Duan siblings were arrested together and turned over to the police in Qidong County, another part of Hengyang. The head of the orphanage in Changning came to their defense, confirming that, yes, these people were in essence working for the government, bringing babies to the state-run orphanage. The police did their job, traveling from Hunan to Changning to investigate the source of the babies. They determined that the babies were indeed being trafficked for sale but that they did not appear to have been kidnapped.

The Duan siblings spent a month in jail after this first arrest before being released. They decided then that selling babies had become too dangerous and that they ought to quit, but the orphanage directors convinced them to keep going. Business was booming. The orphanages competed with one another for babies. Duan Yueneng would later recall that his mobile phone rang constantly with new orders. The orphanage officials invited him to meals and bought him gifts of expensive liquor.

"They couldn't get enough babies. They kept calling," he said.

Duan Yueneng couldn't say no. He used to be a punk, a migrant worker in plastic sandals. Now he was a businessman wearing brand-name athletic shoes and a shiny black leather jacket. He paid for his father to renovate their apartment. He felt rich.

Only later would he realize that the real money was going to the orphanages and what he was getting, as his father would put it, was like "the dregs of the tofu."

When the Duans went on trial in 2006, their attorneys obtained a wealth of previously confidential documents from the orphanages, which eventually found their way to journalists (myself included).

The secrets of the adoption business were spilled out to the public. In the trial, prosecutors were able to present evidence of three hundred babies sold to six orphanages, but the Duans later told journalists that the numbers were in the thousands and that the babies had gone to orphanages all over China. It was a professionally run operation: There were receipts and invoices, ledgers indicating how much the orphanages had paid the traffickers. There were no euphemisms. There were "buyers" and "sellers" of babies. Just like any other trade except that the merchandise was human. "Single eyelid." "Small mouth."

In the end, the Duans took the fall for everybody. Only one orphanage director served any prison time. (Investigators later said it was because he didn't pay a bribe.) Members of the Duan family were sentenced to up to fifteen years in prison. The Chinese government was trying to contain the scandal and preserve the system, pinning all the blame on these lone "evil, greedy criminals," as they were demonized in the state press.

The Duans later said they were just one family among many who were selling babies to the orphanages. They insisted that the real fault lay with a government that harshly penalized families for unlicensed births while failing to set up any legal mechanism for babies to be turned over to an orphanage. Experiments in setting up "baby hatches" for families to safely abandon children were discontinued because virtually all the children were sick or disabled, overwhelming the limited resources of the social welfare institutions. The Duans had found their market niche.

"I would make sure those babies were safe. I would bathe them and feed them," said the mother, Chen, soon after she got out of prison. "You can judge for yourself: Was I a good or a bad person?"

It was true that the trafficking system worked for a while. Babies made it to the orphanages. The orphanages earned money, building hotels, old-age homes, playgrounds. The adoptive parents were thrilled with their daughters. One might say it was a win-win situation. Except that it was all illegal, in violation of international law. And that three-thousand-dollar cash donation for a baby was in effect a bounty that incentivized a wave of kidnapping of female babies and toddlers.

The statistics made clear what was happening. Up until 2001, about three-quarters of the young children abducted were boys, presumably taken by traffickers to sell to families who needed a male heir. After about 2000, the rates began to equalize, according to a study commissioned by the National Bureau of Economic Research. (The study also found that abductions had increased dramatically during the periods when the one-child policy was most vigorously enforced.) The cases were shocking.

In 2004, a man jumped out of a van on a busy road in Dongyuan County, Guangdong Province, and snatched a sixteen-month-old girl from the arms of an eight-year-old cousin walking along the side of the road. The owner of a teahouse in Chongqing walked out to the market in the summer of 2003 without realizing that his twenty-five-month-old daughter had tried to follow him. When he returned to the tea shop and realized she was missing, he and his wife put up missing posters around the town, including at the gates of an orphanage. They got no response. The father asked to search the orphanage for his child but was refused entry. After a few weeks, his wife managed to sneak into the orphanage on the pretext of volunteering as a nanny and recognized her daughter. She had arrived just in time. The orphanage had already started the paperwork to send her out for adoption.

The orphanages weren't charged with direct involvement in the kidnappings. They were more like fences who didn't question the origins of the stolen goods dropped at their doorstep. They disclaimed any responsibility. "We can only take care of the child. It is up to the public security bureau [police] to investigate if that child was really abandoned," said Chen Ming, a former orphanage director from Hengyang, as it happens the only one who served any jail time.

Wang Huachun, the orphanage director who admitted to buying babies from the Duans, made the more ludicrous assertion that the traffickers were responsible for vetting the children. "I told them, 'If there's been any fraud or theft, the consequences are on you,'" he told police, according to the handwritten notes.

Fair enough, but there was another hitch. The orphanages had to explain how they'd come into custody of these babies. To comply with international law, the orphanages were required to look for birth families before putting babies up for adoption. They had to publish notices detailing where the babies were found, what they were wearing, and any other information indicating they had been willingly abandoned, not kidnapped or stolen.

They needed to launder these trafficked babies to turn them into bona fide orphans. That's where the real fraud would take place.

CHAPTER SEVEN

CREATING ORPHANS

A child in an orphanage in Guizhou Province.

LIKE MANY CHINESE ORPHANAGES, SHAOYANG'S WAS HARD TO
find. Housed behind the nondescript gates of the Social Welfare Institute, it was located on a seldom trafficked road in the south where the
city dissolves into farmland. Nowadays the institute is a sprawling compound with an imposing high-rise administrative headquarters out
front. But before extensive renovation a decade ago, it was a squat,
three-story building with a tiled façade like an inside-out bathroom.
The institute was established in 1952, in the early years of the People's
Republic of China. Thousands of these institutes were set up to replace
the Christian charities, foundling homes, and shelters previously run by
missionaries. After the revolution, the Communist Party expelled most
foreigners and shuttered facilities that they maintained "had a strong
feudal flavor." These new Social Welfare Institutes were designed to

showcase the party's concern for orphans, the disabled, and the elderly. Although they were chronically underfunded, they were important to the party's legitimacy and maintained close ties to the military. One wing within the Shaoyang Social Welfare Institute was reserved for disabled veterans. A military hotel stood across the street. Since 1985, the Shaoyang Institute was headed by Jiang Dewei, a respected former officer of the People's Liberation Army. He had won numerous plaudits for his work. Jiang had been honored by the Hunan Province government in 2004 as an "Advanced Worker of the Provincial Civil Affairs System" and again in 2011 when he was awarded the title of "Hunan Advanced Worker."

At least six orphanages in Hunan were implicated in the Duan trafficking trial. Shaoyang appeared to escape unscathed. No evidence was presented at the trial that Shaoyang had purchased babies from the Duan trafficking network. Or that any of the Duans' trafficked children had ended up being resold to Shaoyang. In all the voluminous sheaves of documents released in the discovery process of the Duan trial, Shaoyang never appeared.

One explanation for how it dodged that scandal: It had a more convenient supplier of adoptable babies. These were the babies who had been confiscated from the villages around Gaoping by the Family Planning office. Evidence would later emerge showing that the children were delivered first to the Civil Affairs office, which oversees Family Planning, and from there to the orphanage. In effect, the government was the trafficker. This was an operation run by highly esteemed Communist Party cadres, unlike the disreputable Duans, who were denounced in the Chinese state press as the "hands of evil."

The birth parents would have hardly suspected this reputable institution. Although Shaoyang oversaw the governance of villages around Gaoping, it was more than a two-hour drive from the villages. For parents without access to a private car, it was a full day's trek.

Of the parents, only the indefatigable Yang Libing, the father whose nine-month-old daughter was taken in 2005, suspected the orphanage's involvement. Yang repeatedly traveled to Shaoyang and tried to get inside. He never managed to get through the front gate. The security was designed to keep out people like him.

But Yang was not so easily dissuaded. He decided not to return to southern China to work and to devote himself full-time to distributing the petition demanding the return of the children. With copies of the petition tucked in a tattered suitcase, he set out in early 2006. He only made it as far as Changsha, the Hunan provincial capital, before he was stopped by the police, who hoped to silence him. But somehow this petition got into the hands of Chinese journalists.

This should have been an explosive story for the Chinese press. The publishing climate had become much more permissive under the leadership of the reform-minded Hu Jintao, China's paramount leader. Newspapers and magazines published articles about environmental degradation, land confiscations, a deadly train collision. Several intrepid Chinese reporters tried to pursue the story of the confiscated babies. This subject, they were told by their editors, was too "sensitive" to be published because it dealt with the one-child policy, a pillar of Communist Party rule. But the media had more latitude in Hong Kong, which, although it had reverted from British to Chinese rule in 1997, still enjoyed a measure of self-rule.

In March 2006, a short article ran in the *South China Morning Post*, the territory's English-language newspaper. The article reported that thirteen children had been confiscated by Family Planning, and it quoted Yang Libing and a few others who had signed the petition. The article didn't tie the confiscations to international adoption. And it didn't mention the Duan trafficking case, which had received more publicity both inside and outside China.

The Duan trafficking case and the baby confiscations both surfaced within months of each other in early 2006. The two scandals were unrelated. Family Planning officials weren't working with the Duans. The Duans hadn't sold babies to Shaoyang. But they both circled back to the same market forces, the insatiable demand around the world for healthy, adoptable babies. That demand came from the United States, Europe, and to a lesser extent Australia; and the lubricant was that three thousand dollars in cash, the crisp hundred-dollar bills.

Combined, the two scandals marked the beginning of a very slow reckoning about international adoption in China. They shattered many of the myths about Chinese adoption, horrifying adoptive parents who had been assured repeatedly that the program was corruption-free. And when the birth parents eventually found out, it would be a revelation. They hadn't appreciated the demand for their daughters outside of China. If Americans and other wealthy foreigners wanted these babies so badly, they had to reconsider their own bias against girls. They would realize that, no, daughters were not like spilled water. Their lives weren't as cheap as kittens'. They were so precious that people would steal, cheat, and lie to get them.

THE CHINESE GOVERNMENT temporarily suspended all adoptions from Hunan Province. The county government conducted its own investigation and prepared a report titled "Longhui County's Investigation of Petition to Beijing Arising from Family Planning Work." Dated March 12, 2006, it was never released publicly, although investigative reporter Pang Jiaoming was leaked a copy, which he shared with other reporters.

The investigators didn't interview a single parent, only the Family Planning officials. Predictably, it was a complete whitewash.

Family Planning officials defended themselves, saying they had confiscated only children who had been illegally adopted by villagers. In fact, they had tricked many parents and grandparents, such as Yang Libing's father, into signing false statements claiming the children were abandoned babies they had picked up from the streets. Then they'd tell the parents, *Whoops, sorry, you are not eligible to adopt after all because of the strict requirements in the new laws.* And since the adoptive parents were "unable to account for the adoptees' origins," the child had to be sent to the welfare institution to determine if he or she had been kidnapped.

Not only couldn't the family reclaim the child or visit the child, but they had absolutely no right to know where that child had been taken. "According to the adoption legislation, the City Welfare Institutes have to keep the details of both adoptees and their adopters confidential. Only the Welfare Institutes may know the basic whereabouts of each child," the report stated.

THE ZENGS MOVED back to the village in 2005 as the petition was being drafted. It was nearly three years after Fangfang had been taken, but they were still hopeful she would be returned. They arranged to meet with Old Yuan. Soon after they arrived, Old Yuan hitched a ride up to the village to visit the family. He interviewed both parents at home so that their account could be added to the petition and briefed the family on what had happened with others. Out of character, Zeng Youdong stomped his feet and yelled. He was beside himself, almost shaking with rage. Zanhua, who tended to be the more talkative of the couple, could barely speak.

"She just cried the entire time. She couldn't stop crying," Yuan would later recall.

Zanhua joined the continuing meetings at the carpentry shop. One day she steeled her nerves and accompanied other parents going to complain to the Family Planning office in the yellow building in Gaoping. They figured there would be safety in numbers. When they arrived, Family Planning officials were sitting around playing cards. They barely looked up.

"It was your fault for having too many children," one of them snapped at Zanhua. They went back to their card game.

Zeng had earned enough money in Chongqing to pay off his accumulating fines to Family Planning. Since they hadn't found Fangfang, they focused on their four other children—the older daughters, the twin

Shuangjie, and their newborn son. The younger children still needed *hukou*s so they could attend school. As the children of migrants, they'd received no education in Chongqing other than what Zanhua, with her marginal literacy, was able to provide by reading to them from picture books. They enrolled in the same village school as their mother and older sisters had, except by then the dilapidated wooden buildings had been replaced by concrete.

Life in the village was much improved. Brick houses sprouted at the edge of the rice paddies, rising one floor at a time as their owners gradually accumulated funds from their migrant labor. A small shop had opened selling cigarettes, beer, miscellaneous candies, and snacks. Minivans called *mianbao che*, "bread loaf cars," so named because of their shape, started service to Gaoping.

Like their parents' generation before, the children had responsibilities on the farm. The older girls took turns getting up at 6:00 A.M. to feed the oxen. Although by then the family could have afforded a tractor, the animals were better at navigating the terraced fields—small, irregularly shaped, and flooded with knee-deep water. It was difficult to mechanize this kind of farming. Cultivating rice was a painstaking process: germinating the seeds in bundles of wet rags, planting, and transplanting again. With their young, limber bodies low to the ground, children excelled at the repetitive job of constantly bending into the calf-deep water to plant the young seedlings a suitable distance apart. They used sickles for the harvest and hoes to loosen the earth and pull out the weeds. In the dry land adjacent to the rice paddies, they planted cabbages, carrots, and radishes. The Zengs had about twelve *mu* of land—roughly two acres—to farm, more than some other families because neighbors who had left the village had given them permission to cultivate their land as well. Everybody pitched in, although not at the exhausting pace that had robbed the preceding generation of childhood. China was wealthier now. The children could go to school and still have time left to play.

When the children weren't working, their playground was infinite, the unfenced, unbounded landscape that stretched out far beyond their own terraced fields. They roamed through the mountains, splashed in the streams, and scooped out tiny fish. The bamboo groves offered a variety of diversions for the energetic and creative. Toppled bamboo placed over a cement block could easily become a seesaw. The wood was supple enough that a child could catapult into the air or bounce as though it were a trampoline. Girls strung ropes between the closely spaced trunks for jumping. In front of their grandmother's house, a cherry tree exploded with brilliant blossoms in spring. The mountains were thick with cypress, pine, chestnut, and bayberry trees, squat and bushy, excellent for climbing. Shuangjie, a lively child, once took a nasty spill from one of the bayberries and split open her lip. During a winter with a rare accumulation of snow, she and her brother collected scrap wood to make a sled, although they gave up after a few spills.

The parents took turns working outside the village. Every other year, Youdong would go out to do portering or construction work. Zanhua worked in a noodle restaurant in Guangdong. The arrangement ensured that somebody would bring in cash while the other would take care of the children and Zeng's father, who was by then a widower. Over time, Zeng was more often the one remaining in the village, as he was expert at maintaining the earthen berms that enclosed the rice paddies and keeping clear the irrigation channels that regulated the flow of water. They had plenty of food. They had enough cash earnings that they could keep building the house, which by tradition would be given to their son to carry on the Zeng family line. The family got their first television set in 2007. Not long after came a *sanlunche*, a motorized three-wheeled cart that farmers liked because it was cheap and convenient for carrying produce to market.

Zeng was a devoted father. After Shuangjie started middle school, located in Gaoping, he would often drive her so that she didn't have to wait for the bus. He thought she was the cleverest of his children, with an excellent memory and an uncanny sense of direction. In that way, she was not unlike the twin sister she had barely known.

Fangfang's absence hovered like the shadow of a death in the family. It was a sadness that was rarely discussed but never forgotten. Shuangjie had no actual memories of Fangfang, since they had been separated at six months, but she conjured up images of a little girl who looked just like her. As her older sisters entered puberty, Shuangjie felt left behind, yearning for a playmate her age. She fantasized about what it would be like to have her back. What fun it would be if they could go to school together, switch clothes, trick their friends and teachers.

For lack of any better guidance, Zeng hired a fortune teller who used the traditional Chinese method of examining one's fate by the year, month, day, and hour of birth, the so-called four pillars of destiny. The fortune teller told them that Fangfang was alive and thriving and would have a brilliant future. And that one day they would see her again. Zeng wasn't sure he believed. He'd always disdained superstition. But the prediction gave him encouragement to keep looking.

Zeng wasn't a rabble-rouser like Yang Libing, but he didn't give up on his daughter either. If Fangfang was alive, he figured she had to be somewhere in China, probably nearby being raised by another family. The suggestion that his daughter might be in the United States—one of the many rumors he heard—was as outlandish as saying she'd been abducted by aliens and taken to the moon.

By the time they moved back, Fangfang would have been five years old. He figured she looked just like Shuangjie and that he could easily recognize her. Whenever he was at a market or on a busy street, he would scan the crowd, looking for her. At times, he thought he spotted her. A girl with pronounced cheekbones, twinkly eyes. He studied groups of schoolchildren, round-faced girls with glossy pigtails, and girls being held by the hand by parents who had learned by now to clutch their children tightly. None of them looked quite like his daughter.

WITH THE WISDOM that comes long after the fact, it isn't hard to explain why the birth families remained ignorant for so long about the whereabouts of their daughters. Although Zeng and others would eventually figure out that their children went to the Shaoyang orphanage, they assumed they remained within China—either adopted by Chinese families or sold for some nefarious purpose. Nothing had been published about international adoption that they could easily access. The stories about the Duans in the state press didn't mention that the trafficked children had been intended to go overseas. The county's investigation about Family Planning's confiscations, completed in 2006, hadn't been made public. The birth families didn't read newspapers, much less newspapers published in Hong Kong in English.

Most important: They wouldn't have seen the obscure legal journals in which the orphanages had advertised the finding of orphans. In short, the parents' ignorance was by design. They weren't supposed to know what was happening.

INTERNATIONAL LAW REQUIRED that orphanages conduct a search for the birth family before they offered a baby up for adoption. To comply, the Hunan Civil Affairs Bureau had placed legal notices in local newspapers declaring that children in their care were to be put up for adoption.

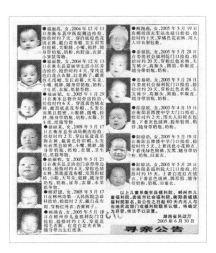

Under the heading "Seeking Family," the advertisements gave sixty days for parents or guardians to step forward. After that, the children were legally classified as orphans.

The ads ran in the back pages of the *Hunan Daily* and the *Hunan Legal Daily*. These newspapers weren't sold in the villages. Parents with imperfect literacy wouldn't have read them anyway. On the minuscule chance that they'd obtained the newspapers, they would not have recognized the references to their own children. The "finding ads" disguised the true circumstances by which the babies had come to the orphanages. Only in later years would they routinely include photographs. And the ads assigned new names reflecting the orphanages where the babies were placed. All the babies in Shaoyang had the same family name—*Shao*. (The dates are given according to the lunar calendar.)

> Shao Mingao, female, picked up at the doorstep of the Shaoyang Welfare Institute on May 1, 2005, dressed in a yellow top with red trousers.

Years later, when the case was investigated, it was confirmed this was Yang Libing's daughter, taken from the arms of her grandmother in the village. Yang had tried to find his daughter in the orphanage the following month—well within the sixty days—but was not admitted.

> Shao Yangfu, female, picked up at Shaoyang, pub mill entrance. September 24, 2004.

She was actually the third daughter of a farmer named Yuan in Fengxing, the same village where Yang Libing lived.

> Shao Minguan, female, picked up at the entrance of Longhui County government building, Gaoping. December 26, 2005.

She was the first child of a young couple, aged twenty and nineteen, who were too young to register their marriage.

And finally, there was

Shao Fuquan, female, picked up in Shaoyang City, Bamboo Arts Factory, main gate. June 4, 2002.

That was Fangfang, taken from her aunt in Shanghuang village.

ALL THE INFORMATION WAS FABRICATED. In order to make the babies legally adoptable, they had to be transformed into orphans. This was the same technique that the orphanages employed to effectively "launder" the babies delivered by the trafficking rings. These were entirely new backstories, spun out of the imagination of some bureaucrat. Somebody—often a friend or relative of an orphanage employee—had found this baby in a basket. Or maybe in a box or wrapped in a blanket. It would be at a market, the side of a road, a factory gate—some plausible location. The fictions were often accompanied by a falsified police report. The same techniques were used with the hundreds, maybe tens of thousands, of babies sold by the Duans and others.

The lies would be recorded in the orphanage ledgers. When overseas parents adopted, the lies would be repeated in the paperwork they were given. Eventually, the adoptees would be old enough to read the documents themselves, as they tried to make sense of their personal histories.

In adult life, these young women, now mostly in their twenties and thirties, would struggle to figure out what had happened to them. *Where did I come from? How did I get here? Who am I really?*

Part Two

BEIJING

CHAPTER EIGHT

MY STORY

Yang family daughters in Tianxi village.

THE WOMEN OF MY GENERATION CAME OF AGE BELIEVING THAT our lives held infinite possibilities. We threw ourselves into everything—careers, creative endeavors, travel and adventure—postponing child-bearing until the point that fertility declined. By the time I was in my thirties, I knew many people who had adopted Chinese baby girls—friends, former classmates, colleagues, a cousin. China was an appealing destination for my circle of friends. Like me, they were people who lived or worked abroad, some also foreign correspondents. They were well traveled, idealistic, and curious about other cultures. They liked the idea of providing a home to a girl who might otherwise have been discarded.

In 2002, I was living in Seoul, South Korea, as a correspondent for the *Los Angeles Times* when one of my best friends adopted a baby girl in China. I wanted to be there with her and her husband to mark the occasion. I packed up the baby clothes of my two-year-old son and caught a flight to Guangzhou, in southern China.

The city on the northern banks of the Pearl River was the clearing point for many American adoptions because the city's U.S. consulate had been designated to issue visas for the babies. The most popular hotel was the thirty-seven-story White Swan, located on Shamian Island, a verdant former colonial concession that had been signed away to the French and British during the nineteenth-century Opium Wars. Now it was full of foreigners again. The hotel's hallways were lined with colorful mats to create rubberized play areas, and hotel rooms were furnished with cribs. Each arriving family found a unique gift in their room— a Barbie doll with platinum-blond hair clutching a dark-haired Asian baby. The dolls had been donated by Mattel: That's how much of a phenomenon Chinese adoption had become. A few wags called it the "White Savior Barbie," but cynicism was not the prevailing sentiment at the White Swan. Most guests were adoptive parents, friends, or family members, all swept up in the enchantment of the moment. The squealing of the soon-to-be-American babies echoed through the atrium. One magazine story called the White Swan "the happiest hotel on earth."

In the lobby of the hotel, my friend and her husband were seated next to an artificial waterfall, practically aglow with the flush of new love. The fourteen-month-old girl they'd just met sat on her adoptive mother's lap, beaming as triumphantly as though placed on a throne. Her knowing smile suggested that she understood it all—that she had been matched with people who would love and cherish her forever. The next day, dozens of parents and their friends and families went to the U.S. consulate, then down the street, for a communal ceremony granting the adoptees their visas. When the consul pronounced, "Welcome to the United States," we cheered and cried. There wasn't a dry eye left in the house. All of us—parents, friends, relatives, consulate staff—were overcome. I found the experience as emotionally charged as giving birth myself.

I didn't then question the convenient narrative that prevailed in the adoption community—that these baby girls had been voluntarily aban-

doned and were being rescued through adoption from institutionalization or worse.

After moving to Beijing in 2007 to become the newspaper's China
correspondent, I became more skeptical. My apartment and office were
both in a large compound run by an arm of the Chinese foreign ministry to house diplomats and journalists. Nearby was the compact but
well-manicured Ritan Park, with children's rides and ponds stocked
with shimmering carp. Watching Chinese parents proudly clutching
the hands of their small daughters on sunny weekends, it was hard to
imagine that cultural prejudices against girls ran as deep as foreigners
imagined. Outside the gates of the compound, recyclers drove flat-
bed pedicabs, collecting the high-value garbage of the expatriate elite.
A recycling culture prevailed. Nothing went to waste. I'd seen how
people picked up items that I couldn't imagine anybody would want—
magazines from the former Yugoslavia in Serbo-Croatian, a language
that ceased to exist after Serbia and Croatia broke up (a story I covered
in the 1990s), obsolete computer monitors nearly as big as dishwash-
ers. Could healthy human babies be tossed away so casually, especially
without remuneration? My doubts were bolstered by stories that were
beginning to trickle out about corruption. The Duan family's trafficking
trial had gotten extensive coverage the year before.

This was a very open period for China, at least relative to both the
preceding decades and what would follow. In the early years of the People's Republic of China, the Communist Party's antipathy to the United
States meant that only a handful of American journalists, like Edgar
Snow, author of *Red Star over China,* had access to the leadership, with
the rest of the press pack sniffing for rumors out of Hong Kong. After
the normalization of relations with the United States in 1979, news organizations set up bureaus in Beijing, but correspondents weren't allowed
to travel outside the capital without getting permission, often ten days in
advance. That had started to change by the time I arrived. Beijing was
hosting the 2008 Summer Olympics, an event billed as a coming-out
party for a new, improved, and more tolerant China. As part of its winning bid, the government had promised to improve its human rights

record and to give journalists more freedom to travel around the country. An ambitious expansion to Beijing Capital International Airport with a rail link to the city center made traveling around this vast country surprisingly easy. Although we didn't appreciate it until later, when the window closed, these were golden years for journalists. "Foreigners in a foreign land, we guzzled at the firehose of China at the peak of its growth and ambitions," a fellow journalist, Alec Ash, later wrote of that period. "The protean beast of China charged forward, and we were fleas clinging to its back, along for the ride."

There was not only freedom of movement but also relative freedom of information. By 2007, most Chinese adults had mobile telephones. The iPhone would soon become the indispensable tool of the country's elite, and Chinese manufacturers like Huawei were making competing products at prices that migrant workers and villagers could afford. Smartphones were a democratizing force. In the past, Chinese literacy had been restricted to elites who had time to be educated. Now people with an imperfect command of the difficult characters (including foreigners like me) could write phonetically in the Latin alphabet or send voice messages. For many, these were their first telephones, since landlines were scarce in the countryside. Chinese people were messaging like crazy, spreading news of happenings in the most remote villages around the country and making it harder than ever for the government to keep secrets. In 2009, the first large Chinese social media platform, Weibo, started operations and quickly became the favored platform for people to gripe about local corruption. They no longer had to rely on the archaic system of petitioning. Critical posts were often scrubbed by censors, but not so quickly that they weren't picked up by journalists first.

We scoured social media constantly for story ideas in places that had been inaccessible to journalists. I traveled deep into the heartland of China to write about the degradations suffered by people who were poor and powerless. I interviewed people who got AIDS as a result of unnecessary blood transfusions pushed by the government and families whose intellectually challenged kids had been kidnapped as slave laborers. I traveled on the Tibetan Plateau and in the far-western, largely Muslim region of Xinjiang. Rural Chinese often saw foreign correspondents as champions of their cause because we weren't subject to censorship. (The government could try to control our movements, but it had no mechanism to block what we filed.) In the countryside, we were often greeted with unexpected enthusiasm. On one assignment reporting on lead poisoning in Henan Province, where I was trying to travel incognito with a Chinese assistant, villagers strung a huge banner across a main street reading "Welcome American Journalists." Predictably, we were trailed by unmarked cars the entire time. A taxi driver was so grateful we were there to do the story that he helped us lose the tail and then tried to refuse payment.

From the time I visited my friends and their newly adopted daughter in Guangzhou, I was curious about the origins of these girls. When I was traveling in the countryside, I'd look at the women I passed in the street and wonder if they could be the birth mother of my friend's daughter or of other adoptees I'd met. I had always wanted to write about this subject, and there wouldn't be a better occasion than the present. I was encouraged by my friend Peter Goodman, who had written a story in 2006 for *The Washington Post* about abduction and child trafficking. His editors had discouraged him from pursuing the subject, so he suggested that I follow up to investigate the involvement of government officials. Peter put me in touch with Brian Stuy, an adoptive father based out of Provo, Utah, who remains today the leading expert on corruption in Chinese adoption. Many emails and telephone calls ensued, through which I learned how he came to his cynicism about Chinese adoption.

Raised in the Mormon church, Stuy entered his thirties trying to reconcile the communal imperative to raise a large brood of children and his own admittedly radical environmental activism. Zero population growth, he believed, was needed to protect the planet from the ravages of humanity, and it was more ethical to adopt than to bring another voracious human into the world. He strongly supported China's one-child policy. He and his wife adopted their first daughter from China in 1998 and applied to adopt another. Although the marriage later broke up (largely over his decision to leave the Church of Jesus Christ of Latter-Day Saints), he proceeded to adopt again as a single father in 2002. In 2004, he remarried, this time to a Chinese woman, Longlan, and soon after they adopted a third Chinese daughter.

Thrilled with fatherhood, Stuy developed an insatiable curiosity about how he'd had the luck to parent these amazing daughters. Although he no longer belonged to the church, he was keenly interested in family history and well schooled in the methods of research, having been raised a Mormon. The Church of Jesus Christ of Latter-Day Saints teaches that people are reunited with their ancestors in the afterlife and is at the forefront of genealogical research. The church maintains what may be the world's largest archive of family history, with three billion pages stored on microfiche and microfilm in the climate-controlled Granite Mountain Records Vault, designed to withstand a nuclear attack. The church owns the nonprofit FamilySearch, and Mormons started the largest genealogy nonprofit, Ancestry.com, headquartered in Lehi, Utah, Stuy's hometown.

Stuy wasn't concerned with ancestry, but he did want to know more about his daughters' birth families. He studied the paperwork for his first daughter, Meikina, and saw the names of two women who had found her on a roadside in southern Guangdong Province. On a trip to China in 2000, he asked the orphanage to arrange an interview with one of them. The woman told him how she and her friend heard a faint mewling coming out of a cardboard box and looked inside to find a baby left with an empty bottle and crumpled bills. Stuy was moved that the woman cared enough to provide so much detail about his daughter's finding.

Later, Longlan went back to investigate further. A native of Guangzhou, she had owned a souvenir shop directly across the street from the White Swan Hotel. They'd met when he bought a painting from her. She was savvier than her husband about how things worked. She tracked down the other woman listed as a finder and extracted a confession:

They had nothing to do with this baby. They'd agreed to be named on the paperwork to help the orphanage and later were asked to repeat the original lie to placate an influential parent.

As Stuy later wrote about the experience on his blog:

> Many [orphanage] directors are actually actively lying to you with a smile on their face, working behind the scenes to prevent you from learning the truth about your child's origins and early life. They will take you in the orphanage van to your child's finding location, point to where she was found, even bring forward the person that found her in a basket with some powdered milk and some clothes. All of this is to assure you that what you have been told is true.
>
> It may be. But it probably isn't.

In 2005, Stuy had started blogging about adoption on a website he'd started, Research-China.org, to help other curious adoptive families. "The majority of families are satisfied with the information they get about their child. They put away the adoption files and don't think about it again. But there is a significant percentage who want to know more, and we can help them," he told me. He became an essential resource for those collecting information about orphanages and helping adoptive families investigate their children's origins. He also has been a resource for journalists like me and played a major role in the award-winning 2019 documentary *One Child Nation*.

His wife, Longlan, proved to be an equally dogged investigator. One of their first missions together was to visit newspaper archives to buy up the back issues with the legal notices that orphanages were required to publish before putting a baby up for adoption. Sometimes they had to buy the papers from recyclers. Those finding ads were not routinely provided to adopting families at the time of adoption. They contained some of the earliest photos of the babies—which the Stuys sold to adoptive families.

Originally, the Stuys thought that the ads might provide clues as to the origins of the children. They soon realized it wasn't necessarily so. Inputting the information from thirty thousand ads into spreadsheets, the Stuys realized there were too many coincidences. Too many babies found on the same day or at the same location. The orphanages were lazy liars. They used the same locations and "finders" again and again in the paperwork.

"You won't have ten babies found at a tire shop. If you start to analyze the data, you realize they are making it up," Stuy told me when we first spoke on the telephone.

At the time we first talked, in 2009, Stuy had mostly focused on the trafficking cases, such as that of the Duan family. But he'd become intrigued by the case out of Hunan Province where Family Planning officials had confiscated babies. Trafficking was bad enough, but ripping babies away from their parents was a horrific abuse of government power. So far, the only confirmed cases had been those thirteen that had been reported in Hunan Province, but he was convinced that these abuses were far more widespread.

"The government tried to depict this Shaoyang case as a rogue operation," Stuy told me. "But I'm sure there are more."

He urged me to go out and find them.

ONE OF THE items a Chinese researcher in my office had seen on social media was about Family Planning confiscating babies in Guizhou, a landlocked province just west of Hunan. Guizhou is poor and mountainous, its karst peaks barely navigable. Its population includes a large share of ethnic minorities, such as the Miao, related to the Hmong of Cambodia, and like other impoverished areas, it is a major source of babies sent for adoption. In the summer of 2009, I traveled with two Chinese colleagues by plane and train to Zhenyuan, a stunning riverfront city that, only by dint of its remoteness, was spared swarms of tourists. In the evening, we strolled over an ancient stone bridge and made our way along the riverfront. Swans glided past rippling reflections of red lanterns hanging from balconies over the river. The next morning, daylight illuminated the destitution of the city and its surroundings. We grabbed a taxi. Within minutes of our leaving the center of town, the pavement ran out and we continued onto a rutted dirt road that climbed into the mountains. At some points, we had to get out of the car and push to get over humps and gullies in the road. At a shallow rivulet, the driver (also keen to see the story reported) stopped and arranged stones to form a makeshift trestle the width of his tires so we could cross. We drove for almost two hours, until the car couldn't go any farther, then got out to hike the rest of the way over a rubble-strewn trail. Our destination was a village called Tianxi (literally "heavenly beauty"), little more than a cluster of about a dozen wooden houses on stilts, hugging the mountainside, looking as precarious as if it were all built of matchsticks.

Despite its remoteness, or perhaps because of it, the Family Planning officers had targeted Tianxi. They'd trudge up that same mountain trail we'd taken, looking for unregistered babies. Almost every family had had a baby taken away. The family we met first lost their six-month-old daughter in 2004. She was the result of an unplanned pregnancy. The mother, Yang Shuiying, told us that her husband had undergone a vasectomy a few days before she realized she was pregnant with this child. The couple already had four children, three girls and a boy. But once the baby was born, they loved her and assumed they would raise her along with her older siblings, who were equally besotted with the newest arrival.

"We don't throw away our children. Once you have a baby, you want to raise her," Yang told me. Family Planning came several times to the village, watching her work in the fields with the baby strapped to her back. They were patient stalkers, waiting for the right time to swoop in. One day when her husband was working in town and her kids were at school, they announced themselves at her doorstep.

The officials confidently informed her that the law allowed them to confiscate babies in excess of the quota and that she would not be allowed to challenge them. "I'm illiterate. I didn't know any better," she admitted. When her husband, Lu Xiande, returned, he was so distraught that he had a nervous breakdown and tried to kill himself with a knife. Scars zigzagged across his neck and torso.

The family was probably the poorest I ever met in my seven years in China. Their house was built of wood weathered to a washboard gray, the same as the bare interior walls. There was just enough electricity to power a single bare lightbulb that dangled on a cord from the ceiling, and a hot plate. They had no animals except for a single duck, which they decided to slaughter in honor of my visit. After the husband slit its throat, perhaps with the same knife he used in the attempted suicide, he came to talk to me, holding the dead duck upside down. I still have the notebook stained with a splatter of blood. When we gathered around a low table for lunch, I had a hard time eating, realizing how rare it was that this family got to eat meat.

Nobody else in this desolate village looked to be any wealthier or better educated than our hosts. We interviewed a thirty-two-year-old with buckteeth and hair growing out of a prominent mole on his chin. He appeared to be intellectually impaired. And we talked to an elderly man chewing on the ends of an unlit corncob pipe. As elsewhere, government officials had sniffed out families that had an infirmity that might make them easy marks to have their children confiscated. But they were not without resources. Several villagers owned smartphones, which they proudly displayed in their front shirt pockets, sometimes taking them out to show or wave about. After a number of children were taken, one of the younger, more literate villagers texted a better-educated cousin who worked as a teacher in Guangdong Province, complaining about the confiscations. The cousin researched the family-planning regulations and laws and quickly realized that the officials were bluffing. They had no right to take away babies. He consulted a lawyer, who told him the villagers should file a police report. The cousin did so, also filing complaints with the Zhenyuan municipality, the county, the province, and an internal discipline commission set up to investigate wrongdoing by Communist Party members. At first, nothing happened.

But then the cousin started posting about the case on the internet. Six officials in Zhenyuan were disciplined for failing to ensure that babies put up for adoption were properly abandoned. *Southern Metropolis Daily,* a newspaper based in Guangzhou, published a story, although the government's statement suggested this was only a minor procedural violation. The families were not satisfied. If they couldn't get their children back (which would prove impossible), they at least expected the perpetrators to receive a robust punishment.

Unexpectedly, we would meet some of Zhenyuan's officials later that same day. After returning from the village, we swung by to visit the Zhenyuan orphanage. This put the authorities on immediate alert. As soon as we introduced ourselves, the orphanage director telephoned the head of the town's propaganda department—what China calls public relations—and within minutes, they drove up in a late-model General Motors sedan.

They insisted that they escort us on any further reporting. It seemed pointless to argue. Besides, we had already interviewed the families. As we were ushered into their nice car, we very much appreciated that it had air-conditioning and that we could grill them about Family Planning. If we had tried to schedule an appointment in advance, it would have been denied and our trip to the town blocked. Although, on paper, our valid journalism cards allowed us to travel around the country, often local officials would stop us, saying that we couldn't enter for our own safety. On this occasion, our detention turned out to be a lucky break. It would be one of the few times that foreign journalists got an interview with the people responsible for family planning on the ground.

IN CHINA, FOREIGN REPORTERS often find themselves in a gray area between hostage and honored guest. Although it was already late afternoon, the officials hastily arranged a packed schedule to keep us otherwise engaged for the rest of the day—meals, tours, a cruise on the river. They brought us to dinner at a restaurant on a terrace overlooking the water, where they tried to ply us with *baijiu* and luxury cigarettes.

These formal dinners in China are carefully choreographed. We were seated at a round table with a lazy Susan in the center that revolved

at roughly the same pace as the spin dispensed by the propaganda officials. The defense boiled down to this: They didn't do it, but even if they
did, it was the right thing to do.

"It's a lie that they took babies away without their parents' permission. That's impossible," I was told by Peng Qiuping, the head of the
propaganda office.

Although relatively young, maybe in her thirties, with a ponytail and
wire-rimmed glasses, she seemed to be the senior official of the group
and in my mind personified the type of female cadres who, despite the
entrenched sexism in China, were rising in the ranks of the Communist
Party.

"These parents agreed that the children should be put up for adoption," she told me. "They understood that they were greedy and had
more children than they could afford."

The revolving platter turned again and another speaker piped up.
"The children are better off with their adoptive parents than their birth
parents," interjected a man named Wu Benhua, who identified himself
as the director of Zhenyuan's civil affairs bureau.

According to the reports we'd seen, the orphanage had sent sixty
children abroad, not just to the United States but also to Holland, Sweden, Belgium, and Spain. He claimed that the money from the adoptive
parents—which should have been close to two hundred thousand
dollars—had gone to upgrades of the Social Welfare Institute—as well
as clothing, kitchen equipment, food, and bedding. He didn't mention
that nice air-conditioned car.

The next day, they came to pick us up again to drive us to the train
station. They were keen to see us off and out of town. Ms. Peng, the
propaganda director, gave us each a gift of embroidered slippers she said
had been handmade in Zhenyuan, although when I examined them on
the train, they had a factory label from Guangdong. It didn't matter. A
story didn't have to be believable or even plausible.

CHAPTER NINE

HUNAN PROVINCE

Zanhua and Shuangjie on the footbridge.

AUGUST 2009. THE NEXT DESTINATION WAS HUNAN PROVINCE, where the first reports of confiscated babies had surfaced. Although the story had been reported in the *South China Morning Post* three years earlier, that article didn't connect the confiscations to international adoption. And it received little attention, aside from an excellent report by Dutch television that made a big impact in the Netherlands but was little seen elsewhere. One of the Dutch journalists passed on the contact information for Yuan Chaoren, "Old Yuan," the former schoolteacher who had helped the families draft their petition in 2006. Not yet fifty years old, he'd been nudged into early retirement from teaching because of his activism. He did various odd jobs to support himself. We asked if he would serve as our guide. We'd need him to introduce us to the families and to interpret. Although the Communist Party standardized Chinese after 1949, local dialects persist. Mao's Hunan accent was difficult for many Chinese to understand, and some of the rural dialects are incomprehensible even to mother-tongue speakers. A younger activist was hired to drive us in his Volkswagen Santana. Our guides came to pick us up in Gaoping township, pulling up quickly near the market so that we could slip in unnoticed. We were just around the corner from the Family Planning office, and we didn't want to be on the radar of officialdom.

Yang Libing, the petitioner, remained the most outspoken of the parents, so we headed first to his place in a village called Fengxing. In mid-August, everything was a luxuriant tangle of vines. When we reached Yang's house, morning glories crawled up a trellis outside and squash spilled out from the bounds of the vegetable garden. Although the house was old and sparsely furnished, the walls almost bare except for the yellowing Mao portrait, the family was well dressed, perhaps in honor of our visit. Yang wore a crisp striped polo shirt and spotless white sneakers. His much younger wife, Cao Zhimei, had on a tube top and a flouncy skirt. Their three-year-old son played with their dog, both of them chasing a chicken in the front yard as we spoke.

It had been nearly five years since Yang's daughter was taken. By then he was certain she had been adopted in the United States. Brian Stuy and his wife, Longlan, the investigators from Utah, had managed to track down the adoptive mother through American adoption circles. She was sympathetic, up to a point, and passed along photos to the Stuys to send on to the birth family. Yang had stashed them in a decorative red tin that held other precious family documents. His young son knew it was one of the family's treasures and rushed to get it for us.

One photo sent by the adoptive family showed a girl about four years old wearing a traditional Chinese dress, a *qipao*. Another showed the same child standing next to a friend, wearing a T-shirt that said "Spicy Hunan Girl."

"My sister," the little boy told me proudly.

Yang's wife teared up.

"Everybody in the village adored her. She had big eyes like saucers and a smile for everybody she saw," she said. "They said she looked like me. I wonder if she looks like an American now."

Yang was realistic. He understood that he could not expect to recover his daughter. Photos were all he could hope for. But he hadn't lost the fighting spirit and wanted the culprits punished. "Our children were exported abroad like they were factory products. Our own flesh and blood," Yang told me with some bitterness.

Yang insisted on accompanying us on interviews with other families who had lost children. We all squeezed into the Volkswagen and headed to another village. Sitting on a stoop waiting for us outside her house was Liu Shuzhen, a woman in her early sixties who looked at least a decade older, her gaunt face etched with grief. I had already read about her case in the petition: She was the one who had been locked up in the Family Planning office and forced to give up her three-month-old granddaughter.

The baby was the first and only child of her twenty-four-year-old son and his longtime girlfriend. She was already pregnant when they got married, celebrating their union with a traditional village wedding. But they hadn't gotten around to registering the marriage before they left for the city to earn money. That's what new parents often did to prepare for the expense of the growing child. The baby was left in Liu's care. Family Planning came for the baby late at night, switching off the headlights of their car so they could barge into the house before the grandmother could call for help.

"Don't hit me. Don't mow me down," Liu said she begged the officials. She was arthritic and sparrow-like in her frailty. Yet somehow she found the strength to hold on to the child. So the Family Planning officials took her as well. They held her overnight, sitting on a hard wooden bench, still cradling the baby in her arms. The next morning, one of the bosses came into the office and insisted again that she had to give up the baby.

"You're too old to take care of her. She'll be in better hands with others," he told her. Before she could answer, another man came from behind, reached over, and grabbed her hand, pushing her thumb into an ink pad and then onto a series of documents. She couldn't read them, since she was entirely illiterate. Family Planning positioned the baby on her lap and snapped a photograph. They then drove her back to the village. She lived alone now, sick with grief.

I heard more and more stories. I interviewed close to a dozen parents—some in person and others on the telephone—whose children had been forcibly removed. Zhou Changqi, a migrant worker in his forties with a much younger wife. The couple had a son in 1999 and two years later a daughter. They named her Baishui, or "white water," after a river that ran through his village in southern Hunan. The birth, though, put them in the crosshairs of Family Planning, since a second child was permissible only if the first was a girl. Family Planning officials demanded not only fines but also that Zhou's wife undergo a tubal ligation. Zhou agreed. The exact sequence of what happened next is in some dispute, but what Zhou told me was that his wife and the still-nursing six-month-old baby were housed in a hotel overnight awaiting the operation. When he came the next day, both had vanished. Zhou was told his frightened wife had run away and that the baby was sent to the Civil Affairs office, which in turn had sent the baby to an orphanage.

Family Planning officers toyed with Zhou for months. He was told he could get his daughter back only after he paid the fines for the excess birth, about five hundred dollars, then another five hundred dollars for the cost of the operation. Since his wife was still on the run, they demanded money to rent a car to retrieve her. They wouldn't tell him which orphanage had his daughter. When he discovered she had been taken to Changsha, he went there but was denied admission. By the time he finally wheedled his way inside, an official scoffed at him, "You're too late. Your daughter has already gone to America."

Zhou kept trying to file lawsuits, selling his house to finance his quest for his daughter. When I spoke to him, he was essentially homeless, living in a shack next to a farm where he was raising pigs. He still had his son, who was helping him with the pigs, but the wife never returned. I thought he was the saddest of the parents I'd interviewed.

Each case was a small tragedy writ large for the family. People had nervous breakdowns and tried to commit suicide. Couples broke up from the mutual recriminations and the trauma of losing a child. Parents and grandparents wept as they spoke to us, and sometimes we did too.

Although at this point, I had to admit, the stories were becoming numbingly similar. Poverty. Illiteracy. Migrant labor. If you're a journalist, you know that you've done enough reporting when the stories begin to repeat themselves.

I had more than enough material now. I could show that the confiscation of babies was systematic around China. I had photographs and detailed notes. I could have headed back to Beijing to write my story. But I was in Gaoping, where the first cases had been reported, and I decided to press on. I often have a superstitious feeling that the last interview—the one you almost passed up—will be the most crucial. That you have to persevere and do one more. And there was another family I wanted to interview. I'd heard they'd had twins.

IN THESE PARTS of China, the farther up the mountain you go, the fewer the facilities, the shabbier the houses, the smaller the agricultural plots, and the rougher the roads. There were no commercial enterprises here, no industry except for an abandoned quarry that looked like a gaping wound in the landscape. It was obvious why people had to leave to earn money. Bouncing along a dirt road between the rice paddies, the Volkswagen came to a halt in front of what looked like a large pothole. We climbed out to inspect more closely and saw what appeared to be a scam—a ditch deliberately dug in the road to extract money from motorists. Two men conveniently stood nearby with planks of wood to cover the hole. We quarreled a bit and then handed over twenty yuan (four dollars). I asked for a receipt. The men just laughed.

Winding through the rice paddies, the road eventually petered out at a stream, just deep enough that the car could go no farther. Three logs had been laid out as a makeshift footbridge.

It was there at the footbridge that I met Shuangjie ("double purity," in recognition of her status as a twin) and her mother, Zanhua. The girl was nine years old at the time, a skinny slip of a child, small for her age, prettily dressed in lime-green polka-dot trousers with matching sandals and a pink T-shirt. Zanhua stood behind her in white capris and a green shirt emblazoned with a decal of Tinker Bell. The two of them correctly anticipated we wouldn't be able to reach the village without assistance and expertly guided us over the rickety bridge. We crossed one by one, followed by a little black dog. Although the bridge was only a few feet above the waterline, and the stream shallow, the logs were wobbly. I was glad I had left my laptop in the car.

At the other side of the bridge, the road continued as a footpath that cut through a thicket of bamboo, the golden sunlight of late afternoon flickering through the slender bars of the stalks. Two barefoot boys about seven years old bounced up and down on a fallen tree placed over a concrete block. Along the roadside, farmers heading home lugged baskets of vegetables swinging from yokes on their shoulders.

The village looked caught in time, stuck between eras. Everything was in the process of falling down or going up. The old wooden homes were being replaced with new construction, houses that were surely sturdier and more modern but unattractively built out of dispiriting red brick leached of color by the sun. Everything looked incomplete, missing a roof or a window.

Zanhua told me about the house her family had been building for the past decade. Her husband, Zeng Youdong, was working in the city, since they needed cash earnings to continue the construction. In the meantime, they were living next to her mother's. She guided us to what was little more than a log cabin, with a door made of corrugated metal and a roof no more than plastic sheeting. Their worldly possessions appeared to consist of what we saw outside: three pigs, one cow, a few chickens, and a duck.

For lack of anyplace else to sit, we settled outside on low plastic stools laid out on the dirt. Shuangjie nestled close to her mother, sometimes resting her head on her mother's knee.

Zanhua did most of the talking. She had a friendly, open face. She spoke with animation but not excessive emotion or self-pity. She went through her whole story. How her father-in-law had pressed her to have a son after the birth of her first two daughters. How she had arranged to give birth secretly in the bamboo grove—which, as it happens, was just across the road from where we were speaking. How she had ended up instead with twin daughters, Shuangjie and the missing Fangfang. The subterfuge they'd used in an attempt to keep both girls. She was apologetic about what had happened. Fangfang wouldn't have been stolen away if she and her husband had not left the village to work in the city. But then again, if they hadn't left to go to the city, they'd never have had the money to pay the fines. She felt bad for her youngest daughter, who grieved for her missing twin, although they hadn't been together since infancy.

"Shuangjie," she told me, pointing to the little girl draped on her lap, "she always asks me, 'When are you going to get my sister back?'"

The little girl, who was shyly clutching the hem of her mother's trousers, looked up and, with some prodding, finally spoke up in a squeaky little voice.

"She would be the same age as me. It would be fun. We could play together. We could wear the same clothes and go to school together," she said.

"Yes, it would be better. You should never separate twins," Zanhua agreed. "If it was possible, we'd want to take her back. I gave birth to her. I still want her. I at least want to know where she is. I don't know which country she is in. She could have been trafficked for her organs." Zanhua's voice trailed off. It was clear she still wasn't aware of international adoption.

"I don't know if she still exists."

By the time we finished speaking, the sun was low enough that we sat in the shadows of the bamboo, crisscrossing the landscape like the bars of a prison. We couldn't stay much longer, as it would be hard to navigate out of the village in the darkness. We started organizing our bags and notebooks and making our excuses to leave, and Zanhua thanked us politely for our visit.

"Come back again, and next time bring my daughter," she told me. I gave a noncommittal nod.

Later I wondered what it was about this particular family. They were distraught, but not shattered like some others. The family was still intact, both parents raising their four remaining children, although one was often away working. Zanhua didn't weep or rant or curse. She seemed like a competent person, strong, stable, holding it together for the four other children she was raising.

Why was I going to help this family find their missing daughter and not the others? Perhaps this was a case of triage. Fangfang had a twin sister, quite possibly an identical twin sister. As they matured, the girls would look alike. I thought just maybe I could succeed.

CHAPTER TEN

MUG SHOTS

Shao Fuquan, formerly Fangfang; referral photo supplied by orphanage.

IN SEPTEMBER 2009, MY ARTICLE RAN ON THE FRONT PAGE OF the *Los Angeles Times* under the headline "Stolen Chinese Babies Supply Adoption Demand." An accompanying sidebar inside the paper focused on the separated twins. A short video of Shuangjie talking about her missing twin ran on the website. The stories were syndicated in newspapers around the country and widely shared on social media.

Although I was not the first journalist to report on corruption in Chinese adoption, the story made a big impact. It added to the growing realization that not all adopted children had been heartlessly rejected by their birth parents. It upended the comforting assumption by adoptive parents that they had salvaged these babies from the garbage heaps of China.

At the time of adoption, babies were given new names, new identities. It was like they were tabulae rasae, blanks without personal histories or baggage. The adoptees celebrated their "Gotcha Days"—the dates that they joined their new families—instead of birthdays. Whatever had happened before their adoption didn't matter. They were, in effect, reborn. Now they had pasts that were very possibly problematic.

For the adoptive parents, these revelations were terrifying. As though the Chinese birth parents thousands of miles away were lurking just around the corner, ready to snatch their daughters back. Practically speaking, from a legal standpoint, they knew it couldn't happen, but the possibility that their children had been kidnapped felt like a question mark over their moral right to custody.

For the most part, these parents were well-educated people who had had viewed China as the most ethical choice for international adoption, unlike Ethiopia or Haiti or Guatemala, where they would have been exploiting the abject poverty of birth parents. China was poor, but the issue wasn't poverty so much as the one-child law. The adoptive parents told themselves they were saving children from death or institutionalization, not becoming end consumers in a repressive system that might have fueled kidnappings. They felt sorry for themselves, sorry for their children and the birth parents whose babies were taken away.

"We feel lied to, scared, upset" is how a mother from Philadelphia, Wendy Mailman, described the feelings. She told me, "As a mother, I can only imagine what it would feel like having a baby taken away."

Mailman had adopted her daughter in 2005 from the orphanage in Zhenyuan, the first place we'd visited. The documents she received said the girl was born the previous September and abandoned in January. "What kind of mother would wait until the dead of winter to abandon a child?" She worried there was only one explanation: that her daughter was one of those confiscated.

"I cried quite a bit when these stories broke. What ever happened to the idea of China being a country where adoptions were aboveboard? My child will have to know this story and the possibility that it could be her story," wrote Moya Smith, who had adopted a girl from Shaoyang, in an email.

As for other parents, she wrote, "it runs the gamut. Some were defensive, some frightened, some in denial."

When parents contacted me, I tried to reassure them that the majority of girls adopted from China probably had been abandoned. That was especially true of those born in the 1980s and 1990s, when Family Planning was most unforgiving and parents felt they had no other choice. Brian and Longlan Stuy would later estimate that perhaps 10 percent had been confiscated, mostly after 2000, when the supply of healthy babies dried up. As for the rest, it was unclear how much coercion was applied before the parents gave up their girls. Parents who gave up their children, when interviewed later, would often repeat the same phrase over and over: *Mei banfa,* "There was no choice."

To say that the babies were simply "abandoned" wasn't accurate. It was more nuanced than people originally thought. And how exactly did those babies find their way into the orphanages? The documents given to adoptive families were unreliable at best.

"Most of the stories we were told by the orphanages were not true," conceded Mary House, an official at Children's Hope International and the mother of a brother and sister adopted from China. "We didn't realize at the time."

By the time my stories ran in 2009, nearly 100,000 babies had been sent out of China, more than half to the United States. (The worldwide number would reach 160,000 by 2024, when China finally ended its international-adoption program.) The adoptees were their own community within the larger immigrant population. Their support groups and cultural exchanges were widely celebrated online. Back in 2009, flush with enthusiasm about social media and less privacy conscious than today, proud parents loved to post photos of their daughters. There they were wearing their *qipao,* form-fitting Chinese dresses, and doing dragon dances at Chinese New Year celebrations. Celebrating their heritage, while also partaking in the delights of American childhood, building sandcastles at the beach or riding ponies. Participating in school plays and graduations.

From my office in Beijing, I scrolled through these photos on social media, using a VPN to access Facebook, which was blocked in China. Sometimes in my spare time, refreshing page after page, I wondered about the daughters of the families I'd interviewed and whether they appeared on those pages.

At first blush, it seemed impossible to track down a single Chinese baby adopted years earlier. This pool of one hundred thousand girls was scattered among sixteen countries. Adoption records were strictly sealed in China and in the countries where they were now living. Even if one had access to the records, my reporting suggested that the orphanages often didn't know the real identities of the children. All there was in the way of public records were the legal notices that orphanages were required to publish before putting a child up for adoption, which often contained misleading information. At that, it was difficult to distinguish one young baby from another in the postage stamp–size, grainy photographs printed in the Chinese newspapers.

Fangfang's case was different: I was certain she had been delivered by Family Planning officials to the Shaoyang Social Welfare Institute. She'd been taken on May 30, 2002. Since it took at least six months for a child to be processed, she would most likely have been adopted in late 2002 or early 2003. She would have been two and a half, a full year older than most adoptees. Now she would be nine, just like Shuangjie. I wouldn't be able to find the other children taken, but those telling details would allow me to narrow down the search for Fangfang. I decided to try.

I had stumbled across a Yahoo! group for families who had adopted from the Shaoyang Social Welfare Institute. Many groups of this sort had been set up by adoptive parents who were raising money to support the orphanages that had fostered their children. The administrator, Moya Smith, the adoptive mother who had corresponded with me, was a family therapist and believed it was crucial for families and children to know the truth of their circumstances. She said she would look through the listings to see if anybody matched the description of the missing twin. Smith identified several girls who looked like possibilities. One child was about the right age and had been adopted in the fall of 2002. The description said she had one leg shorter than the other. Another candidate had crossed eyes. They didn't sound like Fangfang, whose only identifying feature was a small extra bump on one ear.

Then there was another girl, who was described as having been found in front of a factory. The administrator thought that ruled her out as a possibility. Like most adoptive parents, she wasn't yet aware of how much had been fabricated. But she passed on the information anyway, sending me a link to another adoption site.

The link was for a charity called Adopt the World International.

"A Home for Every Orphan," read a blue banner near the top. Underneath was the exhortation to adopt: "There are millions of orphans with no one to call mom and dad. . . . They need you."

The organization gave as its address a post office box in Mineral Wells, Texas. It was run by a married couple who appeared to be devout Christians, which was not surprising given the passionate embrace of adoption among evangelicals. The couple who ran the charity were adoptive parents, quite a bit older than was customary and previously married with adult children. The mother, Marsha, had written an introductory essay describing her path to adoption. "My idea of life at 50 was relaxing, having some quiet Bible studies with a few ladies on my days off, flying to Michigan to visit with my son and his family. After all, I had worked over 30 years by the time I reached 50. I thought life was supposed to slow down, but God had other plans for me and I'm so glad He did."

Marsha wrote that she was inspired to adopt from China after reading an article in *Reader's Digest*. It was about a famous case from 1983 in which a father in Shandong Province reportedly drowned his daughter in a well because he wanted a son. She wrote on the web page:

> The man's wife was pregnant with their second child. This
> father wanted a son so badly, and because of the one child

per family policy, he threw his daughter down a well and killed her. As he threw her down the well, she was scream-ing, "Daddy, Daddy!" *I knew from that moment on I was going to adopt from China. Nothing could stop me. . . .*

Now, we don't "fit" the perfect situation for adoption. First of all, at the time we both had grown children. I was 46 and my husband was 54. We both had health issues. My husband had already had 2 heart attacks and I was diag-nosed with multiple sclerosis in May '84. A year after our first talk concerning adopting, Al had a brain aneurysm and stroke within a 2 week period. To add to all that, we were not financially ready at all. When God births His pas-sion in you, it doesn't matter what the obstacles are.

Despite these impediments, the couple adopted twice. They first went to China in 1999 and adopted a ten-month-old girl whom they named Victoria. Then they went back in December 2002 and adopted a baby they were told was eighteen months old. They named her Esther.

We learned from our agency that Esther had been found outside the gate of a factory. The papers stated that when she was found her face was ashen white. She was terrified because she was all alone, and I cried for days just knowing that. . . . Though it took a couple of weeks for Esther to bond with me, she has since become my little shadow.

I compared the information she'd disclosed with what I knew about the missing twin. Marsha said she'd adopted Esther in December 2002—that would be six months after Fangfang was taken. The age wasn't right: Fangfang would have been more than two years old at the time of adoption. But the orphanage might have whittled down her age to make her sound more appealing to adoptive parents, who preferred younger babies. The age was close enough.

Marsha's website included two photographs. One looked like it had been taken at the time of her adoption. It was a headshot showing a toddler in a white sweater with a Peter Pan collar. Her hair was thin, her eyes downcast, and her cheeks flushed as though she had a fever. In the other, she was a four-year-old, so her features were more fully formed. She had a wide, heart-shaped face, bangs to the middle of her forehead, and shoulder-length hair that fell to the edge of a white puffed-sleeve blouse. Her smile stretched from cheekbone to cheekbone.

Was Esther actually Fangfang? Did Esther look like the nine-year-old Shuangjie I'd met in the village in Hunan? Could they even be twins? Maybe yes. My Chinese colleagues looked at the photos and, like me, couldn't say for sure. I thought the birth parents could tell me.

Borrowing a technique from police procedurals, I plucked random photographs from the internet of Chinese girls of similar age and appearance. Interspersed among them were the two actual photos from the Adopt the World website of the girl I suspected could be the missing twin. I printed out a sheet with eight color photographs side by side— cropped so that they looked like mug shots. This was, in effect, a police lineup. Since postal service was unreliable in the village, I sent the photographs by registered mail to Old Yuan, the teacher who had translated for us. I included a note saying that I'd found some photos of adopted girls from Hunan Province and wondered if perhaps one of these eight photos might resemble the missing twin. I hedged the wording so as not to raise anybody's hopes. I didn't tell them that two of the photos were of the same girl at different ages or that I had other information that made me suspect she was Fangfang.

Old Yuan called a few days later. He told me he had brought the photographs to the village and that Zeng Youdong had immediately recognized his daughter. He had pointed first to one picture, then to the other—both of Esther—and said with confidence, "That's her." He was absolutely certain.

NOW WHAT? I had heedlessly barreled ahead, setting a challenge for myself to find the missing girl, without giving enough thought to the next step or the implications for very real people. I couldn't publish a story exposing a girl still a minor, only nine years old, but I couldn't ignore the discovery. I decided to contact the American family discreetly and tell them there was a possibility that their younger daughter was a twin taken from her birth family. I couldn't find a listed telephone number in Mineral Wells or anyplace else in Texas. Their website listed only a post office box. I started googling.

To my dismay, one of the first items to pop up was an obituary from the *Fort Worth Star-Telegram*. Al, the father, had died at the age of sixty-six the previous year. Obituaries are an excellent source of information, and I learned much more about him: He had recently retired from Lockheed Martin, which had a plant in Fort Worth. I already knew from the Adopt the World website that both the adoptive parents had adult children from previous marriages, and the obituary listed their names, the names of their spouses, and their hometowns. Al had a son and three adult daughters. I found the telephone number for one of them in Washington State and called. The daughter listened politely but was noncommittal. She said she would pass on a message to her late father's wife, Marsha. I also read in the obituary that Marsha had a son living in Lansing, Michigan. I found him on Facebook and sent a message.

> Hello. I'm Barbara Demick with the Los Angeles Times in Beijing. I'm trying to reach you or your mother about your sister Esther. Could you let me know when/where it would be convenient to call you?

There was no response. When I went to the Adopt the World website again to search for more clues, it had been removed. The family must have realized that I was looking for them and felt too vulnerable. Confirming my suspicion, the administrator of the Shaoyang orphanage families group wrote an email shortly after, asking that I no longer contact anybody in the family. "She and her family are still deeply grieving her husband's death and I don't think she is ready or able to deal with this at present," the administrator explained.

This presented an ethical dilemma. Was my obligation to protect the American family? Or to inform the Zeng family about the whereabouts of their daughter? My editors agreed that the highest priority had to be this nine-year-old child, who had lost her father the year before and surely couldn't remember anything of China. I gathered together the information and photographs we had taken in China and mailed them to the family through the stepdaughter, explaining that I just thought they should know. I reassured them through the adoption group administrator that I didn't intend to publish anything.

As for the Chinese family, I told them their daughter had been adopted by an American family and appeared to be in good hands. I didn't disclose any further details—like where in the United States she lived or that her father had died. I'm not sure why I left it at that. I had set out originally to help the Zeng family, but it felt like it would be better for now just to reassure them that their daughter was safe and that she had not been killed for her organs—as that rumor continued to circulate through rural China.

And I was happy to hear from a Chinese journalist that the Zeng family still had the photos I had sent taped to a wall in their new house. That was as far as it would go.

Over the next few years, many journalists and filmmakers contacted me about the twins, pushing for the identity and whereabouts of the American twin. One Chinese journalist who had interviewed the Zeng family was sharply critical of my decision not to reveal more. "They told me you know where their daughter is but refuse to tell them," she complained.

AT FIRST, it seemed all for naught. My reporting hadn't brought the Chinese families any closer to recovering their stolen children. But a peculiarity of the censorship system is that the Chinese government can only control the movements of foreign reporters inside China; once we have a story, they cannot prevent it from being published or aired outside the country. They can try to limit the damage by blocking foreign websites or blacking out television broadcasts, but it's impossible to completely cover up the bad news. Knowing this, Chinese journalists will sometimes even leak their scoops to the foreign press, embarrassingly allowing us to take credit for their hard work. Dogged Chinese reporters knew much, much more than I did about Family Planning's abuses, but they hadn't been allowed to publish. My stories helped to create an atmosphere where the unprintable could now see the light of day.

Investigative journalist Pang Jiaoming had been pursuing the story about confiscated babies in Shaoyang since 2007. He had made his name with an exposé about corruption in the construction of China's high-speed railroad but had been long frustrated by editors who would not permit him to tackle abuses by Family Planning. In 2011, Pang was hired by the well-known and, more important, well-connected editor Hu Shuli, who ran *Caixin*, a business magazine that had taken advantage of a window of liberalization to cover stories previously off-limits. The result was a lengthy cover story that ran in May about the babies taken by Family Planning. (Pang would later publish a book by the same title, *The Orphans of Shao*, which is available in English translation.)

Caixin's story opened the floodgates. Everything before had been published in English or, in the case of the television exposé, in Dutch. That report had had a major impact in the Netherlands and had prompted Ina Hut, the head of the country's largest adoption agency, to quit her job and speak out publicly about corruption. But this report was in Chinese and would be read by a domestic audience. Other Chinese publications ran follow-up stories. More birth parents came forward, saying that they too had had babies taken away by force or trickery.

At long last, Chinese authorities had to take action. In September 2011, Shaoyang City and Longhui County jointly released a report acknowledging that fourteen children had been taken by Family Planning officials. "In five cases," they wrote, "the parties concerned knew the truth about the blood relations of the children and passed them off as 'abandoned.'"

As in the previous unpublished investigation conducted in 2006, the investigators reported no evidence that the orphanage had paid off Family Planning officials for delivering the children.

> The investigation did not find any evidence of the buying and selling of infants. However, the workers involved in this incident did not work practically, and the methods they used were indeed crude.
>
> For these offenses, the current and former heads of the family-planning agency, Zhou Xiaofang and Li Zijian, and twelve others will be stripped of their duties and expelled from the party, among other penalties.

Nobody was going to jail, but it wasn't a complete whitewash like the 2006 investigation. Expulsion from the Communist Party was more than a slap on the wrist. A bureaucrat might find it difficult to secure future employment.

At the very least, the punishment was a black mark on their careers. And on the entire already-embattled system of Family Planning.

CHAPTER ELEVEN

THE POPULATION BUST

Yanyan, whose mother died during a forced abortion.

IDEAS CAN GO IN AND OUT OF STYLE AS QUICKLY AS FASHION. By the dawn of the twenty-first century, the panic about overpopulation felt as vintage as bell-bottoms and sideburns. The apocalypse prophesied in 1968 by *The Population Bomb*'s Paul Ehrlich and his many Chinese disciples had failed to materialize. In fact, the population bomb was turning into a population bust.

Hard to believe, but China was running out of people. China's economic miracle had been conjured up on the backs of hungry migrants from the countryside. Those young workers toiled away long hours in the factories to churn out cheap exports and transformed China into the world's second-largest economy.

In 2011, China's working-age population plateaued at nine hundred million, and it would fall each successive year. (China's overall population would decline for the first time in six decades in 2022, putting it on track to cede the dubious title of the world's most populous country to India.) Too many retirees and too few working people created a squeeze that would depress the entire economy. It was aggravated by an unsustainably low retirement age—set in the 1950s at fifty to fifty-five for women, depending on their jobs, and sixty for men.

For decades, Chinese scholars had been warning of an impending demographic crisis, but cautiously and in the confines of academic journals, as was the prudent course for intellectuals criticizing the Communist Party. Now the voices were growing more emphatic. "China is on a downhill demographic vehicle in terms of low fertility and rapid aging," warned Wang Feng, an outspoken Chinese demographer, in 2011.

The crisis wasn't only economic. The entire society had been thrown off-kilter. The only children of the 1980s—the first generation of the one-child policy—had reached adulthood, and the consequences were as predicted. The lopsided gender ratio—seven males to five females in some areas—meant some young men would be unable to find wives. Raised to perpetuate the family line and sire their own sons, they were destined to fail at their main mission in life. Many would grow up to be unmarriageable bachelors, disparaged in Chinese as *guanggun,* literally "bare branches." Sexually frustrated, angry young men were not conducive to social stability, the enduring obsession of the Communist Party. The party's official mouthpiece, *People's Daily,* opined in 2012 that the millions of unmarried men were more likely to take part in "rioting, stealing and gang fighting." Rural men, less desirable on the marriage market, imported brides from neighboring countries—Vietnam, Myanmar, North Korea, Nepal, and Laos. But the practice raised its own set of social problems, rapes and bride trafficking among them.

The situation for young Chinese women was mixed. Some benefited from better educational opportunities. If they were only children, their parents were likely to invest as much in their upbringing as they would have in boys. But the advantages came with new pressures. These women were supposed to land good jobs, earning enough to eventually support their parents, all the while being solely responsible for providing heirs to the family. But educated young women often balked at marriage and childbearing, which only exacerbated the bride shortage. Many chose to remain single.

What was most surprising was that the Chinese leadership stuck by the one-child policy as long as it did. The policy was, as Mei Fong wrote in her book *One Child*, "born in haste, dragging on past its sell-by date." At the time the policy was announced in 1979, it was billed as a temporary emergency measure. "In thirty years, when our current extreme population growth eases, we can then adopt a different population policy," the leadership had promised at the time.

But population control had become so closely tied to the party's legitimacy, the bureaucracy so entrenched and the fines so lucrative, that the Chinese leadership couldn't enact the badly needed rollbacks. To revoke the policy would be a loss of face in a system inordinately concerned with perception. The Communist Party was paralyzed. It could only react to events, such as in 2008 when an earthquake in Sichuan Province killed thousands of children and teenagers—crushed by the collapse of shoddily built high schools. Rural couples were left without a single surviving heir. Public anger ran so high that the leadership feared an uprising. The earthquake highlighted the "vulnerability of the one-child policy," Gu Baochang, a prominent Chinese professor of demography, most recently with Fudan University, told me. "These people are not covered by any social security program. They rely completely on their children for elderly support. And it's not just money. Once they are old, without children they have no place in society."

The very same Family Planning officers who'd forced people to get sterilized and abort pregnancies now had to do a 180-degree turn: They were mobilized in a campaign to reverse vasectomies and tubal ligations and remove IUDs. They offered fertility treatments to nearly menopausal women. A year after the earthquake, I visited a maternity ward in Mianzhu, a Sichuan city near the earthquake's epicenter, where the director of family planning told me proudly that fifty mothers had already given birth and four hundred were pregnant with what were callously known as "replacement babies."

At the urging of demographers, the Chinese government had been conducting discreet experiments in which it allowed second children in designated areas, testing whether this would result in a spike in births. Since the early 1980s, residents of rural Yicheng County in northeastern Shanxi Province had been allowed to have two children. Not only did birth rates remain low, but this control group reported fewer cases of infanticide, a healthier gender balance, and overall more harmonious relations between the governed and their leadership. In 2006, researchers from the Chinese Academy of Sciences surveyed couples in Jiangsu, north of Shanghai, where the government had allowed a second child if either of the parents was an only child. Only 10 percent of those eligible availed themselves of the exemption.

It was obvious to everybody (except perhaps the ossified leadership of the Communist Party) that urbanization was more effective at keeping down the birth rate than coercion. When families left their villages, moving into one- or two-bedroom apartments, husbands and wives working long hours, they didn't have the space or resources for large families. A maturing, more prosperous China had become more like Asian neighbors South Korea and Japan, and parts of Western Europe as well, where birth rates were plunging in spite of generous incentives offered by governments to keep procreating.

The resistance to population control also came from the ground up. Brutalized for decades, rural Chinese people were sniffing out the weakness of the Family Planning apparatus and fighting back. The petition signed in 2006 by the parents of confiscated children was only one sign of this rising assertiveness.

The early years of the twenty-first century saw the blossoming of the *weiquan*, or "rights defense movement," as idealistic lawyers, previously cowed by the Communist Party, started to step forward, trying to use the law to force accountability. Ordinary, law-abiding citizens were increasingly taking to the streets, emboldened to complain about grievances arising from abuses of government power. There was a groundswell of grievance. The Chinese Ministry of Public Security reported that "mass incidents" had increased to eighty-seven thousand by 2005, up from a mere ten thousand per year a decade earlier—after which it wisely stopped counting (or at least publicly releasing the data). Riots broke out in a rural county in southern Guangxi Province in 2007 after Family Planning cadres bulldozed the house of a penniless farmer who didn't pay his fines. Up to three thousand people trashed the Family Planning office and overturned and set fire to the officers' cars. Most other Family Planning protests were in such remote locations that they didn't get reported in the media.

From outside of China, the scorn mounted. Back in 1979, the international community had hailed China for its courageous move to save the overcrowded planet. Champions of the one-child policy claimed it had prevented four hundred million excess births—a figure disputed by demographers. But human rights had long since overshadowed the environmental benefits of population control. In the 1990s, U.S. immigration law was amended to allow asylum claims from Chinese people fleeing forced abortions and sterilizations. Liberals and conservatives, prochoice and prolife, who agreed on almost nothing else, found rare common ground assailing the abuses committed by Family Planning enforcers.

A new hero emerged in China: Chen Guangcheng, a blind lawyer who had gained international acclaim for bringing a rare class-action suit against the Family Planning office in his hometown of Linyi, Shandong Province. After serving more than four years in prison, Chen was placed under house arrest in his village, where he became a cause célèbre. In 2011, actor Christian Bale, accompanied by a CNN crew, tried to visit Chen, hoping to "shake his hand." Bale retreated after being punched and shoved by plainclothes thugs. ("China vs. the Batman," screamed the predictable headlines.) The following year, Chen scaled a wall around his house, evaded guards and cameras that encircled the village, and sightlessly crawled his way to freedom. He took refuge in the U.S. embassy in Beijing, precipitating a weeks-long diplomatic crisis that ended when he received political asylum in the United States.

*   *   *

IN RETROSPECT, 2012 was the turning point. A cascade of seemingly unrelated events, starting with Chen's dramatic escape, developed into a perfect storm that threatened to kill off the one-child policy once and for all. In mid-May, Chen arrived in New York City to great fanfare, giving a series of press conferences denouncing Family Planning. Then two weeks later, a twenty-two-year-old factory worker, heavily pregnant with her second child, was captured by Family Planning officials, hauled to a hospital with a pillowcase over her head, and injected with an abortion-inducing drug. The woman, Feng Jianmei, had assumed she was entitled to a second child because she lived in a rural area in Shanxi Province, but Family Planning disagreed and assessed the family a six-thousand-dollar fine, which they couldn't pay.

The forced abortion was nothing unusual: For years it had been standard operating procedure for Family Planning. Except that Feng's sister-in-law had snapped a photo with her cellphone in the clinic. The photograph of this dejected young woman, her hair strewn over her face, lying in bed next to what looked like a perfectly formed but obviously dead baby, was destined to go viral.

China went crazy. The gruesome photo lit up the internet. Censors couldn't delete fast enough nearly one million online comments calling for Family Planning officials to be prosecuted for murder. ("Auschwitz in the womb" was one comment.) Local government had no choice but to apologize to the family.

Three Family Planning officials were suspended. Even the *Global Times,* a Communist Party–run newspaper, opined that "forced termination of late-term pregnancies must be condemned and banned."

A WEEK AFTER the Feng Jianmei abortion hit the press, I drove with a Chinese assistant to Lijin in Shandong Province, a few hours southeast of Beijing. Shandong had become notorious for the severity of its family-planning apparatus. Not only was Chen Guangcheng from Shandong, but so was the author Mo Yan, an astute social critic whose 2009 novel *Frog* (translated into English in 2015) described a former obstetrician tormented to madness by the memory of the babies she'd murdered. As it happened, Mo Yan won the Nobel Prize in Literature in 2012.

The village we were visiting was in the midst of gentle, rolling countryside sloping down toward the Yellow Sea, about thirty miles away. The previous year, a thirty-eight-year-old woman, Ma Jihong, had died after a forced late-term abortion, and the case was back in the news as a result of the viral photograph of the dead fetus.

When we arrived at the deceased woman's home, her five-year-old orphaned daughter came outside. She was wearing a pink polka-dot tutu, and she was very articulate, telling the story of what happened to her mother. A posse of Family Planning officials had surprised them at home early one morning. Her mother slipped through a gap in the wall enclosing the house and sprinted down the main road. Her father, who was working in the yard, heard the screams and tried to fight off her pursuers. The girl waved her hands, reenacting what had happened. "But there were too many people," she told me. "He couldn't stop them."

By the end of the day, Ma Jihong was dead. Her family found her lying in a bed at a makeshift clinic, her head resting on a roll of toilet paper used as a pillow, dried blood caked under her nose. The daughter, Yanyan, struggled to understand why her mother had risked her life to have another child. "I didn't want a little brother or a little sister," Yanyan said. It was clear that what she wanted was her mother.

After talking to the family, we went into the village's general store, where a group of men were gathered. At first, they stared sullenly, unfamiliar with strangers, but once we explained we were writing about Family Planning, they couldn't stop talking—about the beatings, the demolished homes, the forced sterilizations, the woman who died. When interviewing people in the countryside who aren't experienced with journalists, one has to be careful not to get them in trouble. I offered not to use their names in print, but one of the older men insisted.

"This is a free country. Use my name," said Ji Shuqiang, taking my notebook to correctly write the characters of his name. "I'm not afraid of those people," he added. Family Planning had lost its teeth.

*   *   *

LATER THAT SAME YEAR, in October 2012, Xi Jinping was anointed head of the Chinese Communist Party at the 18th Party Congress. The son of an early revolutionary and official, Xi is what is called in China a "princeling," a class of privileged offspring who are perpetuating the reign of the Communist Party. Xi has developed a syncretic style that fuses Marxism with the hierarchical framework of Confucianism. Xi's ascension was expected to augur a more assertive leadership than that of his predecessor, Hu Jintao. But when it came to family planning, his government dithered, merely nibbling away at the rules. In March 2013, it weakened the previously all-powerful National Population and Family Planning Commission by folding it into the Ministry of Health. In November 2013, it rolled out a nationwide exemption that would allow all couples to have a second child if either parent was an only child.

The Chinese government didn't finally pull the plug until October 2015. At the end of a Communist Party plenum on the economy, Xinhua, the official news agency, published a communiqué stating that China would "fully implement a policy of allowing each couple to have two children as an active response to an aging population."

The announcement lit up news sites around the world. As it happened, I was riding on a city bus through New York's Chinatown on that day, October 29, 2015, when my cellphone started vibrating with the announcement. All the other passengers appeared to be Chinese. As I glanced across the aisle at two small girls sitting in matching pink parkas, I couldn't help wondering whether their parents were among the immigrants who had left China to escape the one-child policy. I had lunch later that day with a friend who had two nieces and a goddaughter adopted from China. The reverberations of the one-child policy lived on, profoundly shaping our world in so many ways never envisioned at the outset. In its wake were millions of Chinese families grieving, often secretly and in silence, for the children who were never born or who were relinquished under duress.

As for me, I wrote a quick story that day about the end of the policy in the style of a mock obituary. "China's one-child policy died on Thursday, after a long illness. It was thirty-five years old" is how I phrased it.

By that time, I couldn't count how many dozens of stories I'd published about Family Planning, child trafficking, and adoptees during my seven years in Beijing. I had left China for New York the previous year. I was writing a book on Tibet and had started to contemplate other issues. I thought I'd finally extricated myself from the subject of population control in China. I'd never write about this again, I told myself.

That proved to be very wrong. In January 2017, I received the unexpected message on Facebook. The correspondent was a car salesman from Lansing, Michigan, Sam Belanger. He was the son from the first marriage of Marsha, the woman who had adopted the girl once named Fangfang, now his sister Esther. He was one of the people I had contacted back in 2009. I returned the message, apologizing profusely that I had at first forgotten who he was. He explained:

> Years ago, when you reached out to us regarding the story you were putting together regarding our family, we weren't emotionally ready to respond to you, and neither was my sister, given the gravity of the request. Through the years things have changed, though, and we feel that it might be time.

Soon enough, I found myself plunged into an entirely new family drama.

Part Three

T E X A S

CHAPTER TWELVE

MARSHA'S STORY

Marsha.

AS A CHILD, MARSHA DREAMED OF BEING A MISSIONARY. RAISED a devout Christian, she was an adventurer by temperament. The missionary life would allow her to reconcile her faith with ambition. It also sounded like a way to get as far away as possible from Kermit, the Texas Panhandle town where her father worked in an oil field and all four siblings shared a bedroom. In high school, she almost jumped at an offer to work with a church that ran a suicide hotline in Mexico. But life didn't work out as planned. She was as crazy about boys as she was ambitious, and she married as soon as she graduated from high school.

By the time she turned twenty-one, Marsha was a divorcée with a six-month-old son. It was too late to dream of living abroad or of going to college, something her father thought was unnecessary for girls. She worked a series of civil service jobs, including one in a prison, which toughened her up. In 1978, she felt lucky to land a job as a data processor with General Dynamics in Fort Worth, and despite her lack of a college degree, she rose through the ranks to become a planner in the inventory department. She earned a good salary, kept busy with her church, and considered herself a proudly independent woman until just after her fortieth birthday.

She met Al through a Pentagon debacle. In January 1991, the Pentagon canceled an order for the A-12 Avenger II stealth bomber under development by General Dynamics and McDonnell Douglas, throwing Marsha's employer into crisis. She was reassigned as a planner to the team charged with closing out the project. Al, a cost analyst, was on the team, too. They worked together, she inputting his cost estimates into the computer. They sat in adjacent cubicles. The pace of work was slow, and they had plenty of time to talk. Al, eight years older, was also divorced with children. He was a strapping man more than six feet tall whose height was accentuated by a sweep of silver hair. Originally from Bismarck, North Dakota, he had disarming midwestern manners. Although Marsha thought him attractive, she said no when he asked her to dinner.

In middle age, Marsha hadn't lacked for male attention. Her hair's red highlights set off dove-gray eyes. Men were charmed by her soft Texas drawl. But having married young the first time around, she'd adopted a been-there-done-that attitude. She owned her own house, an hour west of Fort Worth, and drove her own car, a Geo Prizm.

"I wasn't playing hard to get. I was just not interested in dating," Marsha told me years later when we first met.

Al was polite but persistent. When she finally agreed to dinner, he selected her favorite Mexican restaurant—despite his own preference for meat and potatoes. They bonded over enchiladas. She'd assumed that a man from North Dakota would be consumed with guns, hunting, and fishing, but Al preferred Disney movies and cartoons. By the third date, Marsha realized she would break her vow to never marry again. She did so only a few months later in a small church on the outskirts of

Fort Worth. Marsha borrowed a dress from her best friend. Her son, Sam, then nineteen years old, gave her away. Al's youngest daughter was the bridesmaid.

Marsha and Al relished the freedom of being a childless, mature couple. They liked to go out to dinner when the mood suited them. They took a Caribbean cruise. They commuted to work together in Fort Worth. If they ran out of things to talk about during the drive—forty minutes each way—Al would do the driving so that Marsha could read.

It was during one of these drives, Marsha later told me, that she first hit upon the idea of adopting. Al had turned on the radio, which was playing a report about Romanian orphanages. The communist dictator Nicolae Ceauşescu had banned abortion and contraception, believing—as did Mao—that a high birth rate would lead to economic growth. After he was overthrown and shot by a firing squad in 1989, aid workers descended on hellish orphanages and discovered more than 170,000 children dumped by impoverished parents, often sleeping three to a bed in their own excrement.

Marsha was aghast.

"Wow, all these babies. This is terrible. It just breaks my heart," she told her husband.

"Well, why don't you adopt one?" he replied. Marsha would later tease Al that it was his idea.

"Just maybe I will," she shot back before returning to her book.

It was something of a joke between them. It progressed to the stage of fantasy, then became a glimmer of an idea. When they had married, starting a new family had been the last thing on their minds. They had five adult children between them—her son and his four. At forty-nine, Al was a grandfather and didn't feel a need for any further children in his life. Marsha was forty-one and had undergone a hysterectomy. Having grown up in a poor family and having struggled through years of single motherhood, she enjoyed the first true financial stability of her life. And yet part of her was unfulfilled. She hadn't entirely lost the idealism of her youth. She felt God had put her on this earth for a reason, and it wasn't to live in a nice house and go on cruises. She thought she had a higher purpose in life and that helping an orphan might be a way of carrying out her mission.

UNTIL WORLD WAR II, international adoption was a rarity, at least as far as Americans were concerned. Pearl Buck, a Nobel Prize winner best known for her novel *The Good Earth* about rural China, had been an outlier, adopting seven children starting in the 1920s and becoming an advocate for transracial adoption. International adoption picked up momentum by the mid-1950s. With the sponsorship of the Vatican, Italy sent more than three thousand babies and toddlers to the United States under the guise of "war orphans," although in reality the children had been taken from unwed mothers. The largest program was started after the Korean War (1950–1953) by Bertha and Harry Holt, an evangelical couple from rural Oregon who brought in displaced children, some of them fathered by U.S. soldiers. The Holts went on to establish the first major agency focusing on international adoption. Eventually more than two hundred thousand Korean children were sent abroad, about half to the United States.

Each new catastrophe, war, earthquake, or coup d'état produced heartbreaking stories of orphaned children. There were the devastating civil wars in Guatemala, El Salvador, Nicaragua, and Honduras. The collapse of the Eastern Bloc opened another new frontier in Romania and elsewhere.

As the Vietnam War was winding down in 1975, the U.S. organized Operation Babylift to evacuate some three thousand babies and children from Vietnam. *Playboy* publisher Hugh Hefner volunteered his private plane for a final leg of the journey, and *Playboy* bunnies carried some of the babies off the plane amid a predictable flurry of self-congratulatory publicity.

From the outset, international adoption was dogged by allegations of coercion. Were these children actually orphans? Had their parents really relinquished them? As one Vietnamese mother, suing to recover her child, expressed it in an open letter published in 1976, "To understand my story, think you are caught upstairs in a burning house. To save your babies' lives you drop them to people on the ground to catch. It's good people that would catch them, but then you find a way to get out of the fire too, and thank the people for catching your babies, and you try to take your babies with you. But the people say, 'Oh no, these are our babies now, you can't have them back.'"

But Americans needed to procure those babies. International adoption compensated for a precipitous decline in domestic adoption. In the post–World War II years, the start of the baby boom, pregnant young women without husbands were forced into maternity homes and made to sign away their babies. At least 2.7 million babies were adopted domestically in the United States between 1944 and 1975, the peak of what critics would later call the "baby scoop era."

By the last decades of the twentieth century, the supply of healthy babies available for adoption shrank dramatically as young women around the world took control over whether they reproduced and who received custody of their children. Schools began teaching sex education in the 1970s. Birth control became more widely available. In 1973, *Roe v. Wade* legalized abortion nationwide in the United States. Single motherhood gained respectability. The number of babies surrendered for adoption in the United States dropped from an estimated 175,000 in 1970 to 129,000 in 1975, according to the Adoption History Project, run by the University of Oregon.

At the same time, more people were joining the queue to adopt. Delayed marriage and motherhood left many women struggling with infertility. The pool of prospective adoptive parents would soon be joined by same-sex couples, their civil unions increasingly recognized by law and eventually accorded the same status as marriage.

People all had their own reasons for wanting to adopt, some religious, some purely humanitarian. Many were tempted by the idea of a multiethnic family. The environmentally conscious, like Brian Stuy, thought adoption preferable to bringing another hungry, resource-consuming human into the world. And there were countless families, many of them with already-grown children, who felt compelled to help the homeless and orphaned, the downtrodden and abandoned. Celebrities added a touch of glamour to international adoption. Starting in 2002, Angelina Jolie adopted from Cambodia, Ethiopia, and Vietnam. Madonna adopted four of her six children from Malawi. Although cynics dismissed these adoptions as virtue signaling, for the most part, the motives boiled down to good intentions. People who heard about abandoned children simply wanted to help.

Stories about suffering children are a staple of international reporting, sure to tug at heartstrings and boost ratings. By the mid-1990s, many of these horror stories were emanating from China. A documentary aired in 1995 by Britain's Channel 4 called *The Dying Rooms* reported that unwanted girls were left to die without medical care or food in a Shanghai orphanage. Although the documentary was criticized as sensational and implicitly anti-Asian—complete with a creepy Orientalist soundtrack and gratuitous footage of a puppy being skinned at a market—it presented compelling evidence that children were badly malnourished and neglected. At the same time, Human Rights Watch released a report finding that mortality rates in Chinese orphanages were as high as in Romania, in some cases higher.

NOT LONG AFTER hearing the radio program about Romanian orphans, Marsha happened to be visiting her mother. Sitting on the sofa, she reached into a magazine rack and randomly pulled out a magazine with an article about China's one-child policy. That's where she heard the story—the one she mentioned on her website—about the man who threw his daughter down the well. It nudged her past the point of indecision and switched her focus from Romania to China.

Marsha contacted several adoption agencies. One tried to steer her to Mexico. Another said she and her husband were too old. And indeed, she did worry about their age and health problems. Although her multiple sclerosis was in remission, she knew she could have a relapse. Besides his heart attacks, Al suffered a potentially fatal cerebral hemorrhage in 1997, forcing them to put their adoption plans on pause. But Al recovered and she resumed her efforts. She discovered Austin-based Great Wall China Adoption, established in 1996 by a Chinese-born woman, Snow Wu. "The caseworker told us that they liked older parents because we're more stable," Marsha told me.

The couple started the onerous process in earnest. They had a home study, background checks, and interviews. The agency collected their birth certificates and marriage certificate. They submitted fingerprints. After his aneurysm, Al had committed himself to a rigorous diet and exercise regime. He wanted to be in top shape to start a new family. They passed their health examinations. Finances were tight because they'd just bought a larger house with a sweeping front porch. But they found a bank that offered loans tailored to adopting parents and borrowed twenty-five thousand dollars. They applied for passports. Although they'd taken a Caribbean cruise and made a trip to Canada, this would be their first serious overseas adventure. Finally, in 1999, all the pieces came together. Al went to the bank to get the three-thousand-dollar donation for the orphanage. He was told it had to be in hundred-dollar bills, as new and crisp as possible. With the cash in hand, Marsha and Al flew through Detroit (to visit with Marsha's son, Sam) to Beijing. Their destination was Nanchang, the capital of Jiangxi Province, which, along with Hunan and Guangdong, was one of the largest sources of babies for adoption. There they met up with other adopting parents; they would travel as a group on what was, in effect, a guided tour—but a tour with an endgame: to become parents.

Parents adopting from China do not select their child, and adoption agencies scrupulously avoid any suggestion of "shopping" for a cute specimen like choosing a puppy in a pet store. The child is assigned by Beijing adoption officials in a rather mysterious process that the U.S. State Department explains as "a proposed match between you and a specific child based on a review of your dossier and the needs of the child."

Marsha and Al's referral was for a ten-month-old girl. Her file said she'd been found as a newborn in front of a hospital. The referral photo they'd received a few months before the trip showed a baby with large, round eyes and delicate features, uncommonly beautiful though bald as a cue ball. She wore a wraparound shirt patterned with pomegranates. There was something improbably glamorous about this little baby, and they decided before leaving for China that the romantic name *Victoria Rose* would suit her. Even before they met, they bonded with the girl, and the moment the Chinese nanny working for the adoption agency placed her in Marsha's arms, they realized the sentiment was mutual. It was love at first sight.

"Most of the other babies cried when the nannies handed them to their new mothers, but not Victoria. She only cried when I put her down," Marsha said.

Back home, Marsha and Al quickly relearned the skills of changing, bathing, and feeding babies. Victoria was a cheerful, unfussy baby. She lapped up the attention of her smitten parents and in return showered them with affection. "It was like it was meant to be. It wasn't really hard." But Victoria didn't take kindly to being put in daycare. She'd had enough of institutions. Fortunately, Al had decided to take an early retirement to spend more time with his new daughter.

Marsha continued to work at Lockheed (which had taken over General Dynamics), while Al stayed home with the baby. He loved having a toddler with whom he could watch cartoons. They indulged their love of Disney together.

It all seemed so natural and easy that Marsha decided they should adopt a second daughter.

CHAPTER THIRTEEN

ADOPT THE WORLD

Victoria (left) and Esther.

IN 2001, MARSHA AND AL STARTED THE ADOPTION PROCESS again. In the middle of it, Al got a lucrative job offer in Atlanta that tempted him out of retirement. They decided to swap roles. He would be the breadwinner and Marsha the stay-at-home parent. Marsha took an early retirement from Lockheed. Their house with the front porch was on land that had been rezoned for commercial development. They were able to sell it at a tidy profit, which allowed them to buy a three-bedroom condo in the Atlanta suburbs and pay the twenty-five thousand dollars in adoption fees. They had to redo their paperwork, since they had a new home to be inspected and approved.

Late the following year, they received the referral for their second daughter. They decided to call her Esther, the name of Marsha's mother and the biblical queen who saved a nation. They had a premonition that this girl would possess a strong personality.

As had happened last time, the referral arrived in a thick envelope. Marsha thought she ought to wait for Al to come from work so they could go through it together, but after a few minutes, she was too curious. She tore open the envelope and read the description.

> Shao Fuquan, female, born on June 8, 2000, was found abandoned at the gate of Qiaotou Bamboo Craft Plant of Shaoyang City on June 4, 2002. The child was picked up by Huang Xiuyun (an inhabitant of Shaoyang City) and was sent to our Institute for nursing by 110 Police Station of Shaoyang Municipal Public Security Bureau on June 4, 2002. We can not find her natural parents and other relatives up to now.

There was a small photo attached to the referral—the one Marsha later posted on her website—that showed an older baby with an ashen complexion and downcast eyes.

At first, Marsha was taken aback. Their first adoptive daughter had been a baby, while this girl was a toddler. Although she didn't expect an orphan to be smiling in such a photo, the dejection on her face was striking.

This child looks very unhappy, Marsha remembered thinking as she examined the photo.

The adoption procedure allows parents to reject their referral, and they could have backed out. But Marsha thought it was appropriate to get a slightly older child, since she was at that point fifty-one years old, and Al soon to turn sixty. And she wasn't the kind of person to be deterred by a challenge. She promptly sent back her acceptance.

"I felt such compassion," Marsha said. "I believed with us she would become a happy little girl."

*   *   *

SHORTLY BEFORE CHRISTMAS 2002, the family set out for China: Marsha, Al, and Victoria, who was then four years old.

The trip did not go as smoothly as their earlier visit to China. The journey took nearly forty-eight hours, flying from Atlanta through Detroit, Tokyo, and Beijing until they reached Changsha, the capital of Hunan Province, about two hundred miles from where Victoria was adopted. Along with other adopting families, they checked in to a large, modern hotel, the atrium bedecked with ornaments and a Christmas village. Although the Chinese don't celebrate Christmas as a public holiday, they love the trimmings. Victoria would later remember her delight basking in the holiday atmosphere, eating a banana split decorated with parasols. Marsha was exhausted from the trip and would soon come down with a respiratory infection.

As had happened before, adoptive parents were not permitted to visit their children's orphanages. They were told it was too far away and that a visit would be inconvenient. Instead, a hotel conference room had been rented for them to meet their new daughters. It is customary for adoptive families to travel as a group, with tour buses, guides, and interpreters hired by the adoption agency, and about ten families were in the same group. There were couples, singles, and a few, like Marsha and Al, with older children in tow. They seated themselves on chairs scattered around the conference room, waiting together for the babies to be brought in. They chatted awkwardly, covering up their nervousness. Meeting a new daughter would be like a first date, but with infinitely higher stakes. There was no turning back. Marsha was contemplating the strangeness of the experience when she heard her name called out.

Marsha was startled that she was first.

And she was even more surprised by the appearance of her new daughter. All the other babies were carried into the room. Esther was led in by a Chinese nanny but walked on her own, not even holding hands. She looked confident. Her gait was that not of a toddler but of a determined young child. She wore a puffy denim-blue one-piece outfit decorated with cornflowers that Marsha had sent ahead. She held a Lucite cube with family photographs that Marsha had included in the package. The nanny pointed to a picture on the cube and then to Marsha.

"Mama," she told Esther. The word is basically the same in Chinese.

She lifted Esther and placed her in Marsha's lap. Esther didn't react. She was neither fussy nor affectionate. Just obedient.

Victoria couldn't contain her excitement. "Can I hold her?" she kept asking her parents. Marsha transferred Esther from her own lap to Victoria's. This time, Esther objected. She erupted into howls of protest. Marsha took her back, but Esther wouldn't be consoled.

From then on, their relationship deteriorated. Esther wouldn't let Marsha pick her up again. Only Al was permitted to touch her, to put her into a high chair or take her out. When Marsha tried to speak to Esther, telling her in the halting Chinese she'd practiced, *Wo shi mama*, "I am your mama," Esther furiously shook her head to indicate no.

Only at night did Esther tolerate Marsha. They had requested a crib for their hotel room, but they thought it would help Esther bond if she slept instead in a double bed with her new mother. She would curl up next to Marsha to sleep, like a cat, accepting her presence as long as Marsha didn't try to pick her up.

Although Esther was nearly two and a half, she was no bigger than the year-old babies the other parents in the group were adopting. The shoes they'd purchased flopped on her feet like skis. She was completely toilet trained, but the smallest girl's underwear they found—size two— was so big it would slide off her hips. Esther wasn't nearly as healthy as Victoria. Her hair was brittle. She was badly congested.

But she was so quick to learn. One of the Chinese caretakers told Marsha through the interpreter that Esther used to help fold laundry at the orphanage. And on the third day after meeting her new family, she was in a play area in the hallway of their hotel when an older American child—one of the siblings brought on the adoption tour—grabbed a toy out of her hand.

"Mine!" she insisted, uttering her first clear word in English.

Marsha and Al were baffled by their new daughter. She was so unlike Victoria, so unlike the other girls who'd been adopted by their group.

Marsha blamed herself for Esther's coldness. She thought she'd made a critical mistake by placing the girl so quickly in her sister's lap, somehow betraying her trust. Al had another theory. "It almost seems like she's been raised by another family," he said.

As Marsha had predicted, though, this sad-eyed orphan would soon become a happy child. By the time they flew to Guangzhou, the city in southern China where Esther would obtain her visa from the U.S. consulate, she and Victoria, just two years apart in age, had become inseparable. They explored their hotel room, giggling as they hid in an empty cabinet designed for a minibar. Victoria pulled out a portable DVD player and showed Esther some of her favorites—*Winnie the Pooh* and *The Sound of Music*.

When they got home to Atlanta, they realized that Esther was too dexterous to be confined to a crib or playpen. She'd climb out immediately. The girls shared a room with bunk beds, Victoria on the upper and Esther on the lower. Contrary to their parents' fears, Victoria displayed little jealousy toward the new arrival. There was no sibling rivalry, few quarrels, although Victoria sometimes bristled when Esther would grab her toys. The girls often wore matching clothes. Flowered dresses. A shirt-and-shorts set emblazoned with Disney's blond Cinderella. People sometimes asked if the girls were twins, even though Victoria—two years older—was more than a head taller.

Outside their bedroom, they had a cheerful playroom with a small table and wooden chairs with their names painted on the back, a toy Playskool kitchen, and a tiny tea set. They had tea parties together. They loved dressing up and dancing.

All of the distrust Esther had displayed toward Marsha disappeared. She'd follow Marsha everywhere in the house, so closely that Marsha sometimes worried she'd step on her. "She was like my shadow," Marsha recalled. Esther became attached to Marsha's mother, so often repeating "I have a grandma, I have a grandma" that they again wondered if she was talking about a relative back in China.

*　　*　　*

IN 2003, the family moved back to Texas to be closer to Marsha's mother and siblings. Marsha had enrolled the girls in a preschool in Atlanta, but in Texas she decided to try her hand at homeschooling. She did not particularly object to the secular education offered by the public schools; she simply thought that she could do a better job of teaching. Marsha hadn't attended college, but she was a voracious reader of literature, nonfiction, and history. She instilled a love of reading in her daughters. Her brother, an engineer who lived nearby, helped with math and science.

Marsha was more passionate about adoption than ever before. She was an enormously energetic woman—homemaking and teaching were not quite enough to keep her intellectually fulfilled. In 2006, she self-published a book about an adoptive family under the title *The Christmas Miracle*.

But still she felt she should be doing more, not only for her own girls but also for the untold numbers she imagined left behind in China, unwanted, likely neglected. That was how she came up with the idea to set up a nonprofit that would advise other potential adoptive parents and raise money to subsidize their adoptions. This would be an outlet for her restless ambition and her humanitarian instincts, tapping into her unfulfilled desire to become a missionary. She enlisted support from her son, Sam, who shared many of her interests. He served as a youth pastor for a church in Michigan. He was also passionate about adoption and would later adopt an African American boy.

In 2004, Marsha, Sam, and Sam's then wife set up the nonprofit Adopt the World, with the website that led me to them. Al and Marsha were listed as co–executive directors, but Marsha was the power and the inspiration.

Marsha took her message on the road. She spoke to fellow parents who had also adopted from Shaoyang. She spoke at churches and chambers of commerce around Fort Worth. Sam arranged for her to speak in Michigan.

Her speeches were essentially an exhortation for churchgoers to adopt. Those who weren't interested themselves could help defray the costs for other families. Marsha had studied speech in high school. When she believed in something, she surprised herself with the eloquence that could tumble out of her mouth. In another lifetime, she might have been a preacher.

"Joseph was the adopted father of Jesus," she would tell congregations. "God believes in adoption." "Our lives have been blessed."

FROM THE 1950S, when the first large wave of Korean War orphans came to the United States, Christian missionaries had played a leading role in international adoption. Many of the leading adoption agencies were started by missionaries. Especially for evangelicals, international adoption ticked all the boxes. It was a natural extension of their opposition to abortion and another way of spreading the good word to children in need of spiritual and material sustenance. The message was a fusion of the Gospel and the Beatles. "All You Need Is Love" became the anthem for many in the adoption movement.

In her writing and speeches, Marsha echoed other devout Christians embracing adoption. The movement gathered momentum in 2004, when thirty-eight church leaders convened in Little Rock, Arkansas, for what they called the first "orphan summit." Out of that was born the Christian Alliance for Orphans, which to this day works to encourage Christian adoption. In 2009, the Southern Baptist Church, the largest denomination in the United States after the Catholic Church, passed a resolution urging the church's sixteen million members to either adopt or support others doing so. Rick Warren's Saddleback Church held regular adoption summits. "What God does to us spiritually, he expects us to do to orphans physically: be born again and adopted," Warren told followers at a 2007 summit.

The premise advanced by the Christian adoption advocates was that there was an "orphan crisis," with tens of millions of children around the world in need of parents. Rick Warren and his wife, Kay, claimed there were 168 million orphans worldwide who could be placed in Christian homes. (Scholars disputed this claim, saying most of these children were being cared for by living relatives.) Christians would be remiss if they didn't open their homes to these children in need. The Christian women's magazine *Above Rubies* likened adoption to "missions under our very own roof." Editor Nancy Campbell put it thus: "When we welcome orphans into our heart and into our home, we actually welcome Jesus himself."

Christians heeded the call to adopt in droves. Throughout the early 2000s, they set up adoption ministries, awarding grants and interest-free loans to adopting families. The most zealous dashed between war zones and earthquakes from Liberia to Haiti, scooping up children so quickly that it raised alarms. At times, the children picked up in disaster zones were not actually orphans; often there were parents or close relatives who were desperately looking for them. Good intentions had run amok. "Orphan fever" is what author Kathryn Joyce branded the phenomenon. In her 2013 book, *The Child Catchers: Rescue, Trafficking, and the New Gospel of Adoption*, she wrote of families that adopted up to ten children, driving up the demand side of adoption. She heard through adoption circles of one family who had taken in fourteen children from Liberia.

In comparison, Marsha's efforts were modest. She adopted just her two daughters and raised about four thousand dollars to help other adoptive families before she had to abandon the effort.

THE DOWNWARD SPIRAL began in 2007. Sam and his wife split up, complicating efforts to keep the nonprofit going, since it had been a joint venture, with his now-estranged wife playing a leading role. In his mid-sixties, Al had committed himself to healthy eating and exercise to keep up with his young children, but unexpectedly he started experiencing debilitating bouts of fatigue. He went to the doctor and was diagnosed with non-Hodgkin's lymphoma. Al's illness put the family in a predicament familiar to many Americans: soaring medical bills and shrinking savings. Al had come out of retirement to return to Lockheed, but now he was too ill to work. Marsha had left her job to raise the children, not appreciating how much her pension would be reduced by early retirement.

Although they were never affluent, they had been comfortable enough, with their own home and two cars. Now they were at risk of falling out of the middle class. They had to cut down on their expenses. They moved to a smaller house that was both cheaper and closer to the hospital where Al was undergoing chemotherapy. Al died in October 2008, barely a year and a half after his diagnosis. Marsha was a single mother again. Her cheerful, giggly daughters were sullen and withdrawn. Marsha thought the death had triggered all the abandonment issues lingering from their adoption. A parental death was even worse for an adoptee, a counselor told her. Marsha was barely able to pick herself up to rebuild her life when her own mother started showing signs of dementia, needing home care.

Bad things come in triplicate, Marsha thought. Their life would get better. They would heal. But the following year, when revelations spilled out about the underbelly of Chinese adoption, it would call into question much of what she had ever believed in.

CHAPTER FOURTEEN

ESTHER'S STORY

Shuangjie and Zanhua; the photo Marsha first saw.

MARSHA LIKED TO STAY UP LATE AFTER THE GIRLS WERE ASLEEP, catching up on correspondence and paying bills. One evening in September 2009, sitting at the kitchen table, scrolling through her email, Marsha came across a message from a woman whose name she recognized from the adoptees' group on Yahoo! Moya Smith was the administrator of the site and was looking for children who matched the description of the missing twin. The email had a link to the September 20 *Los Angeles Times* article I'd written about confiscated babies, and along with it the short sidebar about the twin who had been taken away by Family Planning officials. "A Young Girl Pines for Her Twin" was the headline of the article.

"Could Esther be the missing twin?" Smith had written in the email. Marsha shook her head. There was no possibility. She remembered the referral papers that said Esther had been found outside a factory the summer before her adoption. Marsha wanted to reassure herself. She quickly checked to make sure that her daughters, now nine and eleven, were sound asleep, then pulled out a briefcase from a hallway closet containing the adoption documents. She riffled quickly through the papers until she found the document she was looking for. At the time an adoption is finalized, the parents are given a certificate in Chinese and in English translation attesting to the child's origins as an abandoned child and their legitimate status as an orphan.

CERTIFICATE

(Translation)

To whom it may concern:

Shao Fuquan, female, born on June 8, 2000, was found abandoned at the gate of Qiaotou Bamboo Craft Plant of Shaoyang City on June 4, 2002. The child was picked up by Huang Xiuyun (an inhabitant of Shaoyang City) and was sent to our Institute for nursing by 110 Police Station of Shaoyang Municipal Public Security Bureau on June 4, 2002. We can not find her natural parents and other relatives up to now.

Shaoyang Municipal Children's Welfare Institute

(Seal)

Oct. 28, 2002

Shao Fuquan . . . found abandoned at the gate of the Qiaotou Bamboo Craft Plant of Shaoyang City on June 4, 2002 . . .

We can not find her natural parents and other relatives up to now.

She was relieved. Then she turned to the article online and read more carefully.

The story reported that on May 30, 2002, a dozen officials from the local Family Planning office "stormed the house of the uncle and grabbed the 20-month-old." The article also said the girl had a "distinctive bump" on her left earlobe.

Marsha clicked on an accompanying photograph. The photograph showed the mother and nine-year-old daughter sitting on plastic stools next to the bamboo.

She enlarged the photo so that she could look more closely at the girl. She scrutinized her pouty lips, the knowing half smile, the wide cheekbones.

All the pieces fell into place. Esther's initial indifference to her adopted family. The unexpected remarks she'd made about a grandmother. The sadness Marsha had noticed in the first photos she'd received of Esther. Everything that had happened was suddenly laid out in her mind, the exact sequence of events revealed. The article said that the toddler had been confiscated from her uncle's house on May 30, 2002. Marsha's documents gave a date just five days later when she was delivered to the orphanage, supposedly an abandoned child left at the gates of the bamboo craft factory. The timing fit. There was one obvious conclusion: Everything she'd been told about Esther was a lie.

Marsha cycled through powerful waves of emotion. Fear. Guilt. Betrayal. Sadness for Esther's having experienced such a brutal trauma so early in life, sadness for the mother whose daughter had been taken away, sadness for the Chinese girl who missed her twin. And for herself. She felt betrayed by her own hubris. Here she'd been telling people to adopt all these abandoned babies ("There are millions of orphans with no one to call mom and dad. . . . They need you," claimed the website she'd created) when her very own daughter had been snatched away from her family. She desperately wanted to talk to Al about it. Instead, she called Sam and told him to take down the website immediately. She could see people were starting to post comments on the article saying that the missing twin should be tracked down and returned to China. Could Esther be taken away from her?

The anxiety swept over her in waves, one receding as another swelled, threatening to crash into her. She was terrified that the journalist—I— would reveal Esther as the missing twin. Already she was reading comments on adoption websites demanding that confiscated babies be returned to their birth parents in China. Although this was before Twitter shaming became so common, the public reprobation was bad enough. Her worst fears were for her daughters. She worried that Esther was quietly suffering from this long-ago trauma of her toddler years, a wound that could be reopened if she learned what had happened. And about how it could impact eleven-year-old Victoria, who was deeply depressed by her father's death. Marsha wanted to make sure to keep it a secret until the girls were old enough to understand, not that she fully understood it herself. She vowed to say nothing to anyone except immediate family.

A FEW DAYS LATER, Esther asked to use her mother's telephone to send a message to Sam's girlfriend, a woman named Carrie who later became his wife. Carrie had become one of Marsha's closest confidantes, and the girls embraced her as a big sister. Marsha had an old-style flip phone, and as soon as Esther punched in Carrie's name, the last text sent to her mother popped up on the screen. "It's terrible for twins to be separated," Carrie had written.

Esther was puzzled. She couldn't understand why the topic of twins was suddenly of interest. But she somehow sensed it was an urgent matter and that maybe it related to her personally. Still clutching her mother's phone, she grabbed Victoria's arm and tugged her into the bathroom. She closed the door behind them and whispered.

"I've got to show you something. Don't tell Mom," she told her. "Something is going on."

Victoria read the message with concern. By then, both girls had noticed that Marsha appeared unusually agitated and distracted. When they asked what was going on, she was evasive. There were hushed telephone conversations that fell silent when the girls walked into the room. At one point, Marsha went up to Esther and, without explanation, pushed her hair aside and snapped a photograph of the small bump on her left ear. Esther's tiny ear tag had never caused much concern or interest before.

"I thought that was kind of weird," Esther said later.

That same week, on an evening when Esther and Victoria had just come home from visiting with friends, Marsha summoned them into her bedroom. They plopped themselves on the quilted pillows while their mother stood ceremoniously at the foot of the bed. Esther recalled a feeling of dread. Their mother's formality reminded her of the previous year when they had been summoned into the bedroom to be told their father had died.

"Girls, there is something I need to share with you," Marsha told them. She began a long-winded account of how a scandal had erupted in China about babies confiscated for adoption, and how one of the babies had a twin sister who was looking for her.

Esther listened for a few minutes and then interrupted. "Mom, am I the twin?" she asked.

Marsha was taken aback. She wondered why it was Esther who had asked the question, not Victoria. Was there something she remembered? She stammered that she didn't know anything for sure, and in any case, it was nothing to worry about, probably nothing that impacted them directly. She just thought the girls should know. She urged them to forget about it.

By then, I had reached out to Marsha's relatives, including Sam, and received the email from Moya Smith urging me not to disturb the family further. I, in turn, had passed on my assurance that I didn't intend to write an article.

A few weeks passed without further discussion. Marsha's anxiety seemed to be lifting. She felt confident that nothing further would appear in the media. The immediate crisis had been averted. But Esther was carefully observing her mother. She noted her breezy, cheerful demeanor. She didn't entirely trust it. Although she couldn't articulate her feelings, she sensed that Marsha was affecting this nonchalance on her behalf. She wasn't satisfied by what she'd been told about the missing twin, but she dared not pester her mother with direct questions.

Esther bided her time, waiting until one afternoon when Marsha was napping on the living room sofa, her laptop sitting on the kitchen table. Esther opened it—at first telling herself she was just going to play a game. She was an obedient daughter who didn't want to think of herself as a snoop, but she found herself quickly navigating to her mother's email. At nine, she was adept with computers and didn't have to look hard. She clicked on the *Los Angeles Times* article sent to her mother, noting the detail about the bump on the ear. She exited the article and read more of the frantic exchange of messages between her mother and the administrator of the Shaoyang adoptees' group.

"Could Esther be the missing twin?" the administrator had asked.

It was posed as a question, but the answer was obvious.

Esther closed the computer and quickly walked away, as though escaping the scene of a crime. She felt terrible. She wasn't yet focused on what she had discovered about herself. Her concern was that she'd been spying on her mother. She was a considerate child, respectful of her mother's privacy, and she knew she'd done wrong. She was sure she wouldn't get caught, but it was not her nature to conceal anything from her mother.

When Marsha woke up from her nap, Esther blurted it out.

"If I tell you something, will you promise not to get angry?" she asked, barely waiting for the answer.

"I know now that's it all true. I really am the missing twin."

As it sank in, the revelation rattled Esther's sense of security. If she'd discovered her past later in life, she might have been gratified that her birth family loved her after all and that she hadn't been willingly surrendered. But at the age of nine, her first reaction was alarm. She felt like a freak. She wasn't just another kid from Texas. Or just another Chinese adoptee, like Victoria, who comfortably inhabited a new identity. She had an entire previous life in China, another name, a storied past. And she had a twin—like another half of herself that had been left behind. She didn't want to be a twin. Now China lurked as a threat. Her past was out there with long tentacles that she feared could take her away from what was now her home.

"Does this mean I will have to go back to China?" Esther asked her mother.

Marsha assured Esther that nobody could take her way. She would be her daughter forever, a U.S. citizen forever. Victoria was fearful too, not so much for herself as for the little sister she had sworn to protect. What if somebody from China came after her? What if they tried to kidnap her? Victoria dared not say the name *Esther* aloud if other people could hear. When they were out shopping or at a restaurant, she'd simply call her sister "E"—a nickname that persists to this day. Marsha installed a high wooden privacy fence along the perimeter of their yard. They kept the curtains tightly drawn most of the day.

Being homeschooled, the girls didn't have as active a social life as some other children, but Marsha tried to compensate by filling their schedules with gymnastics and voice lessons. Now their world shrank. Some of those activities fell away. They went less often to church. Although they knew their fears were unwarranted, a pervasive, unspoken unease constricted their lives. Inside their home, they didn't have to deal with the gazes of curious strangers or the questions about where they were from.

Victoria and Esther were already curiosities in their community. They lived in a fast-developing but still-rural patch of Texas with strip malls and horse pastures. Their little town had seventeen churches for some twelve thousand residents. Although it was an easy drive to Fort Worth and barely an hour to Dallas, increasingly diverse cities, nearly everybody in their town was white. The town had almost no African Americans, few Hispanics, and, as best the children could remember, no other Asians. Once there had been a Chinese restaurant in one of the malls, but it had closed. At the mall, they drew stares. Children some-times touched their hair.

Marsha had tried her best to make her daughters feel less isolated. When they were young, she drove them to gatherings of other Chinese adoptees in Austin. She bought the girls books and videos about China. It was a delicate balancing act trying to make her daughters proud of their origins without shoving their ethnicity down their throats. She didn't force them to study Chinese. She understood that school-age children were keener to assimilate than to explore their roots.

Victoria expressed little affection for China. The trip she'd taken as a four-year-old when Esther was adopted had been more than enough to satisfy her. Her memories of China from that trip were vivid and not altogether pleasant. She was disgusted by a fast-food restaurant (she re-membered it as a McDonald's) that served pigs' feet; she hated a smoky tea served at a traditional teahouse. The only thing she'd liked was that banana split decorated with the paper parasols.

Esther's situation was more complicated. She had been not quite two and a half when she left China. She now knew of the tumultuous events that had transpired before her arrival in the United States, but this part of her life was a blank. She searched her mind for fragile threads of memory that she could grasp, as if to transport herself back to the past. She always came up empty. And yet she felt connected to China in a way that her sister did not. Early on, she developed a taste for spicy food—not just the Mexican salsa favored by her mother—and she wondered if it was a vestigial memory from her early childhood. Hunan's food is nearly as spicy as the more famous cuisine of neighboring Sichuan Province. Since the Chinese restaurant had closed, she started cooking herself. She searched the internet for recipes to make dumplings and noodles, smothering everything with chili paste.

Once in her teens, Esther became more self-conscious about being Asian. She studied herself in the mirror, comparing her features and coloring to those of her blue-eyed, now-redheaded mother. Esther had an acute visual sensibility: She paid close attention to the people and landscape around her. At the age of thirteen, she got her first camera as a Christmas present. She fell in love with photography. She took the camera everywhere. She photographed her family, their cat, the people around the neighborhood. She developed an interest in fashion. It was hard to relate to the tall, leggy models. Esther was still well under five feet tall and Victoria only a few inches taller. She discovered Asian fashion blogs and was happy to see models who shared her body type. She had grown up watching Disney animations of pale, blue-eyed heroines—as a child, she had a T-shirt of a statuesque Cinderella with an updo of bright yellow hair—but she decided now that Mulan, the Chinese warrior, was her favorite. She felt herself to be, well, more Chinese than she had as a small child playing dress-up. And she began thinking about her other half in China. She wondered whether her twin looked just like her, what she wore, what she was doing. She wondered if her twin ever thought about her.

Around the time that she turned sixteen, she spoke to her mother about contacting her twin. And Marsha asked Sam to reach out to me for help in connecting them.

CHAPTER FIFTEEN

THE GO-BETWEEN

Al and Marsha, Victoria and Esther.

JANUARY 2017, NEW YORK. WHEN SAM BELANGER CONTACTED me in 2017, I didn't recognize the name. On Facebook, he identified himself as working for a car dealership in Lansing, Michigan. I'd never been to Lansing and didn't own a car. It had been eight years since I'd identified Esther as the missing twin and more than two since I'd left China. I was still working for the *Los Angeles Times* but assigned to New York. The city was heaving with unrest in the aftermath of Donald Trump's election. A women's protest over the weekend in reaction to the new administration had exploded into one of the largest single-day demonstrations in U.S. history. Some four hundred thousand people protested in New York City alone, many carrying "Not my president" placards. The airports were filled with people protesting the new administration's ban on travelers from some Muslim countries. Although my mind was cluttered with U.S. domestic politics, my focus far from China, I was quickly plunged back into the drama of the confiscated babies.

Sam explained the family situation in a series of messages:

> Years ago, when you reached out to us regarding the story you were putting together regarding our family, we weren't emotionally ready to respond to you. . . . Through the years things have changed, though, and we feel that it might be time.

> My mom asked me to contact you concerning her daughter, Esther, and her twin in China. . . . Any advice regarding this would be helpful.

The family was still apprehensive. It had taken them months—if not years—to get up the nerve to contact me. They were more comfortable communicating by email and Facebook than by anything more personal. I could understand how unnerved they were by their situation. Anybody would have been shocked by the revelation that an adopted daughter had been confiscated by a branch of the Chinese government and trafficked, and they were naturally concerned about the implications for the child. But it also represented a loss of face and faith for a family that had poured so much energy into promoting international adoption. Sam had been a board member of the Adopt the World charity started by his mother—the home page listed him as assistant director—and he had arranged speeches at churches around Michigan for his mother to encourage more international adoption.

When we finally spoke on the telephone, nearly three months after the initial exchange of messages, Sam told me they had been mortified to discover they were unwitting participants in a system tainted by corruption. He told me that in recent years he had become skeptical of international adoption. "International adoption became part of such a large moneymaking venture, even when everything was legitimate," he said. Adopt the World had since disbanded. Sam had turned his attention to advising families in his youth ministry about adopting children in foster care. "There is a lot of need in the United States," he told me. He and his second wife, Carrie, adopted an African American boy in 2015 when he was one week old. That made Sam attuned to the identity issues faced by adoptees, especially those who were not of the same race as their parents. His concerns extended from his own son to his adopted Chinese sisters. He thought Esther, because of her late adoption, might have vague, unformed memories that would plague her in future years.

"I think it would be healing for Esther to be in touch with her birth family," he told me.

THE IDEA OF an adoptee meeting her birth family was novel. Until the 1970s, laws in the United States and most other countries ensured it would never happen. In most states, adoption records were sealed under laws purportedly designed to protect the birth mothers and their offspring from the stigma of illegitimacy. Unwed teenage mothers were shamed and coerced into prisonlike maternity homes where they were forced to relinquish their babies at birth. It was common for children not to be told they were adopted. Although professionals usually advised parents not to conceal the truth, adoptive parents often feared that awareness of another set of parents—the biological parents—could undermine the bonding process. Adoption itself was distasteful, with its implications of premarital sex and infertility. These were not subjects to be discussed in polite company.

The sense of loss experienced by many adoptees was rarely acknowledged. They were often told that asking questions would be an affront to the parents who raised them, a sign that they lacked gratitude.

In 1971, a group called the Adoptees' Liberty Movement Association was launched by an adult adoptee to fight the culture of secrecy. Its founder, Florence Fisher, grew up in Brooklyn, New York, wondering why she looked nothing like her parents and shared none of their tastes and interests, and why other relatives often treated her as an interloper. After confirming her suspicions that she was adopted, she spent two decades tracking down her birth parents. It was a painstaking process in a pre-internet, pre–DNA testing era. She spent countless hours scanning microfilms of old telephone books, knocking on doors, and battling the hostility of the legal system. Under the prevailing laws, the birth certificate for an adoptee was replaced by another listing the adoptive parents. The original was strictly sealed. She chronicled the quest in a bestselling 1973 book, *The Search for Anna Fisher,* and argued her case: "What is more natural than the desire to learn something of one's heritage? All children love to be regaled with anecdotes and details about their parents and grandparents. They look at their parents and try to find something of themselves in the way these people walk and talk, in their interests and talents, in their strengths and flaws. Such information provides a frame for their lives, and a continuity with their pasts."

In the gut-wrenching *American Baby: A Mother, a Child, and the Shadow History of Adoption,* published in 2021, author Gabrielle Glaser wrote of a teenager forced to surrender her newborn son in 1961, although she and her boyfriend intended to marry and did so shortly after the birth. The woman spent half a century trying to find the boy, not only to reunite with him and introduce him to three younger siblings but also to warn him of a genetic predisposition to diabetes. By the time she found him, his kidneys were ravaged by the disease. He received a transplant in 2007 after a long struggle to find a donor, a process made difficult by not knowing biological relatives. Mother and son finally met in 2014, a few months before his death at the age of fifty-two.

The veil surrounding adoption has dropped in recent decades. Widespread commercial DNA testing and changing social mores have made it harder to keep secrets. Adoptees and their advocates have argued convincingly that it is a basic human right to have access to their original birth certificates, which in turn allows them to learn their original identities. They've won support from social workers, psychologists, and the courts. As of this writing, fourteen U.S. states allow adoptees to obtain their original birth certificates, according to the Adoptee Rights Law Center.

This relative openness is not to everybody's liking. It is one reason international adoption has been preferred by many families, who reasoned that geography and linguistic differences would prove insurmountable barriers to keep birth families away. Agencies promoting Chinese adoption even advertised the advantage of anonymity. "Because child abandonment is illegal in China, birth parents leave no trace of their identity. . . . During [their] trip to China, [adoptive families] receive a certificate of abandonment that proves the biological parents have relinquished their parental rights through abandonment. There is no legal avenue for the birth parents to reclaim custody," wrote one agency in 2014.

MARSHA WOULD LATER say she wouldn't have adopted Esther if she had known she was stolen from her birth family. But she also understood it was impossible to undo what had already happened. Esther was now an American. Everything had been wiped clean from her bank of memories except those experiences of her American childhood. She didn't speak Chinese. She didn't remember her birth family. She couldn't be returned to China. Marsha would never consider giving up custody. But from the time, in 2009, when she discovered Esther had been confiscated, she vowed to make amends. And one way to do that would be to allow Esther to reconnect with her birth family. And that could happen only if Esther wanted it to.

And Esther did.

Nearly four months after the first message from Sam, Marsha finally sent me an email. She was not exactly apologetic, but she explained the family's inability to respond back in 2009. She had been deep in mourning for her husband's loss. The girls were too fragile to be subjected to further disruption in their lives. Now they were teenagers, on the cusp of adulthood. Marsha gushed about Esther. Only sixteen, Esther had already graduated from high school, finishing all the coursework offered by the Christian homeschooling program and receiving the equivalent of a diploma. She had obtained a business license for her own photo agency and had set up her own website. She was shooting weddings and engagement parties, babies and class photos. She was an excellent cook and baker. In short, she had graduated into adulthood and was, her mother thought, mature enough to deal with the emotional fallout of contacting her birth family.

"Esther has always wanted to connect with her twin when the time is right," Marsha explained. But still, the family wanted to proceed slowly and privately. Marsha knew that Chinese journalists had been chasing the identity of the "stolen twin," and she still had fear, perhaps unwarranted, that the long arm of China might reach into their lives and snatch Esther back. The family trusted me because I'd kept Esther's identity a secret for all these years. "The steps leading up to this must be safeguarded," Marsha wrote in the email. "I appreciate your protection of Esther these many years and ask for your continued privacy."

From our exchange, I understood I might never be able to produce a story about this, and any efforts to reconnect the twins would be a personal favor not connected to journalism. But it would be out of the question not to help. I had intruded in their lives without thinking through the consequences. I understood now how much trauma I had caused the family. They had lived since 2009 with the shadow of Esther's past hanging over them. It seemed odd that I, a journalist, was one of the few people Marsha trusted who knew China and could locate Esther's birth family. They were reluctant to contact their old adoption agency. They didn't know anybody who knew their way around China or spoke the language. My Chinese was limited, but I could read and write well enough with the help of Google to translate a simple letter. I was designated to serve as the go-between—a role I would occupy for longer than I might have expected.

I dug out my old reporter's notebooks to look for the family's contact information. (Like many journalists, I never throw them away.) But the various cellphone numbers I had for the Zengs and for other families in Hunan weren't working. Few migrant workers have landlines. When they lost or changed their cellphones, it was as though they vanished. I knew the family would still be tethered to Gaofeng village, their *laojia*, or "old home," no doubt the place they returned every New Year. But these mountain villages didn't have reliable mail delivery. In theory, we could contact village officials, but it would be better not to. The subject of the confiscated girls was still sensitive. I didn't want to get the family into trouble.

Fortunately, Chinese journalists were still pursuing the story, and I'd continued to receive queries from reporters asking me for the identity of the American twin. Among them were filmmakers working with director Nanfu Wang, whose stunning 2019 documentary *One Child Nation* would later be short-listed for an Academy Award.

In the end, it was easier to find Shuangjie than her parents. At sixteen, she had already moved on from the village. She was a teaching intern at a kindergarten in Changsha, the capital of Hunan Province. She lived in a dorm with other young trainees. And like most Chinese people her age, she was connected to the wider world through social media. She had her own smartphone and an account on WeChat, the ubiquitous app used by more than one billion in China. The filmmakers passed on her contact information. A colleague in Beijing messaged Shuangjie to give her a heads-up that we had news of her twin sister. I friended her on WeChat and she accepted. There was no need to go to the post office or buy an airmail stamp. The lines of communication were open, with me serving as the go-between.

Marsha had suggested that Esther start by writing a letter. A real letter, handwritten on paper. They didn't want to text and they didn't want the Zeng family to have their contact information. I gave Marsha my mailing address in New York. A few days later, a letter appeared in the mailbox. Esther had written on white, lined paper designed for a three-ring binder. As I could have predicted from her mother's description, the handwriting was tidy, the spelling and grammar exact. She made herself very clear.

> *Hello Shuangjie. I'm Esther. Please allow me to introduce myself. As you already know, I am 16 years old. . . .*
> *I am short, standing just under 5 ft tall, but I actually don't mind in the least. People guess my age to be around 13 or 14, which I think is funny.* ☺ *How tall are you?*

I recently started my own photography business. . . . I love
to cook/bake and I like fashion and art and listening to music.
In January, we celebrated the Chinese New Year for the
first time and we all wore red and I made orange chicken and
fried rice which we ate with chopsticks. We also watched
Disney's Mulan and decided to make it a tradition for every
New Year.

Just to avoid raising expectations that she was planning to move back
to China, Esther added a pointed, though gracious, rejoinder.

I am very happy and want you to know that I have a caring
and lovely family whom I love dearly.

I KNEW THAT Esther preferred sending letters. That would be a way to
control the pace of everything happening. But even with Shuangjie now
living in the city, sending a letter by mail would be unreliable. With their
permission, I scanned the letter. A friend helped me translate it. With a
few swipes, I uploaded the scan and hit Send. And prepared to wait.

It took only a few minutes. Shuangjie wrote back almost immediately. One text message after another.

"Do you have pictures of her?"

"I want to see her."

"Can you give me her contact information?"

Esther was not on WeChat and wasn't about to disclose her contact
information. I suggested that Shuangjie follow Esther's lead and write a
letter in response. Within a few days, she sent me a scan of the letter.
Like Esther, she had written it by hand. Although the response was in
Chinese, I could see by the way she wrote "Esther" that their handwriting was similar.

Dear Esther, hello. My name is Shuangjie. I am 16 years old
and an outgoing girl. I am about 150 centimeters tall and the

slightly chubby type of girl. I like playing ping-pong,
badminton. I like to listen to music and do calligraphy. My
favorite colors are white and black, and my favorite season is
the fall: The temperature of the season is just right, not cold or
hot. We very much want to see you and hope you and your
family are not afraid. We won't snatch you away from your
family. We understand. I hope we will keep in touch in the
future. I really want to wear the same clothes as you, go
shopping together, and listen to music together. I think it's a
magical thing that two people look very much alike. In school,
teachers would call the wrong name because they can't tell us
apart, and our friends would also be confused as to who is who.

THE GIRLS BECAME pen pals, with me as the courier in the middle, translating and relaying messages. Esther wrote to me by email, which Shuangjie didn't use. Like most Chinese, she preferred texting on her telephone. Esther still didn't want to set up a WeChat account. She hadn't told Shuangjie her surname or where she lived.

Esther did send photos, and Shuangjie reciprocated. They looked alike. Flat, wide noses, flared at the nostrils, well-defined eyebrows, eyes crinkled at the edges when smiling. They both had bright, infectious smiles, although Shuangjie's was less confident. Their most striking feature was their cheekbones, so pronounced and wide they reminded me of boomerangs.

Their styles were very different. At least in the photographs, Esther was glamorous; Shuangjie was cute. In one, Esther posed in a wide-brimmed red hat with a matching dress, in another wearing a black velvet dress. She wore vermilion lipstick and her hair rippled to her waist. Shuangjie wore her hair cropped to shoulder length with bangs hanging over her forehead.

I put the photographs side by side and showed some of my friends, asking if they could guess which twin was American and which was Chinese. Most of them guessed incorrectly that Esther—who looked more exotic with her long hair and evening clothing—was the Chinese twin and that the schoolgirlish Shuangjie was American. Only a Chinese friend got it right: A Chinese girl wouldn't show as much teeth in her smile, she said.

The photos prompted more questions. Shuangjie sent one in which she was standing playfully in front of a colorfully painted wall, grinning with glasses posed on top of her head. Esther inquired with concern. Did Shuangjie need glasses? No, she didn't, but she used them in the photograph for comic effect. Esther seemed relieved. As a photographer, she valued her perfect eyesight. They enjoyed pointing out what they had in common. They both liked fruit. They both had nosebleeds when they were young, but Shuangjie's had stopped as she got older. Esther had bad allergies—she was allergic to coconut, avocados, bananas, and soy—while Shuangjie did not.

More photos followed. Esther sent pictures from her childhood. She requested that Shuangjie do the same, although there were very few from the presmartphone era, since cameras were not so common in rural Chinese households. There were the shots I had taken in 2009 and those by the Chinese journalists who wrote about the case later. (A poignant photo of Shuangjie appeared on the cover of Chinese journalist Pang Jiaoming's 2014 book *The Orphans of Shao.*)

Esther was more forward in their exchanges, peppering Shuangjie with questions. How tall are you? What is your favorite color? What is your favorite season? What do you like to do? Where did you go to school? How far away was it? What are the names and ages of your brothers and sisters? Shuangjie dutifully answered. But she seemed reluctant to ask direct questions in return, although Esther encouraged her: "Please don't hesitate to ask if you have any questions."

At times, it felt like the cultural divide loomed ever larger. I stumbled over translating a letter from Esther in which she referred to her love of colors.

I like gray a lot, I even painted my bathroom gray and
decorated it with pink accents. I do like to wear colors in the

spring and summer though. My favorites right now are
pastels—light pink (blush), mint green, and baby blue.

I was trying to imagine what Shuangjie would make of this letter. Esther was not at all wealthy, but she would sound entitled referring to her "bathroom." I'd been to enough Chinese homes to know Shuangjie wouldn't have her own bathroom, and that the toilet might be a wooden outhouse. I suspected she didn't have enough clothing to switch colors by the season.

The correspondence plodded on like this for a few months. With a limited means of communication and a language and cultural divide, the conversation revolved around an endless loop of hair, school, hobbies, fashion, and food. Perhaps these are the topics that interest teenage girls, but I could sense that both twins were getting a little bored. The dialogue was starting to peter out—the novelty wearing off with the subject matter so limited. They were like pen pals without real intimacy, struggling to find common ground. Esther was still nervous about revealing too much of her identity, although I did finally convince her to get her own WeChat account so that the messages wouldn't have to go through me. The app has a built-in translation function, so I could be replaced by artificial intelligence. It went against my instincts as a journalist—I always wanted to know what was going on. On the other hand, I didn't like the feeling that I was in the way of the twins' ability to develop their own relationship.

This might have been the end of my involvement in this story. But over the summer, I was planning a trip to China, and it wouldn't be so complicated to route myself through Changsha to see Shuangjie in person and maybe revisit the village. I could also set up a video chat with an interpreter between Shuangjie and Esther, since it seemed unlikely they could arrange it on their own. When I suggested it, they both jumped at the idea.

CHAPTER SIXTEEN

VIRTUAL REUNION

Shuangjie on a video call with Esther.

CHANGSHA, AUGUST 2017. CHANGSHA IS ANOTHER OF THOSE Chinese megacities you've probably never heard of, even though it has a population of ten million, larger than New York City or London. Its most famous son, Mao Zedong, born nearby, attended secondary school in the city and formed a study society, many of whose members later joined the Communist Party. A 105-foot-tall Mount Rushmore–like bust of the young Mao rises from a public park that runs along the banks of the Xiang River. Changsha has become better known in recent years for its enthusiastic embrace of capitalism. Not to be dismissed as just another provincial capital, the city in 2012 gave initial approval to a 222-story tower called Sky City that was supposed to take the title of the tallest building in the world, surpassing Dubai's Burj Khalifa. Although the project was canceled the following year due to feasibility concerns,

Hunan's capital retained its bristling ambition to rival China's most famous cities. At least it had a comparable level of congestion. When I flew in on a Monday evening in August at about 5:00 P.M., the traffic along the four-lane airport highway proceeded at a crawl. Rather than stall, the taxi driver switched off his air-conditioning. I cracked open the windows to admit a blast of the 104-degree air. The hotel was outside the city center barely ten miles from the airport, but ninety minutes elapsed before we arrived.

I had booked a newly opened, high-end hotel, figuring that we would need fast Wi-Fi for a video call. Shuangjie agreed to come for the call. The hotel was fashionably sleek, dimly lit (think a Park Hyatt crossed with a love hotel), and maddeningly high-tech. A colleague had come from Beijing to do the interpreting, and it took some time for us to find each other, since we were booked on separate floors where each other's key cards didn't work, and even more time elapsed before Shuangjie could get upstairs to meet us. When we finally managed to convene in my room on the eleventh floor, we were all flustered and sweaty. We looked around to find the light switches recessed in the wall. I was eager to get a good look at Shuangjie.

The sixteen-year-old Shuangjie didn't bear much resemblance to the nine-year-old I'd met clinging to her mother's knee in the bamboo. But I recognized her from the photos she had exchanged with Esther—the striking cheekbones, large eyes that crinkled at the corners, wide and expressive face that made me think she'd be an excellent stage actress. Like many Chinese teenagers, Shuangjie seemed younger than an American the same age. Her dress and mannerisms were still girlish. Her hair was tied back in a ponytail and her bangs were plastered on her forehead by sweat. Her complexion had a luminescent glow of youth, flushed from the heat. She wore very short denim cutoffs and a black T-shirt that had "California Roll" written across the chest. She wore no makeup or jewelry other than a red string tied around her wrist for good luck.

Shuangjie was not as confident as she sounded in the letter. She had brought a friend with her for support. They both stood awkwardly, ill at ease in this modern hotel room. I had to coax them into sitting down in the hotel's oversize cream-hued armchairs. I'd learned early in my time in China you don't usually ask somebody if they'd like a beverage—you just give it to them to avoid a ritual of back-and-forth refusing—so I reached into the minibar to grab two cold cans of soda and thrust them into their hands. We made small talk about the unusually hot weather, the customary traffic.

We had arranged in advance not to start the video call until it was 7:00 P.M.—that was 6:00 A.M. in Texas—so we had time to catch up. I reminded Shuangjie that we'd met before, in 2009, but she didn't remember. Since our initial meeting, she had been interviewed by many journalists, Chinese and foreign. Shuangjie gave me a quick update on her life.

Although she was only sixteen, Shuangjie had lived away from home for four years. She'd left the village when she was twelve years old to board at her middle school—the normal pattern for rural kids, since the villages have only elementary schools. Then she had attended a vocational school in Shaoyang to study early education. She'd been doing her internship in Changsha for the last year. Her friend was one of her roommates.

We kept looking at our watches. When it was finally time, my colleague, Nicole, perched at the side of the armchair to interpret. I sat on the bed to stay out of the way. Shuangjie's friend, Yaodi, held up the smartphone so that Shuangjie would have her hands free for the call.

We opened WeChat and hit Video. The technology worked without a hitch; just like that, Esther's face popped up on the tiny screen. The girls stared at each other from seven thousand miles and thirteen time zones apart.

For what seemed a long time, they just examined each other. Neither said a word. Shuangjie had her mouth agape, a look of awe on her face in suspended animation. Then she broke into a big smile and spoke up.

"I'm so happy I can finally see you," she said.

Nicole interpreted.

"I can see you too," Esther replied.

Another interpretation.

"You look so much like me," Shuangjie said.

A long pause ensued. Esther made a joke.

"I was going to put on makeup, but I figured you already know what I look like."

Everybody laughed.

From my angle, I couldn't see Esther, but I heard her. She spoke in a bright, peppy voice. She sounded more like she was from Southern California than Texas. As in their text exchanges, she was bursting with curiosity. The questions spilled out as quickly as my colleague could interpret.

Shuangjie was still smiling, so lost in the intensity of the experience that she seemed unable to speak. "She is a little overwhelmed. She needs time to think of questions," Nicole apologized. Although we had decided in advance to interfere as little as possible, we started offering Shuangjie some prompts. I could hear that in the background Esther's mother, Marsha, was doing the same, coaching her daughter through the conversation.

When Esther asked Shuangjie what music she liked, she answered without hesitation—soft music and folk music. She then went silent.

"Now you should ask her what music she likes," Nicole whispered in Chinese.

Shuangjie obliged. Esther responded that she liked country music and bluegrass. They determined that they both played guitar, although Shuangjie somewhat more seriously. They compared their taste in sports, which followed predictable cultural norms. Esther liked swimming. Shuangjie didn't know how to swim but played ping-pong and badminton.

The girls related best through gestures. Esther held up her waist-length hair and pulled it back to look more like Shuangjie. Shuangjie showed Esther a birthmark on her back, which Esther lacks.

This disjointed conversation was made all the more awkward by the need for interpretation. They became tangled in language and cultural differences addressing the simplest of queries.

Even their birthdays. They were born on the ninth day of the eighth month in the Year of the Dragon, but that was by the lunar calendar used in rural China; it took some back-and-forth to confirm the date: September 6, 2000. They discussed their weights. Esther said she weighed ninety pounds, Shuangjie fifty kilos. That took more time to resolve.

"What did you do today?" Shuangjie asked Esther.

Esther had to explain that it was early morning and that she'd just woken up.

She planned to go to a library.

Then she asked Shuangjie, "What do you plan to do today?"

It was Shuangjie's turn to explain that it was past 8:00 P.M. in China, so the day was done. She told Esther she had had a long and exhausting day. Although the children were on summer break, she and other interns had to canvass residential neighborhoods, handing out flyers advertising the school to prospective parents. It wasn't pleasant work in such hot weather.

Before I'd left New York, Esther had mailed gifts for me to deliver in person in China. I'd taken them out of the original packaging with the return address (Esther was still afraid to reveal her address, for fear she could be forced back to China) and put them in a colorful gift bag.

"Have you opened your gifts yet?" Esther asked, trying to keep the conversation going.

It was another awkward moment. In China, people customarily don't open gifts in front of the gift giver. But Shuangjie obliged, pulling a notebook and several items of clothing out of the bag. She held up a white blouse.

"I hope it's not too small. I need a large," Shuangjie said. It was the second comment she'd made in the conversation about being too fat, although by almost any standard she was fit and slim, other than having a schoolgirl chunkiness in the legs. (She weighed 105 pounds and was about five foot two.)

Shuangjie pulled out of her bag her own gift for Esther. It was a clay figure of Dory, the fish from *Finding Nemo*. She'd made it in school.

At that point, the girls had spoken for more than an hour. I remembered that Shuangjie and her friend had come straight from work, me straight from the airport, and none of us had eaten. I suggested a dinner break, which everybody agreed to with great enthusiasm. We were all hungry. We also needed a break from the tension. The long silences had been excruciating. The lobby café, as dim as the rest of the hotel, seemed to cater to furtive romantic encounters, so we pushed through the revolving doors, exiting the air-conditioned lobby to the outdoors, where heat was still radiating off the sidewalks after dark. Far outside the city center almost everything was closed, but we turned a corner to see a small Muslim noodle shop illuminated as brightly as an aquarium in a darkened room. We took seats on backless wooden stools. A boy, maybe younger than the girls, was making noodles by hand in the back.

I'd expected to spring for a fancier dinner, but the girls were thrilled with their wide knife-cut noodles in a simple sauce of tomato and egg, and delicate, long noodles in a cilantro-flavored chicken broth, all delicious and inexpensive. (The whole meal was nine dollars for the four of us.) Shuangjie pulled out her phone to snap pictures. We were all happy and relaxed after the stress of the video call, and the girls opened up more with their thoughts about the status of females in rural China.

Shuangjie's friend did much of the talking. She told us how much she hated her name, *Yaodi,* which translates literally to "want little brother." She had been branded with that name by her grandfather. The cruelty is hard to fathom, and yet this affliction is not uncommon for Chinese girls. A researcher examining official registrations among just five common surnames in China once counted 16,557 women in China with the similarly insulting name of *Zhaodi* ("seeking younger brother").

Shuangjie said she hadn't experienced such blatant discrimination in her family. "My father treated us the same," she insisted—something I would hear later from other members of the family. And yet I wondered if Shuangjie's self-esteem had been battered by her position in the family. Birth order is important in China, and Shuangjie was technically the fourth daughter, since she was born minutes after Esther. I didn't understand this until Yaodi brought it up that Esther's reentry into the family had nudged Shuangjie slightly further down in the hierarchy. To adhere strictly to tradition, Shuangjie would be expected to address Esther as her *jiejie*, an honorific term for "older sister."

"You know, you don't have to call her *jiejie* until you know her better," Yaodi advised Shuangjie. She seemed to take some comfort in that.

In contrast to Esther, who seemed to have that stereotypically can-do Texas attitude, Shuangjie frequently made self-deprecating remarks, which could in part be attributed to a cultural aversion to boasting. Chinese people frequently deflect a compliment with the rejoinder *Nali, nali,* roughly meaning "Not at all." It was not just her weight. She felt she wasn't clever enough, although her parents would say she was the smartest among the children, with an unusually precise memory for detail. But coming from a poor, rural elementary school, she hadn't done quite well enough in middle school to follow a high school track preparing her for university. She was still well educated by the standards of her community. In Shaoyang, fewer than half of the children finish middle school, and only about 17 percent finish high school, according to a 2020 census. She was adept with technology and had wanted to pursue a career in high tech. But her mother thought she needed a career with more security and encouraged her instead to go to a vocational high school for teacher training.

Shuangjie was unsure about her chosen career, as well as the role she would be expected to fill as a young woman. Both of her sisters—although then twenty-two and twenty years old—were already married and had children. "I don't want to get married so young and be burdened with a family. I want my freedom. I'd like to travel," said Shuangjie.

We all chimed in to ask her if she hoped to visit her American sister. She seemed startled by the question.

"America? I can't imagine. I've never been on a plane." The places on her wish list were closer to home: Yunnan Province in the far southwest of China and Dalian on the Yellow Sea near the Korean border.

After dinner, we strolled back to the hotel and resumed the conversation with Esther. She had just finished breakfast. It was more relaxed this time, but we broke off after less than an hour, promising to do it again.

We were all exhausted, physically and emotionally. And there was one more piece of business to attend to.

We had come this far on coincidences of timing and physical resemblance, but I felt we needed positive proof that the girls were twins. Science could provide that quickly and cheaply. I had purchased a simple collection kit online from a DNA-testing lab. It consisted of a couple of cotton swabs a little longer than Q-tips and test tubes. Shuangjie rolled hers around inside her cheek for a few seconds and we put the swab back in the test tube and sealed it. We did it again with a second swab just to make sure.

Then we offered to escort the girls back to their dorm in a taxi. They were frightened about taking a taxi late at night without an adult chaperone, and also mindful of the budget. The taxi drove us into one of Changsha's older residential neighborhoods with narrow, tree-lined streets, the leaves arching so tightly overhead you couldn't glimpse the sky. The neighborhood of low-rise buildings was shabby in a way that was pleasantly reminiscent of vintage 1980s China. We offered to walk them down the alley leading to their dormitory, but they refused. Shuangjie was embarrassed by the attention she was receiving and didn't want too many of her classmates to know.

CHAPTER SEVENTEEN

THE AMERICAN DAUGHTER

Zeng Youdong looking at a photo of Esther.

As long as I've worked in China, it still surprises me how quickly the veneer of modernity slips away when you leave Chinese cities. The morning after the video chat, Nicole and I hired a driver, who took us along a wide boulevard that paralleled the Xiang River, one side developed into a nicely manicured riverside corniche, the other lined with new office and condominium towers with silver façades glinting in the sunlight. After we crossed the river, I could see the gleaming skyline receding in the rearview mirror. The landscape opened up into expanses of fields flooded for rice cultivation. In the distance were squat hills rimmed with pine trees.

We were headed to Gaofeng village, where the twins were born. Shuangjie couldn't join us because she was working, but I wanted to see her family again. Since she was still a minor, I would need a parental signature to do the DNA test. And I wanted to explain to them in person, as I understood it, the complicated sentiments of their American daughter.

Our driver was a high-strung young man with a missing tooth who chewed betel nuts, staining his remaining teeth red. He nervously flicked the directional signals the whole drive (perhaps protesting my insistence that he not smoke in the car) but otherwise applied his nervous energy to making good time. The road was excellent—eight lanes wide—probably because it led to one of the most hallowed locations in China, Mao Zedong's birthplace in Shaoshan, a popular destination for Chinese engaging in what they call "patriotic tourism." We took a quick break to buy steamed buns at a rest stop attached to a large souvenir shop hawking busts of Mao, some almost life-size and others small enough for your dashboard. After about three hours, the highway petered out and we navigated through small towns, finally reaching Gaoping, the township seat, where the Family Planning office was located along with other government offices. Gaoping is a messy market town: wooden tables stacked with multi-hued synthetic clothing, much of it with misspelled English slogans, pyramids of watermelons, chickens squawking in wire cages, an internet café, where we gestured for a young man to remove his big black headphones so we could ask directions. There were no street signs in the mountains, only propaganda slogans on billboards affixed to brick houses and electric poles: "Eliminate gender discrimination and promote family harmony." "Sweep away crime and rectify social practices."

The road climbed and curved. This was also rice-farming country, but not as prosperous as the flatlands around Shaoshan. The paddies were smaller and irregularly shaped, shoehorned into the curvature of the mountain terraces. In a few weeks, the rice would fade to yellow, signaling the start of the harvest, but it was now at its peak, the stalks tall and plump, the perpetual humidity of late summer accentuating the colors. The rice paddies glistened summer green, the earth a deep oxidized red. When I'd visited in 2009, it had also been August, and the memories flooded back. But so much had changed.

We were able to drive the entire way, without pushing the car over a ditch or navigating a footbridge. The roads were paved until we reached that last rutted patch into the village. As before, there were few cars. People drove three-wheeled motorized carts and motorcycles—one rigged to carry a refrigerator in the back. Women still carried buckets of vegetables on poles balanced on their shoulders. But the brick houses were taller, rising three or even four stories incongruously from the edge of the rice paddies. Villagers often built as much as they could cram onto their little lots, and some houses were so big they seemed to over-hang the road. After some wandering about and asking more directions, we found ourselves in front of the Zeng family house, looking upward with amazement. It looked more like a small hotel than a single-family home. When I'd visited before, the family had been living in the Chi-nese version of a log cabin with a plastic tarpaulin for a roof. Now there was a substantial brick house, two stories high and climbing, with Juliet balconies peeking out over the rice paddies. Like many houses in China, and for that matter elsewhere in the third world, it was a work in prog-ress. Although the upper floors were incomplete, the scale reflected con-fidence in the future.

Zeng Youdong came out to greet us. Last time, I'd met only Zanhua. They alternated shifts—one working in the city to bring in cash, the other minding the home front. This time it was his wife who was work-ing, in a noodle restaurant in southern China. Their land, and that of the neighbors, which they'd been allowed to farm, brought in an abundance of rice, sweet potatoes, and vegetables, but a job in the city was still es-sential to provide cash for the schooling of their son, now fifteen. Youdong had been working in the fields earlier but had changed into a crisp polo shirt to greet us. He wore gray cotton trousers and brown leather shoes. He had the slight stature of a person who'd come of age in an era of inadequate nutrition, but his arms rippled with muscle. He had boyish wisps of mustache on either side of his mouth. He had a gentle smile.

Youdong ushered us inside, ignoring a pair of baby chicks that trailed after him from the yard. We entered through a narrow kitchen, the walls blackened by smoke from the cooking. The house was not yet fully furnished. The floors were bare concrete, red peppers from the garden strewn about to dry for storage. What served as a dining room had a square wooden table and stools, sacks of grain, and farm tools propped up in the corners. A band of blue-and-white-flowered tile along the wall was the only decorative element. The home and the family—they were all about practicality. Youdong gestured for us to sit on the stools. He set out tall bottles of soda and plugged in a standing fan to blow away the flies.

Since Shuangjie spoke to him regularly, he knew the twins had been in touch. But Youdong was the head of the family, and in deference to his position, I wanted to hear his views about their contact and his expectations. Was he thinking that Esther would come live in China? Was he angry that I had withheld information about her whereabouts for nearly eight years? I told him how I had used social media in 2009 to identify Fangfang. And about the difficulty I'd had weighing the American family's insistence on privacy against my responsibility to his family. I apologized that I couldn't do more sooner. Youdong was also more apologetic than angry. He told me he was relieved to know his daughter was alive and in safe hands with the Americans. He was intuitive enough to understand that Americans might think he hadn't done enough for his daughter, favoring instead the son who was born the same year she was taken.

I'd been told ahead of time that Youdong was very reserved and that it would be hard to have a conversation. That was true only to a point. Unlike most other rural Chinese men I'd met, he spoke softly and deliberately. He was confident in what he had to say and wasted few words. Contrary to what people might think, he didn't value boys over girls, Youdong told us. "I was so happy when the twins were born. It was my wife who felt pressure to have a boy, more than me."

"I treated the children the same. I paid for their education just the same," he told us, repeating what Shuangjie had told us earlier.

Youdong needed to tell me his side of the story. He admitted that he'd not been very clever about searching for Fangfang. He'd known nothing about international adoption, since it wasn't publicized inside

China, and he couldn't imagine that she'd be as far away as the United States or Europe. He'd assumed that she'd been sold to a family living somewhere in Hunan or a nearby province, and that his only hope would be to recognize her on the street. It was not until 2009, when he identified her in the spreadsheet of photographs I'd sent, that he understood what had happened.

"That was the first time I realized that she wasn't in China anymore," Youdong told me.

I had brought along my laptop and I opened it to show him more photos of Esther. The same shots she'd sent to Shuangjie—posed photographs in which she was modestly but elegantly dressed. There was a shot of Esther leaning against a wall in a lacy pale-green dress with her hair tossed over one shoulder. Another in a black dress, wearing a thin gold necklace and magenta lipstick. She had an open, wholesome smile. Zeng couldn't peel his eyes away from the screen. He just kept staring with a quiet grin at the girl with the long, shiny hair, his American daughter.

"You should tell her not to be afraid," he said finally. "I understand she is not coming back to live in China. Just to see her makes me happy."

That was what I needed to convey to Esther and her American family. Her main fear was that her birth parents would try to bring her back to China.

We didn't discuss what might happen next. I told Zeng Youdong we should wait for the results of the DNA test before we proceeded any further. He quickly read the release statement, which we'd translated into Chinese, giving permission to test Shuangjie's DNA sample. His handwriting and signature were better than I'd expected. It was then that I realized he had more education than many of his counterparts in the countryside.

We went next to the family who had raised Esther as a baby. Her uncle, Guoxiong, Zanhua's oldest brother, lived a mile down the road in the adjoining village. The twins were born there in the bamboo grove, and Fangfang had spent the first year and a half of her life with her uncle, trying to evade Family Planning.

When the uncle volunteered to take in the baby, it was naturally his wife, Xiuhua, who took on the burden of childcare. This was the duty of Chinese wives, but she didn't mind.

"She was like my daughter. I had two boys and I always wanted to have a daughter," she told us. Xiuhua was an exceptionally tall woman with short-cropped hair, no makeup or jewelry. She looked like she could be a member of a women's volleyball team. She had a no-nonsense air about her. But when she saw the photos I'd brought, her face crumpled into tears and she struggled to speak. Her aunt by marriage, Xiuhua was more emotionally invested in Fangfang than anybody else in the immediate family. It was a reminder that love runs so much deeper than bloodlines.

Fifteen years had elapsed since Fangfang was taken, but the pain was still raw. Xiuhua reenacted what had happened in that room where we were sitting. (The house had since been rebuilt, but the layout was the same.) How the cadres had terrorized the entire family, dropping in at unpredictable hours looking for the girl. How Xiuhua's young sons had fought for Fangfang. How eventually she had been forcibly removed from their home, never to be seen again.

Xiuhua was nearly as boastful about the girl she knew as Fangfang as Marsha was talking about Esther: how quick she was to walk and to talk, her sensitivity to other people's feelings.

"She could read people's faces and expressions," Xiuhua told us. "My own sons couldn't walk until two years old. She was so smart."

The older son, Yuan Zan, twenty-eight, married with his own child, was at home and didn't seem offended by the comparison. Tall and lanky like his mother, he demonstrated how he had grabbed Fangfang, dashed up a staircase at the back of the house, and climbed a ledge over the bathroom. He mimed the way his younger brother had jumped first while holding tightly onto the baby. "She was like our sister. We weren't going to let them take her away." He also seemed on the verge of tears.

"In the end, they got her. We never saw her again."

Later that afternoon, I met Li Guihua, the midwife who had delivered the twins. She had heard I was looking for more information about Esther and stopped by Zeng's house. Now in her late sixties, Li had graduated from a nearby nursing school and worked as what Chinese called a barefoot doctor, somebody who didn't have full medical credentials but could provide primary care. She had delivered almost everybody in the village under the age of forty, including, she thought, Zanhua, although she couldn't quite remember back to 1973. The birth of the twins, though, was fixed in her memory because it was so unusual to deliver babies in a shack in a bamboo grove and twins were rare in this village. Li had curly hair and gapped teeth and was boisterous in voice and appearance. She was dressed in a multicolored pantsuit with a geometric pattern and wore a green jade pendant around her neck. Although she had a remarkably high level of education for a rural woman of her generation, she was hardly a feminist. Nibbling on the watermelon that Zeng had put out on the table, she bluntly volunteered her opinions. She claimed that villagers never willingly abandoned their daughters, but then seemed to contradict herself. "People aren't happy if they have a daughter. A girl will move out after she gets married—she belongs to other people. You need to have a boy if you want security in your old age."

Li glanced at the computer screen with the photograph of Esther and shook her head dismissively. She didn't seem to view the situation as much of a tragedy. "I think Fangfang is better off in America," Li continued. "Maybe when she grows up, she can help her family financially."

I tried to question Li more. I knew that midwives were often compelled to work with Family Planning officials, sometimes to perform abortions, at other times to tip them off about unauthorized births. Li made it clear she didn't want to talk about any of that, and we drove her home. Her house was by far the grandest in the village, perched on higher ground, surrounded by large balustrades and elegant columns, and I wondered how she earned so much money treating patients in such a poor village. Later Zeng told me he suspected the midwife had tipped off Family Planning about the twins' birth because they hadn't paid her well, but others disagreed. Aunt Xiuhua believed the snitch was one of the neighbors who had admired Fangfang's intelligence. Everybody wanted that girl.

THE SUN SETS early in eastern China because Mao decreed back in 1949 that all of China should follow a single time zone, no matter that the country is wider than the continental United States. By late afternoon, I was eager to leave the village and head down the mountain. When reporting, it was best not to stick around in one place for too long. I was still in touch with the filmmakers working on the documentary about the one-child policy, and they told me they had been chased by police while shooting in the area. I hadn't wanted to alert too many people to our presence. Apart from the family, nobody had seen us except a few retirees outside a small clinic across from the Zeng house. For lack of a café or public park, that was where they gathered to socialize.

As we came out to leave, several of them approached us with excitement. There was an elderly man bent over a cane, wearing what looked like his preretirement work uniform, and a woman carrying a woven bamboo basket of vegetables, which she put down to come closer. They surrounded me, clamoring to see pictures. They had heard I'd found one of the missing children. Since I had already packed up the laptop, I pulled out my iPhone and flipped through the photos until I found the portrait of Esther in the black dress.

"Look, look, that's Shuangjie wearing makeup," the old man exclaimed.

"No, don't you understand? That's Fangfang. Fangfang in America," the woman retorted.

As they quibbled, I smiled and put away the phone. I had the cotton swabs with the DNA and Zeng's signature on the consent form, but somehow it felt like the senior citizens outside the clinic had told me all I needed to know.

CHAPTER EIGHTEEN

TEXAS

Marsha and Esther at home in Texas.

FEBRUARY 2018. WHEN I RETURNED FROM CHINA, I PACKED UP
Shuangjie's DNA samples and overnighted them to a laboratory in Fort
Worth. Esther promised to do a sample at home and send it in as well.
Although it seemed obvious at this point that the girls were twins, we
needed confirmation. From the photos and the glimpses I'd seen of Esther during the video chat, there were noticeable differences that tran-
scended culture. Shuangjie's face was broader, her lips fuller, her features
more pronounced. Esther was more delicate. Only Esther had the extra
bump on her ear. And, assuming they were twins, it wasn't at all clear
what kind.

Identical twins are born from a single fertilized egg that divides in
the womb. They remain rare—about three out of one thousand births.
Births of fraternal twins are at least three times more frequent and have

increased in recent decades as a result of fertility treatments. Fraternal twins, produced by separate eggs and fertilized by different sperm, share no more genetic similarity than ordinary siblings born to the same biological parents. But fraternal twins of the same gender can look very similar, especially as small children, and professionals warn that assumptions are often wrong.

The Zengs were not aware of the distinction. The midwife couldn't say with absolute certainty, but she remembered they had separate placentas, which is more common with fraternal twins.

With Shuangjie and Esther, it seemed best to skip the more commonplace DNA tests that determine paternity or other family relationships, and go straight to the more complex procedure known as zygosity testing—that is, to determine if they were from the same zygote (fertilized egg). The lab examined twenty-two pairs of autosomal chromosomes and compared them using a relationship index made up of unrelated Asians. The results came back within a week.

"The Cumulative Relationship Index is 4,940,264,021.1711. It is 4,940,264,021.1711 times more likely [they] are related as identical rather than non-identical twins. The probability that Shuang Jie and Esther Elizabeth are identical twins is 99.9999%."

On the twenty-two pairs of chromosomes examined, the sequence of the genes matched up perfectly. These were genetically identical human beings—only one was Chinese and one was American. I immediately forwarded the results to everybody involved, adding a translation into Chinese for Shuangjie and her parents.

Nobody but me seemed excited by the lab results. Shuangjie sent me an emoji.

"All along I knew it," Marsha wrote back to me. She later told me she had no doubt from the first time she had seen my video of Shuangjie.

AT THIS POINT, I'd never met Esther or her family in person. We communicated almost entirely by email. I had done my part to reconnect the twins and satisfied my own curiosity. Yet again, I thought my involvement in this saga of the separated twins was finished. But that next February, 2018, six months after my trip to China, I was invited to give a talk about North Korea at Baylor University in Waco, Texas, about eighty minutes away from Fort Worth. I'd planned to fly into Dallas Fort Worth International Airport, and I thought I might as well swing by to say hello and tell the family more about my encounters with Shuangjie and her family.

Marsha quickly invited me to come and spend the night with them. I was happy to visit Texas. Early in my career, I'd lived for a year in Dallas working as a business reporter for the now-defunct *Dallas Times Herald*. But this swath of the Bible Belt felt more foreign to me than Asia, where I'd spent more than a decade, and a world apart from New York, where I was then living.

Driving from Waco to Fort Worth, I saw billboards flash by decrying the evils of abortion: "Babies die, mothers cry" and "Planned Parenthood = Murder in the Womb." Getting off the highway, I-35, I drove past saloons and barbecue restaurants, gun shops, a few strip malls, agricultural feed shops, and pastures of horses and Shetland ponies. Esther's family lived west of Fort Worth, just beyond the point where the suburbs devolved into farmland. It felt nearly as rural as her birthplace in Hunan Province, but without the lushness. The landscape was flat and brown, the grass desiccated by the bite of midwinter. I turned into a cul-de-sac, following the directions on my phone. When the maps application indicated I was in front of the house, I glanced again at my phone in confusion. I realized that the property was concealed behind a high wooden privacy fence. I telephoned Marsha. The electronic gate slid open. Behind the imposing gate was not some mansion but a small, single-story manufactured home painted gunmetal blue with a wooden porch out front. I remembered how intent the family was on keeping their privacy.

Marsha was standing at the front door. As I walked inside, I spotted Esther out of the corner of my eye. She had been watching my arrival from behind the drapes that covered the front window in the living room. So confident on the WeChat call, she now looked like a child peeking around a corner. Truth be told, I felt a little shy myself meeting her. At times, journalists will latch onto the germ of a mystery and get somewhat obsessed. I'd spent so many years wondering about the missing twin, and finally now here she was in person. She came out and introduced herself. Now seventeen years old, Esther was wearing a black sundress with a denim shirt over it. Her hair hung to her waist.

As I'd observed in the photos, her features were softer than Shuangjie's. In keeping with the American fad for eyebrow shaping, hers were fashioned into delicate half-moons. But when Esther smiled, the contours of her face arranged themselves into the image of her twin sister. People look most distinctive when you see them in motion, the way their lips part to emit speech or in small gestures like the backhanded flip of a hand to brush away a lock of hair. Shuangjie had an endearing smile, like the start of a laugh that radiated from her cheekbones to the corners of her eyes. I studied Esther's face like a facial-recognition app, comparing and contrasting with what I remembered of Shuangjie, trying hard not to stare.

Marsha relieved any awkwardness. She put on a fresh pot of coffee, settled herself in her recliner, and gestured for me to settle into a plush green sofa next to her. Marsha had reddish-blond hair that curled around her face and pale eyes framed by dark lashes that glistened when she would tear up. Just as when we'd spoken on the telephone, her words spilled out rapidly. She did most of the talking, as would be the case for the next day and a half. She had an urgent need to disgorge the complicated emotions she'd been processing since she'd learned about Esther's history in 2009.

She would tell me for the first of many times, "Esther has been the light of my life. But I wouldn't have adopted her if I'd known."

Marsha had spent years analyzing the factors, economic and psychological, that led to Esther's removal from her birth family and adoption into her own. She accepted that she had unwittingly played a role in Esther's separation from her birth family, swayed by her good intentions and belief that a higher power was commanding her to adopt, no matter that she and her husband were well past the usual age to become parents.

Al had been fifty-six years old when they adopted their first daughter, Victoria, and sixty at the time of Esther's adoption. Wishful thinking had led Marsha to believe that careful eating and exercise would allow her husband to overcome earlier health problems and raise their daughters to adulthood.

Marsha was also questioning her decision to homeschool the girls. Both were diligent students—Victoria was gifted at math and Esther leaned toward the arts and literature—but they had shown little inclination to continue their education. Marsha thought a traditional high school would have provided guidance counselors who steered them to college. Instead, Esther, almost eighteen, and Victoria, nineteen, were working part-time at a supermarket.

People might have judged Marsha's choices harshly, but two things I couldn't question were her devotion to her daughters and her mothering skills.

The girls were polite and articulate. They appeared to be better read than many of their peers in college. Esther told me she had set a goal of reading a book every week. She made up for her lack of formal education with initiative. Self-taught as a photographer, she was starting to get paid assignments shooting weddings. Her photos were romantic and soft-focus, close-ups of gauzy veils and dresses, often in an artistic black-and-white.

Just as Esther was passionate about art and photography, Victoria was taking singing lessons at a community college. She didn't participate, however, in school musicals, because she didn't have her own car, making it difficult to stay late after classes.

Marsha and her daughters lived a frugal but comfortable lifestyle. Their home was barely the size of a few rooms of the Zeng family's oversize house in Hunan, but it was cozy and clean, with low popcorn ceilings of a type popular in the 1970s, thick mauve carpeting, and etched glass dividers between the rooms. Plenty of books, many Christian themed, but novels and nonfiction as well. Judging from the bookcase, they had done their reading about China.

The house exuded a familial warmth in an abundance of tchotchkes, porcelain teacups, an antique doll collection Marsha had inherited from her mother, and a grandfather clock. A fat brown-and-white cat sprawled in front of the hearth. There were many, many photos of Esther and Victoria together in decorative frames stamped with the words "sisters" and "best friends." As toddlers with their arms around each other's shoulders, a little older in matching Easter bonnets decorated with pink roses around the brims. Photographs of their late father with his brush of silver hair and aviator glasses, beaming as he posed with his young daughters, were on prominent display.

The grief over his 2009 death lingered. A vintage yellow MG sports car sat in the front yard covered by a tarpaulin. Marsha told me her daughters didn't want to sell it because it reminded them of their father.

What mattered in the end was how happy the girls seemed with their mother. Having an occasionally surly son, I envied the warmth of their relationship. Adoption is sometimes likened to the ultimate blind date, where complete strangers are bound together in perpetuity. Often adoptees complain they have little in common with their parents. But in this case, the girls—both of them—seemed to adore their mother. They voiced not a hint of regret that they hadn't been adopted by wealthier or younger parents. Victoria was a little defensive about any suggestion to the contrary. "I had a fairy-tale childhood," Victoria told me emphatically.

As though to provide evidence, the girls wanted me to see videos from their earlier childhood. We gathered around a television next to the fireplace, sitting on the carpet as Marsha popped in a series of videocassettes. There were the girls dancing together, wearing matching Disney T-shirts emblazoned with a cartoonish blond Cinderella. In another, they were dressed in frilly gowns, twirling scarves overhead like whirling dervishes as they sang "Jesus Loves Me."

As children, they occasionally wore matching clothes and were sometimes mistaken for twins, although, other than being Asian, they looked nothing alike. Victoria was taller, with a slim, angular face, large eyes, and a complexion that was more Southeast Asian, making it likely that her birth family was from one of the many minorities scattered through southern China and across the borders into Myanmar and Vietnam. She wore hip, geometric eyeglasses. Her hair was even longer than Esther's. There was something ethereal, almost otherworldly, about the two of them. Esther might have lost her identical twin in China, but Victoria filled the same role. In psychological studies, they would be referred to as "virtual twins."

I stayed with the family for a day and a half. They couldn't have been more welcoming—all except the cat, Lucky, who hissed whenever I drew near. Esther did the cooking. She made chicken tetrazzini and a double-layered coconut cake. They prayed before we ate, Marsha thanking the lord for my help reconnecting Esther with her birth family. She insisted that I take her bedroom, and I slept comfortably under a colorful patchwork quilt, the doll collection arranged by the side of the bed. When I got up, Marsha was already awake. She brewed a pot of hazelnut coffee and we settled into our respective seats—she in her recliner and me on the couch.

Ahead of the visit, I'd fretted about how we would get along, she an evangelical Christian from rural Texas, me a secular New Yorker and a journalist. Through my work overseas (I had written a previous book about North Korean defectors), I had spent a fair amount of time with Christian missionaries and considered some to be friends. But in politically divisive times, I worried that a gulf of potential pitfalls now stood in the way of Marsha and me having an amicable relationship. As we chatted, though, I learned we had more in common than I had imagined. Marsha was a freethinker who didn't shy away from politics that were sometimes unpopular in her community. Even while living in a small, rural town, Marsha followed what was happening in the world, an extension of her earlier dream of becoming a missionary. Her bookshelf attested to her curiosity about the outside world. I expected Marsha to disapprove when I told her that I was a single mother, unlike her, never married. I wasn't taking notes during that visit because I didn't expect to write anything, but I remember verbatim how she responded.

"I'm a Christian, not a saint," she told me with a laugh.

*   *   *

THE MOST SPARSELY decorated room was Esther's, which was strangely tidy for a teenager. She had a double bed with a white chenille bedspread, white and turquoise pillows neatly placed at the head of the bed, a modernist print of a chandelier, and a large cross above the window. There were no posters of movie stars or rock bands. She said she liked to keep the walls bare so that she'd have a place to hang up her own photos.

Since Marsha and Victoria did the talking, it was hard to get a sense of Esther. She wasn't withdrawn, but she wasn't inclined to volunteer opinions either. Mostly she asked questions, displaying the same insatiable curiosity that had characterized her interactions with Shuangjie. She was hungry for details about my trip to China.

"How old was I when I was taken away?" "Did they say anything about what I was like as a child?" I told her what her aunt had said about how precocious she was and how she spoke at an early age, obviously in Chinese.

That seemed to frustrate Esther more. She couldn't remember a word of Chinese. It was a reminder of how much she had lost. Infantile amnesia, the psychological term, is a well-studied phenomenon that in the words of Sigmund Freud "veils our earliest youth from us and makes us strangers to it." Almost without exception, adults cannot retrieve memories of anything that happened before the age of about three. Languages spoken fluently as toddlers disappear. This isn't an affliction but an entirely normal effect of the brain's development process, but it is especially painful for people who lost loved ones at an early age or adoptees who yearn to see the faces of their birth families. When she left China, Esther was already twenty-six months old, a talking, walking, sentient child whose newsworthy early life now lay just beyond the reach of accessible memory. All of it vanished—*poof*—like a dream the next morning.

Esther was fascinated with a 2007 Disney movie, *Meet the Robinsons,* in which a twelve-year-old orphan, looking for his birth mother, invents a machine that allows people to scan their memories. "It's a machine where you can tap into your hippocampus. Even if you think you can't remember, your brain does. It is almost like you can type a date into a machine, and it will bring that memory onto a projector. That's what I would like," she would tell me later.

I could only pull out my laptop and show her the photographs and videos I'd taken in China. Although nothing would jog those memories, she studied the photographs for clues. She liked the shots of Shuangjie and her friend eating noodles in the Muslim restaurant. The house belonging to her uncle and aunt where she'd spent most of her first two years. The talkative aunt who had raised her, and her sons—then children, now adults—who were her first babysitters. The midwife who had delivered her.

The best was the photo of Zeng Youdong, her birth father, seated at the square wooden table in the village, smiling as he looked at my laptop displaying the photograph that Esther had sent me. Now she looked at that same laptop, staring at the photo of him looking at her. For a moment it felt like their eyes had met.

CHAPTER NINETEEN

CHINA BOUND

Changsha skyline.

IN RETROSPECT, IT WAS INEVITABLE THAT ESTHER WOULD GO back to her village in China and that I would be the one to bring her there. Although that possibility hadn't been on the table before I went to Texas, once we started talking, it all made sense. Esther had opened a portal to her past that couldn't be closed. She had to keep going forward. Video chats wouldn't be enough to satisfy her. "I couldn't go through life without meeting them," she would tell me later.

Marsha too felt compelled to go to China. She wanted to apologize in person for the role she'd unknowingly played in Esther's abduction. And she wanted to go soon, while she was still young enough for what could be a strenuous journey, physically and emotionally.

The family couldn't put a trip like this together on their own. They didn't speak Chinese and didn't know anybody who did. None of them had current U.S. passports. When Marsha had traveled to China in 1999 and again in 2002 to adopt the girls, she and Al were effectively on a package tour, with their adoption agency handling every last detail, including the visas, hotels, and transportation. Having lived for seven years in China, I had the expertise to organize a trip. I knew where the village was, and although I wasn't fluent in Chinese and struggled especially with the Hunan dialect, I knew how to find somebody who was.

A trip to China also wouldn't be cheap. As soon as we started discussing it, Victoria said she would come too. Marsha said she wanted to include Sam Belanger, the adult son who had first contacted me. This was becoming mission creep.

Although the family was by no means indigent, they lived on a fixed budget cobbled together with pensions, Social Security, and the daughters' modest earnings at the supermarket. When we went out for Mexican food the day I left for the airport, Marsha insisted on treating. I noticed that they carefully packed up the complimentary salsa to take home.

I was willing to assist, but only up to a point. Until then, I had been helping out of a sense of obligation for having inserted myself in their lives through my reporting. But my finances weren't flush either. I was working full-time, on deadline finishing a book about Tibet, and preparing to send my son to college. If they permitted me to write about their story, we could cobble together the money with the help of family and my newspaper and publisher. American journalists are not supposed to pay their interview subjects, but I could cover at least some of the transport and the interpreter. We discussed what my coverage would entail, and there we found ourselves in agreement. Marsha and Esther didn't want a television spectacle. In 2017, ABC's *Good Morning America* had staged a theatrical reunion between identical adopted twins where a screen (decorated with the show's logo) slid open to reveal them to each other, dressed in matching pink outfits. Nothing like that would be acceptable to them.

And yet, Marsha felt that Esther's story would be instructive to other Chinese adoptees struggling with their identity and sense of abandonment, another of the missions about which she was so passionate. Although she didn't exactly put it this way, it would be one more way of undoing any harm caused by the adoption. "I've known for some time that this story would have to be made public," she wrote once. "It was a question of when."

We thought about going as early as September, after the oppressive heat of summer had subsided but before the gloom of the dark, wet Hunan winter. But Zeng Youdong would be busy with the harvest and the other family members would have difficulty getting vacation time. Shuangjie had her job at the kindergarten in Changsha. Zanhua was still working at the noodle shop in the South. One of the sisters was living in Hubei Province.

To anybody familiar with the Chinese calendar, the timing was obvious. We would have to wait until the Lunar New Year, the fifteen-day reprieve known as Chunjie, or "spring festival." It is the only pause in the relentless quest for growth, productivity, and money—the time when factories, offices, schools, and government offices all close. Hundreds of millions of Chinese migrants travel back to their home villages, often the only time they will see their families the entire year. Ambition, for a moment, takes a back seat to tradition.

New Year would also be a convenient time to visit the village without attracting undue attention. Like every other entity in China, the security agencies operate on skeleton staffs. With millions of people on the move for the holiday, people don't pay as much attention to unfamiliar faces. Because she was active in Christian circles, Marsha was concerned about her personal security. She had read about pastors and worshippers arrested for their involvement with churches not officially sanctioned by the Communist Party. The demolition in January 2018 of the evangelical Golden Lampstand Church in northern China had received extensive publicity in Christian publications. An official five-year plan, issued later that year, called for "patriotic education" and "socialist core values" to be taught at churches and for sermons to enforce party leadership and reject foreign influences. I thought it unlikely that an American tourist like Marsha needed to worry, but overall, I agreed that we wanted to make our travels as discreet as possible.

In the preceding years, China had become more open about international adoption. The Chinese government even subsidized tours for adoptees, whom they described as potential goodwill ambassadors for the country. "Through root seeking," explained a Chinese government website, "the adopted children deepen their understanding and comprehension of China, and have a healthy growth." But "root seeking" was more about culture than about seeking out birth families. Adoptees are encouraged to study calligraphy, Chinese paper cutting, and dumpling making. They are not expected to ask hard questions. In a few cases, adoptees visiting their home villages were greeted with big welcoming parties and fireworks. But Esther's visit would be of an entirely different nature. Esther had been a confiscated child, and her homecoming could reopen the scandal over abuses committed by Family Planning. Although the one-child policy had been lifted three years earlier, in 2015, the subject of confiscated children was not to be discussed openly. I had stayed in touch with Old Yuan, the teacher who had written up the petitions. He warned me that he remained under surveillance. The culprits responsible for confiscating the children were still working nearby in local government jobs, and they could try to make trouble for us or for the Zeng family.

It was not just a question of logistics. Esther had continuing bouts of fearfulness. She understood that she was a U.S. citizen and could not be compelled to return to China, but she worried that her birth family would apply pressure for her to stay. At one point, I showed her a clip from an upcoming documentary in which the teenage Shuangjie made a brief appearance. Teary-eyed in the video, Shuangjie spoke of her fantasy of her twin moving back to China, going to the same school as her, and wearing the same clothes. That frightened Esther, making her think that any contact would lead to disappointment, since she didn't intend to stay. When she'd finally gotten up the nerve to create her own WeChat account, one of her Chinese sisters sent an unsolicited message addressing her as Fangfang. Again she got scared and started to back away from having further contact with her birth family. Practically speaking, she knew she couldn't be kidnapped and returned to China against her will, but she feared being entangled in a familial relationship that she couldn't easily escape.

I was traveling in Asia for work in 2018, so I went again through Hunan Province to try to pin down details for a reunion. It was more relaxed this time. Shuangjie came to meet me and we went to a stylish restaurant to eat *hongshaorou,* a pork dish reputed to be Mao's favorite. We returned to my hotel for another video call with Esther. All the awkwardness of the previous visit had dissipated. Esther and Shuangjie had celebrated their eighteenth birthdays the month before, giving them new confidence as adults. Esther had copied a "happy birthday" message from a Chinese calligraphy book, which pleased Shuangjie.

Esther asked Shuangjie about how she'd spent a recent national holiday that marks the founding of the People's Republic of China. But for all her effort, the gulf between them yawned wide and was, if anything, more apparent than in their initial video chat.

When they discussed their favorite childhood memories, Esther told Shuangjie she had liked "playing dress-up."

Shuangjie was mystified. Nobody in her family had fancy clothing, scarves, or jewelry that girls could play with.

Esther spoke of a summer when she was sent to a farm camp and how much fun it was.

Shuangjie explained that she lived on an actual farm and helped with the planting and harvest.

"I can take you to the field for some work on the farm to harvest cabbages and radishes," she offered.

"That would be cool," Esther replied gamely.

We discussed the fact that Shuangjie's family grew most of their own food, emphasizing that it was fresh, organic, and delicious.

"Farm-to-table is very popular in the United States," Esther said encouragingly. Shuangjie murmured under her breath, "Oh, this is embarrassing." She didn't like to tell people she grew up on a farm. The farming life in China carries no cachet, only a stigma of backwardness and poverty.

I made note of the potential pitfalls if Esther and her family really went to China. Jealousy. Unrealistic expectations, cultural miscues. Would Shuangjie be afraid to open up to American visitors? Would she think that Esther was a spoiled American, living a very privileged existence? Even the midwife had suggested that Esther should send her birth family money. It was hard to explain that Esther's family was far from wealthy—not by an American standard, not even by a twenty-first-century Chinese standard.

Shuangjie told Esther about her grueling work schedule at the kindergarten—7:30 A.M. to 6:00 P.M., six days a week—and duties that included cleaning up after young children's toilet accidents. She inquired pointedly whether Esther's work as a photographer was taxing.

"I guess it's hard to carry all those cameras," she told Esther, making what was maybe a concession or possibly a microaggression.

If that was a slight, Esther let it roll off without bristling. They switched to safer topics, such as their shared love of trying new foods. Shuangjie briefed Esther on Changsha's cuisine, promising to bring Esther to her favorite—a snack bar serving a famous specialty, *choudoufu,* "stinky tofu."

"But I'm allergic to tofu," Esther replied.

THE MISUNDERSTANDINGS WOULD have to be cleared up in person. I visited the village again to pin down plans for a reunion. As expected, it was the height of harvest season, the fields faded to greenish yellow, sweet potato leaves drying to feed the pigs. Hunan's famous citrus fruits were in season. Zanhua handed me pomelos as big as basketballs from her family's orchard. This was a rushed visit, since the Zengs were too consumed with the harvest to chat. But they gave their enthusiastic endorsement to a New Year's visit. Practically and symbolically, this would be the appropriate time for Esther to be reunited with her family.

With that last question of timing settled, all the pieces fell into place quickly. Esther and her family received their new passports, then their Chinese visas. We decided jointly this would be a short trip—little more than one week—skipping the usual tourist destinations. Shuangjie had never been to Beijing or Shanghai, and it would seem unfair if Esther saw more of China's top attractions than her twin. I booked hotels and found surprisingly inexpensive flights to Changsha routed through Shanghai. We would travel in February 2019, arriving a few days after the start of the holiday, giving the Zeng family time to conduct the obligatory visits to other relatives. That would allow them to be more attentive to Esther and her family. Our visit was confirmed for the Year of the Pig, the final sign in the twelve-year cycle of the Chinese zodiac. Like the Year of the Dragon, it is by tradition an auspicious year to be born.

Only later did we appreciate that it would also be an auspicious year for Americans to travel to China. By December 2019, Chinese doctors were puzzling over a previously unknown respiratory virus infecting workers and shoppers at a wet market in Wuhan, two hundred miles away from Changsha. Before long, it would turn the world upside down and plunge U.S.-China relations into a period of animosity reminiscent of the early 1970s. Had we delayed the visit much longer, it probably would not have happened.

Part Four

GAOFENG

VILLAGE

CHAPTER TWENTY

HOMECOMING

The twins' first meeting in person.

FEBRUARY 10, 2019. THE CONFUSION STARTED AS EARLY AS John F. Kennedy International Airport. We had booked a late-evening flight to make it easier to sleep. We stood in a long, snaking line waiting to board a China Eastern flight to Shanghai. Few business travelers or ordinary tourists visit China at this time of year, so our fellow passengers were almost all Chinese. Among more than one hundred people in line, only a handful were Caucasian—including me and Marsha and her son, Sam, now forty-seven, tall and goateed with the remains of blondish hair. The crowd looked to be mostly students who had booked cheap tickets by flying a few days after the start of the holiday. The lingua franca of this section of the terminal was Chinese. In the queue of Asian faces, Esther and her sister clutched their blue U.S. passports, as though fearing the fragility of their American identity. Sure enough, the airline agent addressed them in Chinese when asking for their boarding passes but, seeing their consternation, rapidly caught himself and switched to English. It would be the first of many times that would happen over the next week.

There had been a few days for acclimation. Esther and her sister, along with their mother, had arrived in New York City earlier in the week and stayed with me. My apartment was close to Columbia University, which has a large Asian student population. Esther and Victoria felt comfortable being in a city where nobody gave them a second glance. A Chinese adoptee roughly the same age came to dinner at the apartment and gave them a briefing on returning to China. She prepared them for that unaccustomed feeling of vanishing into a sea of familiar faces, the pangs of longing for a place that should feel like home but wasn't. Regret alternating with the relief that they had escaped what they imagined would have been a life of poverty and repression. All those conflicting sentiments would keep their emotions churning over the coming week.

WE STEPPED OFF the plane into the blinding light. It was just after 8:00 A.M., and sunlight streamed through the soaring atrium above the arrival terminal at Shanghai Pudong International Airport. We squinted as we pushed our hand luggage down the glass-roofed corridors, exhausted and exhilarated to finally set foot in China. It was hard not to be dazzled by the modernity gleaming off of every surface, precisely the desired effect. The airport was designed for the express purpose of impressing foreigners who might otherwise dismiss China as a backward country.

We all queued at the "foreigners" line of immigration—no confusion here about the nationality of the adoptees. Our passports were quickly stamped, giving us a few hours to kill before our flight to Changsha. We inspected the luxury shops and modish restaurants before selecting one that had a fusion menu of Chinese and Western food. Marsha, Victoria, and Sam all wanted fried eggs and toast. But Esther gamely opted to start the day with a Chinese-style breakfast of noodle soup. I noticed, watching her eat, that she was wearing a black-and-white-checked flannel shirt—almost identical to a shirt Shuangjie had worn the last time we had a meal.

From Changsha's equally futuristic airport, a minivan drove us through canyons of high-rise office towers and condominiums. We were staying at a newly opened apartment hotel—again ultramodern—that occupied the upper floors of an office building at the center of the city. Our bedrooms had little kitchenettes and floor-to-ceiling windows that would have induced vertigo were it not for the impenetrable mist hugging the building. Jet-lagged and befuddled, we made our way to the hotel restaurant on the fortieth floor for a light dinner. Unable to use chopsticks, Victoria asked the waiter for a fork, which he immediately handed to me as one of the few Caucasians at the table. We laughed. Outside we could hear the car horns from the traffic jam far below that we couldn't see through the clouds.

THE NEXT MORNING, Esther and her family embarked on what could only be characterized as a journey back in time. We were leaving China's newly spiffed-up cities for the countryside. And Esther would peel back her identity as an American teenager to reveal the Chinese orphan within. Joined now by a photographer and an interpreter, we piled into a minivan. Esther and Victoria took the back seat together. Our soundtrack was a loud, robotic female voice from the driver's GPS giving directions. We drove along the corniche that runs along the Xiang River and crossed a bridge near the giant Mao statue. The girls, in the back, started watching movies on an iPad. I had expected them to be glued to the car windows, surveying the landscape of their ancestral homes (Victoria came from adjacent Jiangxi Province). I understood later it was their way to ease the anxiety.

We zipped along the eight-lane highway, making such good time that we added in a couple of bathroom breaks and food stops. Down the highway past the exit to Mao's home village (Marsha had made sure the girls knew the basics of Chinese history, but we had to explain to Sam who Mao was), we bought dumplings and pancakes. We turned off the highway and made our way to Gaoping. In the middle of the holiday, the township was more congested than usual, the main intersection a tangle of honking cars, pedicabs, and pedestrians laden with their New Year's shopping, nobody willing to yield an inch to anybody else. People padded down the streets wearing heavy quilted pajamas in childish shades of pink and turquoise, often patterned with cartoon characters. This is a quirky New Year's fashion in southern China, popular for adults as well as children. They're worn indoors as well, since, according to a regulation set more than six decades ago by the Communist Party, there is no central heating south of what is roughly the thirty-third parallel.

Although the New Year's holiday is known as Spring Festival, heralding the end of winter, the weather in this part of China is usually wet and miserable, with none of the frosty white elegance of a northern winter. The ground was soggy, with red wrappers from spent fireworks stamped into the mud. Dangling from storefronts were colorful paper lanterns that folded out like accordions. We thought these festive accoutrements were on sale for the New Year's celebration, but we later realized they were used for funerals, when we saw them carried by mourners in white, marching to the sound of drums in procession.

Trapped in the gridlock, we got out of the van to explore the market. At tables covered with green tarpaulins, butchers sold freshly slaughtered meat still dripping with blood. Vendors sold crab apple–like fruit coated with caramelized sugar on long bamboo skewers—candied hawthorn, or *tanghulu,* a popular wintertime snack. A sparkly new bakery with English signage advertising cake and bread looked somewhat incongruous in the heart of this old-fashioned market. Needing a gift, we peeked inside at cakes frosted in oversaturated colors, some topped with gold-wrapped chocolate coins to signify good fortune for the New Year, another with frosting molded into a buxom bikini-clad redhead. The cakes looked too lurid, so we ducked into a supermarket—neon bright, with blaring music that jostled the jet-lagged brain—to choose from big bins with perhaps a hundred varieties of candies wrapped in colorful, crinkly paper. We tossed some into a plastic bag, along with a large plastic jug of cooking oil—a popular gift in the Chinese countryside.

Enough stalling. We piled back into the van and began the ascent into the thick mist obscuring the mountains. The asphalt gave way to rutted roads choked with mud. With each pothole, we needed to brace our hands against the interior roof of the van so we wouldn't bump our heads. The girls turned off the iPad and giggled.

At this point, I had been to the village three times, but never in winter. The lushness of my previous visits had given way to a dreary monochrome landscape of dead leaves and bare trees. Everything was washed out of color except for the red paper scrolls hung for the New Year—horizontally over the doorways and vertically along either side—with propitious sayings. ("Dragon and phoenix bring prosperity" and "Spring returns. The land becomes warm" were two of the more popular.) It was hard to distinguish one village from the next, a repeating loop of muddy fields and houses built of the same bleached red brick. The driver took a shortcut onto a makeshift road following the narrow dikes that enclosed the rice paddies. There was knee-deep water on both sides. He kept up a steady speed, unconcerned that a slight miscalculation would have toppled the van into the muck.

I used my sleeve to wipe the condensation on the inside of the window, but it barely helped. The GPS had run out by now. We had come in from a different direction and I wasn't sure if I was in the right place or if I could recognize the Zengs' family house. I was about to suggest that the driver ask for directions when I saw her.

Shuangjie was standing alone in the middle of the road. She wore a black parka with a fake fur hood and pink suede boots that gleamed against the drabness. Her stance suggested she knew what to do. She gestured to the driver to pull up the van alongside the house. As though she had intuited exactly where in the van Esther would be seated, she put her face close to the glass and peered into the back.

The side door slid open. Esther climbed out.

Shuangjie lightly touched her arm to help her out.

"*Esta,*" she said softly, unable to pronounce the final syllable of her name.

Victoria came next. Then Marsha and the rest of us. Shuangjie offered an arm to help them out in turn. She didn't look directly at Esther. Esther seemed to avoid her gaze as well but smiled politely and gave a little wave to the family members who had come out of the house. They both were playing it cool, reluctant to stare.

When everybody was out of the van, the two of them stood next to each other, side by side, facing the photographer. Nobody embraced. Nobody spoke. I imagined the twins as a bride and groom in an arranged marriage, meeting for the first time, willing to pose for the photographer but not yet able to engage in conversation.

Shuangjie took charge. She ushered Esther into the house.

"Go, go, go," she commanded with her limited English vocabulary.

The rest of us trailed slowly behind. We walked through the blackened kitchen and into the dining area. The square wooden table where I'd sat before was now covered for the holiday with a red plastic tablecloth. A double-tiered porcelain dish like one my grandmother had owned held delicacies for the season—apples, mandarin oranges, almonds, sunflower and pumpkin seeds.

I'm not sure what I had expected. Tears and hugs, of course, perhaps somebody fainting or collapsing on the floor begging forgiveness. That's what had happened when I covered a reunion in Beijing a few years earlier of an adopted Chinese boy with his relatives. In one of the video chats between the twins, they had shared fantasies of what it would be like to meet for the first time. ("It will be like magic," Shuangjie had said.) None of the imagined scenarios prepared me for the long silences and reticence. I would soon learn that this was not a family prone to histrionics. They did not readily display emotion. We all stood around awkwardly, wondering what to do. Even Marsha was uncharacteristically quiet. Esther and Shuangjie stood on opposite sides of the square table, still avoiding direct eye contact.

Shuangjie led a round of introductions, using the precise Chinese terminology to explain family relations. There was the number one *jiejie*, the oldest sister, Ping, twenty-three years old, wearing padded pink pajamas. The second sister, Yan, twenty-one. Then Jialiang, the *didi*, or "little brother." This was the long-awaited son, now a lanky sixteen-year-old with bangs hanging over a handsome if acne-marred teenage face. He nodded his greeting before ducking into another room. Ping poured hot water from a thermos into red paper cups with the character *qing*, meaning "to celebrate." Under the table was a charcoal brazier to warm our legs. There was no other heating in the house. It was cold enough inside that we could see our breath. Nobody took off their coat or hat.

Throughout the introductions, the parents hung back. The father, Zeng Youdong, stood quietly in the doorway between the dining room and kitchen, watching with a private smile—the same expression I remembered from when I first showed him photos of Esther. The mother, Zanhua, hadn't come out to greet us, instead busying herself in the kitchen, from which billowed clouds of smoke so pungent with red pepper that it made our eyes water. Only after she had carried out dish after dish of food—pork, fish heads with hot pepper, spicy cabbage, stir-fried egg with tomato, duck—did she finally speak.

"Eat, eat, before it gets cold." Those were the first words she spoke to her long-lost daughter.

Since the square table wasn't large enough, the sisters and their husbands, the teenage brother, and assorted children were shuffled off to an adjoining room. The rest of us—me, Marsha and Sam, Esther and Victoria, an interpreter, the birth parents, Shuangjie—crowded onto the backless wooden benches around the table. We ate with red chopsticks out of white porcelain bowls. Nobody asked for a fork.

That first meal felt like a formal banquet. Esther and Shuangjie stole glances at each other but didn't dare look each other straight in the eye. Unlike many Westerners, Chinese don't consider meals a time for conversation, but the silence felt stifling. Esther tried to break the ice with what I would come to admire in her—impeccable manners and grace.

"You are making me feel so welcome," she said, instinctively pausing for the interpreter.

"I am having a good time in China."

"I'm glad to finally meet you."

Again, a pause.

Toward the end of the meal, everybody was starting to warm up, gradually letting down their guard. When the photographer pointed the camera at Shuangjie, she flashed him that distinctive smile and raised her fingers in a victory sign. Yes, she'd done it. She'd gotten her twin sister back. Esther gave her version of the same grin. As we sat, side by side, it was for the first time possible to compare. Esther's hair was longer and parted on the side, while Shuangjie had bangs over her forehead, emphasizing the roundness of her features. Her upper lip curled up a little more, which she attributed to a fall from a tree as a child. Esther had a smattering of freckles, probably because as an American, she wasn't as concerned as many Chinese women about avoiding the sun. The most striking difference was size. Shuangjie was a larger person, taller by almost three inches and proportionally heavier, although not at all overweight. That hadn't been evident during video calls and wasn't cleared up by all the discussions of inches and centimeters, pounds and kilos. It's not uncommon for identical twins to vary in size. But Esther was larger at birth, as is usually the case with the firstborn twin. One would have expected Texas-raised, firstborn Esther to be larger in adulthood. It seemed that the six months she'd spent in the orphanage had cost her several inches in height. But they were otherwise close enough in appearance to revel in all that they shared. "It's like seeing another me in the mirror," Shuangjie exclaimed.

WE DIDN'T STAY long that first day. Sunset would be earlier than when I had visited in the summer, and we needed to navigate our way off the mountain. The family had invited us to stay with them, but I thought the lack of indoor heating and an American-style bathroom would be too difficult for Marsha. And we needed a psychological break. I had booked rooms in Shaoyang, about ninety minutes away. We promised we would come back the next day. We piled back into the van, carrying a bag of bread that Shuangjie had given us for late-night snacking. We hardly spoke at all on the drive back. At our hotel, we rode the elevator up to our rooms with barely enough energy to mumble good night at our respective floors. Over breakfast the next day, I asked Esther how she had slept. She told me that she and Victoria had watched *Kung Fu Panda 3* before falling asleep. "I didn't dream at all. It was all dark."

CHAPTER TWENTY-ONE

MEMBERS OF THE FAMILY

The first family meal.

EVEN WITH ITS PRECISION WHEN IT COMES TO FAMILY RELA-
tions, the Chinese language lacks the terminology to refer to the adoptive mother of your stolen birth child or the various foreign half-siblings
and adoptive siblings thrown in the mix. Not to speak of a foreign journalist. But we all were beginning to feel like members of the family.

We came back to the village every day for the rest of the week, filing
into the house, chattering amiably, taking the same seats at the wooden
benches around the square table. We'd walk through the kitchen, which
was the main entrance of the house, our eyes tearing from the hot pepper
wafting out of the wok.

Marsha and Victoria figured out how to use the chopsticks. They
managed to tolerate the spiciness. As promised, it was true farm-to-table

cooking, since the Zeng family grew almost everything, including their rice. On our second visit, we watched Zanhua hacking away at a rabbit with a cleaver. Each time, it seemed another animal was dying on our behalf. We were served a variety of six or seven dishes, sometimes one or two left from the previous day but always something fresh that they somehow managed to cook up on a single gas burner.

For their part, the Zengs had grown accustomed to the Americans and their strange habits. Marsha said grace before every meal. The Zengs listened respectfully but didn't join in the prayers.

They were still speechifying, but the words flowed more easily, tripping off the tongue of the interpreter, who could barely get a chance to touch her food. No more small talk. They got quickly to the gist of the visit—the circumstances under which Esther was taken from her birth family and eventually returned.

Marsha gave the speech that she had, in effect, rehearsed for nearly a decade, ever since she'd learned about Esther's past in 2009.

"Esther's name means 'star.' She has been a bright star in my life," she began. "But I would never have adopted her if I knew she was stolen from you."

"It was the situation. It was the government," Youdong replied.

"Still, it gives me pain knowing that my gain was your loss," Marsha said.

"I'm overjoyed just to be able to see her again."

"I'm happy that she can come here and be with her birth family. I want that connection to remain," Marsha replied.

"I'm grateful to you. I can see that you raised her very well," Youdong replied.

Marsha and Youdong went back and forth this way, each deferring to the other with fulsome utterances of praise and gratitude. Although we were seated on the crude wooden stools, the formality of the discourse made it feel like one of those stilted U.S.-China summits, the leaders facing forward, sunk into oversize armchairs with a flower arrangement and interpreter strategically placed between them. Nobody quarreled, but there were underlying tensions that bubbled to the surface, squeezing through the niceties. As in any family, money and favoritism were the touchy subjects.

Youdong couldn't understand why Marsha and her husband, at a relatively advanced age and with adult children, came to China to adopt. And he was confused by the role played by Sam, who was almost exactly the same age as him.

"I'm surprised that Sam did not object to the adoption," Zeng said at one point.

That took Marsha and Sam aback, both a little offended by the assumption that an adult son would have power over his mother, especially one as independent as Marsha. Sam tried to reassure them about how much he loved having Esther and Victoria as sisters. Zeng inadvertently offended again by saying it would be good in the future for Esther to have Sam for support. The implication was that Esther would need a parental figure after Marsha died. It reminded me—Chinese are more direct than Americans when it comes to discussing age and death.

About the finances of the adoption, Zeng was even blunter, so much so that the Americans in the room cringed at his question.

"How much did you pay for her?"

Marsha looked to the interpreter for guidance as to whether the translation was accurate. It was. Zeng was using the Chinese words for "buy" and "sell." Zeng knew nothing of international adoption, even less of the niceties of the Hague Convention, which was designed to guard against the outright sale of children. Marsha didn't lose her composure and answered as though she had anticipated the question. She explained briefly the laws and answered directly. The adoption had cost about twenty-five thousand dollars, she explained. Except for the three-thousand-dollar contribution to the orphanage, the fees were paid through the government's China Center of Adoption Affairs, so it was not as though they'd been dealing with child traffickers. She and her husband were able to afford it because they had sold their house.

It was an artful answer—it gave Marsha a chance to explain that Americans weren't just buying babies. And also to emphasize gracefully that American adoptees weren't necessarily rich. Her family, in particular, was not.

They then touched on a subject so sensitive that nobody dared voice it aloud. I had wondered if the family would have scraped up the money to pay the Family Planning fines for a boy, and I sensed that Marsha and her family might have the same suspicion. (I thought back to something one of the other families had told me back in 2009 when I was reporting the original story: "We don't throw away our daughters, but if somebody tried to take our sons, we'd kill them.") Youdong seemed to anticipate this line of inquiry: He explained that Esther was already gone by the time they could have raised funds. He apologized for the fruitlessness of his efforts to find her.

"It was a dream that I would find you, but I didn't know where to look. It seemed impossible. The world was so big, with so many countries. How would it have been possible?" Youdong said, addressing himself to Esther.

WITH THE UNCOMFORTABLE questions out of the way, we started to relax. Each day, the visits became easier, the interactions more natural. Chinese people generally are not as touchy-feely with strangers as Americans, and they don't engage in casual hugs or handshakes with people they've just met. But I watched as slowly, tentatively they began to touch one another. The second sister, Yan, took Esther's hand and placed it under the table to teach her how the brazier below would keep her warm. Esther pulled out her Canon camera to show Shuangjie, and so they were finally sitting close to one another, their shoulders touching. Shuangjie soon got up, stood behind Esther, and began braiding her hair.

Marsha brought out an album of photographs she had prepared for the family, showing Esther's childhood in the United States. There were many shots of Esther in various outfits, Easter bonnets, a *qipao,* a snowsuit. Esther and Victoria sipping from toy teacups at one of their pretend tea parties. Esther opening presents with colorful wrapping paper.

After being confined to the dining room, we were finally welcome enough to get a tour of the house. It was bigger than I expected, but it seemed to be in a perpetual state of incompletion. The third floor was more an aspiration than an actuality. The staircase was bare concrete, treacherous without a banister, and petered out after the second floor. That second floor opened off the staircase into a large central room, which held a new sectional sofa and coffee table. On the floor sat a bulky cathode-ray-tube television, recently displaced by a large flat-screen model on a small table. Off the main room were three bedrooms with double beds covered with fuzzy red quilts. Each room had a decorative band of tile running horizontally around it. Juliet balconies with white molded balustrades overlooked the rice paddies. It was a working farmhouse with various farm implements here and there. There was a large blue contraption for milling rice, and sacks of rice were stored in every corner and piled up against the walls. The only animal in the house was a friendly white dog with pinkish eyes. Unlike on my earlier visits, I didn't see the chickens wandering in and out of the house—I suspected they had become part of our delicious meals. The bathroom was reasonably modern by the standards of the countryside, with a fairly new sink and vanity, although it was not connected to running water. To wash your hands, you took water with a dipper out of a large plastic drum. The kitchen had a traditional Chinese kang stove—a massive box of bricks into which you shoveled wood for fuel. But the family seldom bothered with the old-fashioned stove. Whenever I visited, they were cooking in a wok on a single-burner stove fueled by a gas canister, somehow managing to serve up five or six dishes for every meal.

In a garage area beside the house was their motorized three-wheeled cart, the clunky contraption favored in the countryside. Parked behind it was a new white General Motors car, albeit one of the less expensive compact models, the Baojun, manufactured in China. It belonged to one of the sons-in-law.

Not for the first time, I wondered if the Zeng family might have a higher net worth than Esther's adopted family. It would be hard to compare, because the economic systems of the United States and China are so different. But the Zengs had the land they farmed. Although the nominally communist system didn't give them outright ownership, the land provided fresh food and a safety net. They didn't have mortgages or car payments. With Zanhua working at the noodle shop and every other member of the family bringing in at least a little, they had disposable income. Since 2000, when Esther was born, the Chinese per-capita income had risen tenfold. The Zengs had clearly prospered in recent decades—as evidenced by the large house and the accumulation of furniture and appliances. Had a baby been taken away now, they could have easily raised the thousands of dollars to pay the fines.

During those same decades, Marsha's family had experienced an all-too-common American adversity—too little retirement savings and inadequate health insurance. The reversal of fortunes of these families was not unlike what was happening on the world stage, a rising China nipping at the heels of the United States.

Like China itself, the Zeng family was caught in that cusp between tradition and modernity, poverty and prosperity. They were still tethered to the village life, the *laojia*, "old home," but were, step by step, extricating themselves from the old ways.

For the holiday, most village houses displayed red scrolls over the doorways with auspicious rhyming couplets welcoming the New Year. The Zengs' was one of the few left bare. But inside, almost an entire wall of a back room behind the dining room was covered with a family shrine made out of shiny red tiles. In the center, a vertical column of tiles formed a central banner dedicated to the ancestors of the Zeng clan. Other red tiles etched with gold writing contained various auspicious verses similar to the couplet "May the merits of the ancestors last for generations and bless the offspring for a thousand years." Other colorful tiles were drawn with pictures of lanterns and the character *fu*, which simply means "fortune." It was their nod to tradition.

We were fascinated by this extravagant display of veneration of the ancestors and wanted to know more. We learned that *Zeng* is the thirty-second-most-common surname on the mainland, meaning "high" in ancient Chinese. This particular branch of the family had been in Gaofeng village for hundreds of years, and before that they had lived in another nearby county. Youdong couldn't tell us much more. Genealogy wasn't his thing. He didn't even know all of the Zengs who lived in his own little village. We pressed him for information about any distinguished ancestors—a soldier, a war hero, a minor official, or even a bandit—but as far as his knowledge stretched back, there was an unbroken line of farmers eking out a living by growing rice, something Americans knew only from Pearl Buck's *The Good Earth*.

Youdong was more informative about the transformation of rural China in his own lifetime. He was unsparing about the hardships of his childhood in the 1970s.

"We ate rice and vegetables, rarely a little pork," Youdong told the American family. "When I was small, there were still people dying of starvation."

Youdong wasn't the type who would bad-mouth Mao, but he did allow that after Mao's death in 1976 and the end of collective farming, they were able to eat. "Mao has his rights and wrongs, but at least he laid the foundation for the new China," he said, reciting an accepted spin on China's founding father.

Esther and her family listened intently. This was a crash course for the Americans in modern China. The economic liberalization of the 1980s enabled new freedoms—the right to cultivate their own fields and to travel outside the village. But it meant that both Zeng and his wife had to leave home to earn money when they were still children themselves.

Zanhua reminisced about selling bags on the street starting when she was just thirteen years old.

"It was hard. The bags didn't sell well." After she was married, she and Youdong teamed up to sell together. "When he came along, business improved," she told us, which prompted Sam to high-five Zeng in an attempt at male bonding. Youdong looked mystified.

I'd heard these stories before, but the couple added fresh details for the benefit of Esther and her visiting family. As an American, Esther was accustomed to posing direct questions, asking about personal matters not often discussed in China. What interested Esther the most were the events that led up to her birth, how the couple met and decided to marry. The Zeng sisters listened attentively, squeezing closer around us at the wooden table to hear the answers to questions they had probably never dared ask their parents. Zanhua told the story of the matchmaker who fixed her up with the soft-spoken boy from the even-poorer village farther up the mountain, and how she was won over by his abstemious habits and gentleness.

As she spoke, I glimpsed knowing smiles between them, a sweet touch in a culture that frowns on public displays of affection. I knew from my reporting elsewhere in China that the migrant life was not conducive to domestic harmony. Husbands and wives who lived most of the year apart spent their time together fighting—about money, children, infidelities, you name it. A colleague and I were once assigned what was supposed to be a cheerful feature about a migrant worker returning to his village for the Lunar New Year, only to find that his wife was threatening to kill him because he'd lost money gambling.

The Zengs were not like that. They genuinely appeared to be a happy family.

"They have a good relationship, my mother and father," said the second sister, Yan. "My father can get angry, but he never hit us. I wanted to marry somebody just like my father, who didn't drink, smoke, or gamble. . . . My husband is like him, except that he smokes."

Almost in a chorus, the sisters praised their parents. How hard they worked. Their cooking skills. Their attention to the children. Even when he was busiest with the harvest, their father would drive them to middle school in Gaoping in the three-wheeled cart. The girls faced no discrimination, they insisted.

Even though he was the youngest in the family, the baby, their brother didn't receive favored treatment in the household. He had the same meals. The same chores. He wore the same type of clothing, although as a boy he couldn't be expected to wear his sisters' hand-me-downs.

"Our parents have the same expectations for the girls as for the brother," Yan continued. "Maybe even more for us. They wanted us to live independent lives."

Still, I wondered. Shuangjie had told me that she would have been very angry at the family if she were Esther. She seemed to think they should have done more to keep her. And she recounted a conversation she'd had with her mother about their house, which they intended for her brother to inherit.

"Why can't I get the house?" she had asked her mother.

"If you were the one to support us in our old age, it would be your house," her mother had retorted.

Tradition still reigned. The Communist Party hadn't abolished the old ways. Girls married out. Boys stayed in the village. Over the course of our visit, we found it was pointless to ever ask a question that began with the word "why." During one of these conversations about gender equality, their paternal grandfather ambled into the house. The sisters jumped up to help him to a stool.

At ninety-three, the older Zeng had a starburst of wrinkles emanating from his puckered lips, but his face was otherwise surprisingly unlined. He walked with a cane and wore a black leather cap with the brim turned sideways, which gave him a jaunty look.

"You have to have a son. It's the traditional way," he insisted when we asked about the underlying reasons for the son preference. He spoke in such a heavy dialect that nobody in the family but Zeng could understand him, and we eventually abandoned efforts to elicit more nuance.

It was basically that you needed a son because that's the way it always had been.

CHAPTER TWENTY-TWO

THE PIGEON HOUSE

Walking to the bamboo grove.

TO THE EXTENT THAT THERE WERE ANY LANDMARKS ALONG THE main road through the village, it would be the house belonging to Zanhua's oldest brother, Yuan Guoxiong. It was located in what had been a separate village, Shanghuang, which means literally "on the yellow," referring to the tawny hue of the earth. But due to the declining rural population, it had been merged with Gaofeng into a single administrative unit.

The house itself was unremarkable—two stories of the same faded red brick as everything else—but it was distinguished by row after row of wire pigeon coops. The wire cages were stacked four rows high, covering the front of the house. Behind the house were more cages. When you approached the house, you could hear the collective cooing of hundreds of birds. Locals simply called it "the pigeon house."

Since the 1990s, the family had been raising pigeons to sell to nearby restaurants. Pigeon is a delicacy in southern Chinese cuisine, served at weddings and holidays—roasted, fried with spiced salt, minced and wrapped in lettuce leaves. Shuangjie and I had dined at a pigeon restaurant in Changsha during my last visit. Pigeons and pomelos had made the Yuan family more prosperous than other villagers, one reason they had been designated as Esther's guardians when she was in hiding from Family Planning.

In the complicated equation of the family, the uncle had been Esther's de facto father. He was the person who had chosen her name, *Fang*. When she was taken, she carried the surname *Yuan*—not *Zeng*. We understood that the uncle should be treated almost the same as her biological father. Marsha, a quick study in the fine points of Chinese etiquette, had brought a set of gifts for him, including another book of photographs of Esther's childhood. It wasn't just a matter of courtesy to visit the uncle. This had been Esther's home for most of her first two years. And it was this family who could explain to Esther the circumstances under which she was taken away.

Although it was walking distance from the Zengs' house, we decided we would take the rented van instead, so as not to attract too much attention. We squeezed into the van—the entire delegation of us; me; the interpreter; the photographer; Esther with her adoptive mother, sister, and brother; the birth parents and their other three daughters; and a few children, perched on their parents' laps.

When we pulled up in front of the uncle's house, we were prepared for an emotional welcome. Instead, the uncle, Guoxiong, politely invited us into the house but stood off to one side, watching. He was a stocky man of right angles—square jaw, square shoulders encased in a black leather jacket, and a haircut popular among Chinese men that made his head look square. He had a cigarette behind one ear and expressive eyebrows that he raised with skepticism.

I could sense what he was thinking. Of course, Esther looked like Shuangjie, but not exactly like Shuangjie. He was doubtful about Esther's identity and the very premise of this visit. In New York, we had seen the musical *Anastasia,* about a woman claiming to be the daughter of the last Russian czar. Guoxiong seemed to suspect that Esther could be a pretender, somehow looking to claim the family's fortune, such as it was.

We took seats at a table in the center of the main room, laid out for the holidays just like at the Zeng home, with a red tablecloth, a dish of nuts, and mandarin oranges.

Guoxiong approached Esther from behind and lifted up her long hair to inspect her ears. Then he laughed at himself. "I can't remember what ear it was," he said before correctly examining her left ear. There he found what he was looking for—the telltale bump—barely larger than a grain of rice but the distinguishing feature nonetheless.

Guoxiong trusted his instincts more than the DNA test. At last, he relaxed.

"Welcome home," he told Esther. "It is sixteen years since you were in this house, and now you are home."

Now the family crowded around so that Esther could be properly introduced to her family. There were the sons, who as boys used to babysit for Esther. Now grown men in their twenties with children of their own, they greeted her quickly before backing away, suddenly shy, or perhaps nervous about using the English they'd been forced to study in school.

Xiuhua, Guoxiong's wife, had no such reticence. Dressed for the holidays in padded pajamas, hers emblazoned with the misspelled words "Ney Yobk City," Xiuhua took command of the narrative.

Esther had as many questions for the aunt as she did for her birth parents. She was keen to hear stories about herself as a toddler, as though trying to recover those early memories lost to childhood amnesia. Her aunt delivered. She was as emotional as Esther's parents were restrained, recounting Esther's early years with tears and cackling laughs. She described Esther's precociousness—how quickly she learned to walk and talk and navigate her surroundings—and her equally prodigious appetite.

"She would drink a whole bottle of milk, very quickly, then fall right asleep. She would eat an egg with every meal," she said.

"Not once a day?" asked one of the relatives.

"No, every meal. She liked to eat," the aunt replied.

That prompted a laugh, as everybody knew Esther to be the gourmet of the family.

Esther was already twenty-two months of age when she was taken away, Xiuhua remembered, not only weaned from the bottle but also talking and walking around the house, sometimes venturing outdoors.

Then she turned to Esther. "You were my daughter. I tried to take care of you like a daughter," she told Esther fondly, before adding a pointed rejoinder. "More trouble than my own sons."

Xiuhua started tearing up and we knew what was coming. She was getting to the story of how the Family Planning officials had been hunting Esther. She showed us the staircase in the back where her sons jumped out the window with Esther to escape from Family Planning. She reenacted what happened in June 2002 when they were able to storm through the front door.

"They had my arms. They had my legs. I couldn't move at all."

She pantomimed the way she had struggled to free herself from the men who were immobilizing her.

Xiuhua addressed herself directly to Esther. "You tried to hold on. You grabbed the bottom of my shirt. But they picked you up and carried you off to the street.

"After they took you, I was going crazy. All I could think about was how to find you and get you back," the aunt told Esther. "You were like my own daughter."

The second sister, Yan, who had been four years old at the time and living nearby with the maternal grandmother, remembered running down the street screaming. "It was like we were robbed. They robbed you."

The room was silent for a few moments. Many of the family members had tears welling up in their eyes. It was a story they knew well, the most traumatic episode in the collective family's history. It was not only the violence of Esther's abduction that was so painful but also the humiliation; the incident was a testament to their vulnerability and poverty as poor farmers without *guanxi*.

Esther didn't cry. She listened quietly and attentively, nodding at times. It had to be a strange experience to hear a story about a defining moment in her life about which she remembered absolutely nothing.

What was clear from the narrative was that she had been taken, not dumped in a cardboard box on the street. She could rid herself of the stigma felt by other adoptees of having been dumped. She had been loved. That was the essence of what the Chinese family wanted her to know.

THE BAMBOO GROVE where the twins were born was a short walk from their uncle's house. Thankfully, there was a brief respite in the rain, long enough for Zanhua to take Esther to see her birthplace.

All of us went outside, following a dirt path still muddy from the days of rain. It led down from the main road, behind the house, to a narrow valley wedged between the village and the terraced paddies.

Zanhua led the way. She was flanked by her daughters. She held Esther's hand tightly and linked her other arm with her oldest daughter's, Ping, who in turn held the hand of her own three-year-old daughter, who was festively dressed in red padded pajamas and carrying a green balloon. Esther linked her free arm with Shuangjie's, who kept her hands in her pockets for warmth. Behind this foursome, Yan walked with her son. The rest of us trailed farther back, Zanhua's elderly mother in the rear guard.

Beside the path was an embankment studded with pine trees, on the other a stone wall supporting a terraced field. The path petered out near the bamboo. This winter afternoon the trunks were bars silhouetted against an irregular patch of gray sky. The pomelo trees interspersed among the bamboo still had their bright elliptical leaves, although the fruit was finished for the season.

Zanhua told the girls about how she had been washing vegetables in her brother's kitchen the day she went into labor in 2000, then how she rushed to the secret hiding place that had been prepared for childbirth.

"There was the shed," she said, pointing into the thicket. It had been demolished a decade ago, having served its purpose. Back in the 1990s, when Zanhua's father first planted the orchard, the pomelos were such a valuable commodity that somebody had to be stationed in the shed to guard them against thieves. But now the family had enough other income that it wasn't necessary. They often gave away the pomelos as gifts rather than taking them to market. And their neighbors were solvent enough that they didn't need to steal fruit.

The bamboo grove was no longer the secret hideaway it had been when Zanhua gave birth. Development encroached. A backhoe was parked next to the beginning of a long driveway that would provide access from the main road. Next to a murky pond was a new three-story house painted lemon yellow, a bright patch in the neighborhood of dispiriting red brick. But the transformation was most apparent in the family.

There was Zanhua, wearing a fire-engine-red parka and leather boots, her hair neatly tied back in a bun. All four of the daughters to whom she gave birth and their children in new boots, woolen coats, and parkas. The long-awaited son, smiling, though with the aloofness of teenage boys. Later in the day, we all lined up for a series of family photographs in various combinations, including us foreign visitors—me, Marsha, Sam, an incongruous sight standing in back. Victoria, as another Chinese-born adoptee, blended in more easily. Then came Zanhua's mother, the *waipo*, the "outside grandmother," whom I had met briefly in 2009, wearing a mauve woolen coat and pink crocheted hat.

Later that was the tableau that I would remember from our trip— four generations of Chinese women, smartly dressed for the holiday, together again in their home village.

CHAPTER TWENTY-THREE

SHAOYANG

Shaoyang Social Welfare Institute.

THE HERITAGE TOUR OF CHINA IS A RITE OF PASSAGE FOR young Chinese adoptees. Although relatively few were as fortunate as Esther in meeting their birth families, thousands made the return trip before her, often as teenagers. They followed a standard itinerary arranged by niche travel agencies offering what they called "heritage travel." They would visit the Great Wall and Beijing's Forbidden City or Shanghai's riverfront walkway, known as the Bund. Then they would depart for the provinces to see the orphanages where they were fostered. The government-run China Center of Adoption Affairs, which sometimes subsidized the trips, would arrange meetings with foster moms and nannies and provide souvenir gifts like inexpensive jade jewelry or plush panda toys.

The other mandatory stop for many adoptees was the location where their paperwork said they were found. This, for most adoptees, would be the closest they would come to their roots. It was their first recorded presence in the world. "The holy finding spot," as one adoptee described it in an unsigned 2023 blog post on an adoption site, was "the mythical place where your birth mom last saw you, last kissed you good-bye and held you close." She wrote of other adoptees who considered this location so holy that they had the GPS coordinates tattooed on their skin.

In Esther's case, the paperwork stating she was found at the gate of a bamboo arts factory was obviously a fabrication. I'd gone on an earlier trip to the address, which was on a busy, recently redeveloped commercial strip in downtown Shaoyang. There had once been a factory that manufactured baskets, trays, and other handicrafts out of bamboo, but it had since been replaced by a modern bank. The only business that remained dating back to 2002, when she was purportedly found, was a photo studio directly across the street. The longtime proprietor said there was never a baby found there.

I asked Esther if she wanted to see the location, just to better understand the lay of the land. She didn't. There was no point in visiting a now-defunct bamboo arts factory where she was *not* found, since she'd been to the actual bamboo grove where she was born.

The orphanage was more relevant. Esther had definitely spent the last six months of her life in China in the Shaoyang orphanage. If there was any wisp of a memory left of China, it would be at this place, where Esther had helped the nannies fold the laundry—so Marsha was told when she adopted her in 2002. Marsha hadn't been allowed to visit the orphanage on that trip and very much wanted to go now. But we hadn't applied for advance permission because we wanted to travel under the radar. It would be tricky. Orphanages were run by a branch of the government. When I'd first reported on this issue in 2009 in Guizhou Province, visiting the orphanage had triggered an immediate telephone call to the government propaganda office, which had in turn sent a team to escort us for the rest of the visit.

We were already returning every night to Shaoyang, sleeping in a comfortable high-rise hotel. From the upper floors, you could see the city swallowing up the fields and rice paddies, expanding outside its former limits. Shaoyang was what in China is termed a prefecture-level city (a prefecture being one level smaller than a province) with an urban population of 1.4 million, spread out along the junction of the Zi and Shao rivers. Shaoyang had a reputation for toughness, earned during World War II, when residents were said to have seized hoes, sickles, and kitchen knives to fight the Japanese, mounting a fierce but futile resistance. The city was burned and flattened, obliterating its history and leaving little to delight the eye. A memoir by British author Nick Holdstock, who worked as an English teacher in Shaoyang, dismissed it as famous only for murders and clementines. Our driver was equally contemptuous. "It's only known for dog-meat restaurants," he told us. As in many lower- and middle-tier Chinese cities, Shaoyang authorities had worked hard to gussy up the landscape. The streetlamps were festooned with red ornamental lights in the shape of Chinese knots, the medians of the larger roads planted with topiaries. The cosmetic upgrades were most successful at night, when colorful illuminations etching the outlines of the buildings and bridges lit up the city like a Christmas tree. The broken sidewalks, the shabby architecture, and other imperfections disappeared beneath the distraction of the twinkling lights.

We strolled around the riverside, looking at the streaks of lights reflected in the water, before stopping at a hot-pot restaurant—where you cooked the food yourself in a boiling cauldron in the middle of the table. After a few days like this, exploring Shaoyang, we began to feel less intimidated. Our trip to China had so far proceeded without incident. I had been conferring through the week with Marsha about the risk of going to the orphanage, and we finally decided to brave a visit.

THE ORPHANAGE WAS a forbidding institution. From the outside, there was nothing to suggest it was a charitable institute, certainly no evidence of the presence of children. In front was a decade-old thirteen-story building with a granite façade, solid enough to withstand a major earthquake. The requisite red Chinese flag flapped over the entrance. If not for the large marble plaque engraved with the name "Shaoyang So-cial Welfare Institute," it could have been mistaken for a well-secured military compound.

When we arrived, the entrance was protected by a steel accordion gate with a guardhouse at the driveway. But the guards apparently were accustomed to receiving overseas guests. The orphanage had started in-ternational adoptions in 1994 and sometimes received families who were cleared to visit, unlike us, of course. After our driver gestured to point out his Caucasian passengers, the gate slid open to admit the van. We parked out front.

Behind the administrative building was a lovely park that could have been the centerpiece of a luxury resort, fussily landscaped with a small pond surrounded by weeping willows and stone benches. We won-dered whether the proceeds of the adoptions—those three-thousand-dollar donations—had financed the elegant landscaping. The compound stretched over thirty-five acres. We wandered around the garden past a low-rise building that looked like it housed elderly residents. I'd read that the institute had begun a for-profit assisted-living facility for senior citizens. This was a new phenomenon in rapidly urbanizing China, where many young people had left their villages and didn't wish to re-turn to care for their elderly parents, as had been the tradition in the past. Across from the pond was an inviting playground with a jungle gym and slides in bright primary colors, looking state-of-the art and brand-new. But no children were in sight. We finally found them inside a low-rise building behind the headquarters with a white tile façade and barred windows. We peered in the windows. There was a classroom that looked clean and cheerful enough, decorated with hand-cut paper dolls, al-though the bars on the windows added an ominous touch. The children were about preschool age, equal numbers male and female, and most appeared to be disabled, confirming what I'd read about the recent or-phanage population. We went to the entrance, where a woman, one of the nannies, held in her arms a toddler with pigtails. She advised us that we couldn't tour the building without getting permission from the of-fices. She was friendly enough, and so we decided we might as well try.

Until then, we had attracted little attention. But our presence in the administrative offices raised alarms. A tall, young official in the director's office confronted us, asking us in a not-too-hospitable tone what we were doing there. He was not only angry; he was aghast that we had dropped in.

"Nobody ever, ever has come here without an appointment. Eight years I've worked here, and nobody has dropped in like that." He was practically sputtering.

Marsha explained that her daughter—indicating Esther—had been adopted from this orphanage and we wanted to visit. She didn't introduce me as a journalist, just said that she was touring China with family and friends. She had heard from other adoptive families that they'd been allowed to visit. The photographer remained in the van so as not to raise alarm.

The man continued to berate us.

"You have to make an appointment through Beijing."

Marsha did her best imitation of a clueless American. She was so terribly sorry. She hadn't known the procedure. She apologized for inconveniencing him. She would immediately call Beijing to make sure she did things properly. Instinctively, she reverted to her Texas accent, relying on the charm of the southern belle. She was so adept at disarming the official, it occurred to me that she would have been an excellent foreign correspondent.

Her contrition persuaded the official to back down. He passed around plastic bottles of mineral water and gave us a forced smile.

He turned to Esther and asked what year she was adopted. When she answered 2002, it seemed to raise his suspicions again—that was the height of the wave of confiscations. It had been a major scandal, the subject of magazine articles abroad and in China. Although he was probably a student at the time, he surely knew about it.

When he asked Esther what name she was given at the orphanage, she deferred to her mother.

"*Shao*," Marsha answered. "Just *Shao*. I don't remember the rest."

It was a dodge. All the babies from the orphanage were given the same family name, *Shao*. Had Marsha revealed the full name, the man could have figured out that Esther was one of the stolen babies at the heart of the scandal.

"I'll make a call to the director to see if he can help you with this," the man offered.

At that point, we decided it would be advisable to leave. We didn't want to be questioned or detained. Marsha made a hasty excuse—we were pressed for time. She would contact Beijing next time.

Instead of waiting for the elevator, we skipped down the stairs to hasten our exit. On our way out, we ran smack into the orphanage director. He was an older man with thinning gray hair and a kinder demeanor than his assistant. He looked exhausted. He already knew about our presence and apologized that they had not been more welcoming. We again murmured our own apologies and headed for the door.

I feared for a moment that we might be trapped inside the parking area, but the same guard on duty waved and pushed a button, and the gate slid open. As we drove away, I wondered how unnerved the orphanage officials must have been by our visit. The man we'd met coming out was a new director, although he could have been there at a lower level in 2002. He might have suspected that Esther wasn't just an ordinary adoptee in search of her roots.

The issue of the confiscated children has never been satisfactorily resolved. Although fourteen Communist Party officials were fired and stripped of their party membership in 2011, nobody from the orphanage was implicated or disciplined. They claimed that they had no idea that these adoptees weren't willingly abandoned children and that there was no exchange of money or favors with Family Planning. It strained credulity.

As one director of a large orphanage, in a rare moment of candor, explained to the Stuys in a 2009 interview, "If you don't pay any money, how would you find any babies?"

CHAPTER TWENTY-FOUR

ESCAPE FROM THE VILLAGE

The family shrine.

THE NEW YEAR HOLIDAY WAS WINDING DOWN WHEN WE RE-turned to the village. Although the Chinese calendar revolves around the holiday, and people look forward all year to the fifteen-day vacation, it can drag on for too long. And these village houses with their thick concrete walls that retain the cold are uncomfortable for a younger generation softened by life in the city. The villages were the *laojia*, the "old home," full of sentiment and history but not a place you want to stay longer than absolutely necessary.

The sisters and their husbands were itching to get back to their everyday lives. Their children were listless, playing games on their parents' cellphones. Zanhua was getting ready to return to her job at the noodle shop in southern China. Shuangjie's school would open the next week, and she had to report back a few days early to prepare the classrooms. Zeng Youdong alone would stay in the village to mind the farm. It would soon be time to plant the rice, and he had inherited the knowledge passed down through so many generations past of how to prepare these thousand-year-old terraces.

There would be a long goodbye before we could leave. There were more photographs—this time posed in front of the tiled family shrine. Over our last meal, Youdong made an exception to his policy of not drinking alcohol by serving us warm rice wine, brewed at home with rice grown in their own fields. He assured all of us that the alcohol content was very low. We had a series of toasts and a few more speeches.

"From now on, I will call you 'Mom' and 'Dad,'" Esther told her Chinese parents through the interpreter. Marsha nodded her assent.

Zanhua toasted me as well. She spoke of the visit I had first made in 2009 to the village, when, according to her recollection, I had promised her I would bring back her daughter. I couldn't remember making any such promises, as it had seemed so improbable that I would not only find the missing twin but also bring her to China. But I drank to it anyway.

Youdong rustled into the cabinet to pull out a stack of red envelopes, used in China for gifts of cash. This is a New Year's tradition in China— the red color symbolizes good luck—but it feels awkward for Americans, especially for journalists, who are not supposed to accept gifts, especially not cash. I'm not sure how much was in the red envelope, as it's bad form to open it in front of the gift giver. I asked if I could give mine to one of the sisters' children, which seemed to be acceptable etiquette.

Now we truly felt like family. I remembered that the first day we'd arrived, Zanhua had recoiled when Marsha tried to hug her. But now the two women had a long embrace, celebrating their collaborative motherhood. I wished that they could have really talked to each other about their lives and frustrations as young women, their sacrifices. And yet they seemed to intuit what they had in common. I thought I might have detected a tear in Zanhua's eye at saying goodbye again to her daughter.

*   *   *

WE HAD DECIDED in advance that Shuangjie would drive back to Changsha with us, which would give her more time to spend with Esther. Yan, the second sister, also wanted a ride for herself and her son. We stuffed the van with our suitcases, the New Year's gifts, toys, bags of fruit, then climbed over our parcels to take our seats, the driver barely able to close the sliding door behind us.

Until then, Esther and Shuangjie had had little opportunity to talk to each other. They had snatched a few seconds here and there, like when we rode back and forth to the uncle's house, but most socializing had taken place with the large entourage we had accumulated, the various siblings and other relatives and their children, the crowd hovering over every communication.

The driver was still edging the van out of the driveway when Esther asked the first question.

"Have you ever been on a date?"

The seating had been arranged so that Esther was next to the young female interpreter, Shuangjie just behind them so that she could lean over the seat and converse. Marsha and Sam were up front. It was the only way Esther and Shuangjie could have a modicum of privacy.

No, she hadn't been on a date. Esther hadn't either.

They both agreed that they wanted to travel before settling down.

"I don't want to have the life of my sisters, marrying so young," Shuangjie told her.

From the middle seat, cradling her sleeping three-year-old son, Yan weighed in to the conversation. She wasn't insulted by Shuangjie's remark. She advised Shuangjie to avoid marriage for as long as she could and, when it came time, make her own choice without the intervention of a marriage broker.

"And whatever you do, you better not marry a farmer from the village."

Yan had married a co-worker when she was not quite twenty years old. Although she was happy with her husband, she regretted being tied down at such a young age with a kid.

Although the Chinese government was by then encouraging women to have more children, Yan had no intention of complying. It wasn't hard to understand why the birth rate was declining in China.

"One is enough. I would only have another kid if I was sure it would be a girl. I don't want another boy."

Though not exactly an intellectual, Zeng Yan was the most analytic of the family members, with a trenchant critique of the family, marriage customs, and the overall structure of village society. Yan adored her parents—her father's even temperament, her mother's uncomplaining industriousness, the strength of their marriage. But she didn't like the traditional way of doing things.

Yan resented that she had been left behind in the village so that her parents could earn money. "I so craved parental love. I was so jealous when I saw friends whose parents were helping with their homework."

She criticized the way villagers, including her parents, spent so much of their lives working long hours far from home, earning money to build houses they barely lived in because they were always working in the city. The cycle perpetuated itself. And the sons who were supposed to inherit the houses didn't want to live in the village either.

"People build these big houses in the villages, but they only use them once a year during the New Year holiday," Yan told us. "Then they leave."

It was true. The few other vehicles on the road were heading in the same direction, down the mountain toward the city, away from the villages, which the people were fleeing to go back to their jobs and modern homes in the city.

We made our way into Gaoping, and the van slowed to a crawl in the tangle of cars, carts, and pedestrians all jostling to reach the market. This was a busy time, with people spending the cash they'd received as gifts in those red envelopes. "Market days were always so much fun when we were kids," Shuangjie told us. Her tone was wistful, nostalgic. There was no reason to stop, since there would be better stores in Changsha, not to speak of the thriving culture of online shopping.

Once we reached the highway, the landscape was of less interest, so the sisters decided to teach each other words from their respective languages.

Older sister. *Jiejie.*

Younger sister. *Meimei.*

To eat. *Chifan.*

Hair. *Toufa.*

Happy New Year. *Xin nian kuaile.*

THERE IS A clichéd image of life in modern China—a Chinese migrant type pedaling a cart laden with recycling past a billboard advertising Gucci or Louis Vuitton, and like many clichés, it contains a kernel of truth. The contrast between the old rural China and the new wealth is so pronounced that it never fails to amaze. I'd read in some of the biographies of Mao that Changsha was considered one of the most pleasant cities in China in the early twentieth century. It had been suitably impressive when we'd arrived fresh from New York City; after a week in the village, we were in awe.

We checked back in to the same apartment hotel, perched high above the city on the upper floors of a skyscraper. Recovered now from jet lag, we started to explore. Downstairs was a cavernous multilevel coffee shop—bigger and more stylish than any café I'd seen in New York, with chandeliers dangling between the floors, fake books, and metal spiral staircases between the levels. It had every conceivable flavor of macchiato and excellent Wi-Fi. Young people hung out, tapping away on their laptops.

When we descended to the subway, the doors glided noiselessly open, aligned perfectly with glass barriers that would keep people from falling or being pushed onto the tracks. The cars were spotless, free of graffiti. A pleasing electronic voice, female, announced the stations.

Riding in a taxi at night, we were bathed by spotlights emanating from high-rise shopping malls with their billboards flashing ads for luxury brands. Neon crawled up and down the sides of the mirrored skyscrapers. Past the luxury malls were a maze of pedestrian alleys with shops brightly lit and beckoning with ramen, bubble tea, and ice cream.

"It's like Times Square," Victoria said.

Actually, it was much cleaner, brighter, louder, safer, more futuristic, more like Tokyo's Ginza than any place I'd been in the United States. We went to a lively restaurant where you ordered and paid using QR codes. (This was in 2019, before the coronavirus pandemic made it commonplace elsewhere in the world.) It felt like we had time-traveled to the future.

We cruised the shopping mall downstairs from our hotel. It was filled with young, fashionable clothing boutiques, toy stores catering to young adults with novelties inspired by K-pop and anime. This year, stuffed pigs and pig key chains for the Year of the Pig. Esther and Victoria spent the contents of their red envelopes on inexpensive gifts for family back home.

The girls were enjoying themselves in Changsha. But it was clear that they were not ordinary tourists. They blended in with the crowds of Chinese students, invisible to the curious gaze, which seemed to make them as anxious as being stared at in Texas, since they felt no more Chinese than anybody else from back home. As adoptee blogger and podcaster Grace Newton has observed, Chinese adoptees are often assured they have two cultures available to them, but they don't fit entirely into either: "We adoptees live in this in-between space between worlds."

I wondered if they were more intimidated by China than they would have been if they didn't appear Chinese. Chinese tend to treat foreigners, at least Caucasian foreigners, more politely than they do one another, behaving as though they are hosts and that it would reflect badly on China if they were rude. Chinese adoptees don't get that deference.

The adoptees were constantly required to explain themselves, which they couldn't because they didn't speak Chinese. It was complicated even in English.

When we entered the Hunan Provincial Museum, the guard kept asking Esther and Victoria in Chinese to open their bags for inspection, and wouldn't stop until I loudly informed him, "*Tamen shi Meiguoren,*" "They are American."

On one of the rare occasions that they ventured out unescorted, it was to buy lunch at a kiosk outside the hotel that sold tasty grilled sandwiches and panini. A young man behind the counter spoke serviceable English but naturally tried to take their order in Chinese.

"We don't speak Chinese. We're American," they informed him.

"You don't look American," he challenged them.

Almost in unison, the sisters responded: "What does an American look like?"

It was an excellent retort. And a question we would all ponder over the remainder of the visit.

CHAPTER TWENTY-FIVE

TWIN TALK

Esther (left) and Shuangjie in Changsha hotel.

SHUANGJIE USED TO SPEAK OF HOW MUCH FUN IT WOULD BE TO have her identical twin come to school, confusing people who couldn't tell them apart. That was a fantasy, perhaps nurtured by the countless novels, films, and television shows with contrived plots revolving around twins—from the 1961 teen comedy *The Parent Trap* with Hayley Mills (later remade with Lindsay Lohan) to William Shakespeare's *Twelfth Night*. When it came to real life, she balked. As had happened earlier, Shuangjie didn't want us to come to the residence where she lived with the other teacher trainees. I wasn't sure if she was embarrassed to have us see her accommodations or if she didn't want her colleagues to see us. We also couldn't visit the school, where she was setting up the classrooms for the new term.

But she came to meet us for at least a few hours every day at our hotel. Since the rooms were suites with small kitchenettes, the twins had space and time to kick back and relax together.

The first day Shuangjie came, Esther and Victoria cleared off the kitchen table and brought out a deck of cards. With gestures instead of words, they taught each other card games. Spoons was their favorite. They reverted to patty-cake and clapping games. Esther taught Shuangjie how to do a thumb war. Although they were already eighteen years old, they just played. It was fitting that they got to experience a small piece of the shared childhood that had been denied them.

The entire wall behind the table was mirrored, so it turned into a makeup studio. Esther and Victoria traveled with an ample collection of makeup, and they laid out eye shadow, eyelash curlers, mascara, lipstick, powders. As is typical of American teenagers, Esther wore more makeup than Shuangjie, nothing garish, just discreet blushes and shadows. As they streamed music from a laptop, Edith Piaf singing "La Vie en Rose," Esther applied Shuangjie's makeup. When she started contouring her face to make the cheeks less pronounced and the eyes larger, the differences in their appearances melted away. They were indeed cosmetic. It was easier to see the girls as identical twins without the distinguishing trappings of their respective cultures and upbringings. Esther wore her waist-length hair parted in the middle. Shuangjie's hair was just below her shoulders, with bangs. But when they plaited each other's hair in French braids, their appearances converged again. Their style of dress was similar—clean, sharp designs, nothing fussy or flouncy. They exchanged shirts—a black mock turtleneck of Esther's swapped for a magenta blouse with a gathered neckline.

We went to meals together. We slurped a soupy lunch in an unheated noodle shop, huddled together for warmth on wooden benches. In the mall under the hotel was a lively Korean barbecue restaurant with a Flintstones theme. Shuangjie and Esther held hands as we navigated our way through the mall. During these excursions, the conversations skipped around various subjects, ranging from unicorns (which they both loved) to Halloween. Esther came from an evangelical tradition that frowned on the holiday, but Shuangjie was fascinated by it. Shuangjie had a taste for horror movies and had given some thought to what she would wear if she dressed in a costume. "Something scary," she concluded. These were seemingly unrelated topics, but it all circled back to what the twins had in common and what they did not.

They reveled in their commonalities and puzzled over their differences. Why was it that Esther had so many allergies—not only to tofu but also to other forms of soy, avocados, bananas—when Shuangjie didn't? I suggested that might be because Shuangjie was breastfed longer. Or if growing up in the sterility of an American home had made Esther more sensitive to allergens, a theory advanced by many researchers. They had both suffered from nosebleeds as children, although Shuangjie had outgrown hers.

In the fancy coffee shop under the hotel, Shuangjie drinking a caramel macchiato and Esther a mango juice, they went through lists of what they had in common. They loved fruit. They both enjoyed cooking. They shared a talent for art and design, though Shuangjie did calligraphy, a distinctly Chinese art form. Esther made charcoal sketches of elegant young women and fashion, perhaps an offshoot of her work as a photographer.

To the amusement of people sitting next to us in the coffee shop, the twins discovered they could both roll their tongues laterally. We took photos with our smartphones and all laughed. Tongue rolling might not be the most rewarding of skills, but it is of some interest to geneticists, who have studied identical twins to determine whether the trait is heritable. (It is not entirely.) But the rest of us couldn't do it, which thrilled Esther and Shuangjie.

Beyond what they superficially had in common, there were core personality traits I'd noticed. Both girls were deliberative and thoughtful, with little of the excitability often associated with teenage girls. They weren't prone to giggling. Or crying. Or excessive talking. They didn't rush to express or display their emotions. In that way, they took after their parents, especially their father. On first meeting they had seemed detached, even cold, but on further acquaintance, we came to appreciate their dignified reserve. Esther and Shuangjie remained calm under

stress. They soldiered through the family reunion with few tears or little melodrama. "I think we are similar, emotionally. It's easy for me to
laugh. I don't cry very much," Shuangjie said.

"But I think Esther is much braver than I am," she added. Yan, who
had joined us, nodded in agreement. I had observed in their video chats
as well that Esther had more confidence. Shuangjie had many fears—of
drawing too much attention to herself, of getting lost or being kidnapped. I wondered if that was because she knew her twin sister had
been stolen. Perhaps this was residual trauma from their childhood. She
would take the same bus home from the hotel each night but was scared
to ride in a taxi by herself.

FOR THOSE OF us witnessing the reunion of the identical twins, it was
a magical experience, truly like something out of a storybook. But I realized that Esther and Shuangjie were under considerable pressure. They
were onstage under constant scrutiny. We couldn't help but analyze
their appearance, their mannerisms, and their personalities.

The gaze was unremitting. People have a fascination with identical
twins, what author and psychologist Joan A. Friedman has called the
"twin mystique." They are assumed to have a profound spiritual connection that transcends ordinary familial relations—somewhere in the
paranormal—where they can read each other's minds and feel each other's thoughts.

There was an assumption that Esther and Shuangjie were fated to be
together for life, as though they would be stunted and incomplete without each other. "You should never separate twins," Zanhua had told me
the first time we met, in 2009. The first clue that Esther had about her
history was the text she read on her mother's mobile phone with the
same message: "It's terrible for twins to be separated."

My presence and that of a photographer contributed to the pressure,
but the families were also watching closely, nudging and questioning.
Yan asked if Esther and Shuangjie could communicate through telepa-
thy. They just laughed. They didn't know. She seemed somewhat disap-

pointed that they didn't look more alike. "I thought they would be exactly identical." By fiddling with their hair and makeup, they had tried to erase their differences. Shuangjie resolved to grow out her bangs and lose weight after the holidays. Esther said she would cut her hair. They didn't want the rest of us to be disappointed.

I have a few friends who are twins, and when I told them the subject of this book, they rolled their eyes with dismay. They grow weary of attention, the comparisons and the questions.

"Identical twins have it rough," wrote British author Aatish Taseer in an essay published in 2024 in *The New York Times Style Magazine.* "As soon as we see them, fetishizing their likenesses and dissimilarities, we turn them into proxies for ideas. We revel in our ability to tell them apart, as if it were up to us to impart individuality unto them. We marvel at the sureness of our eye, treating them like human trompe l'oeils."

Reuniting after a long separation can also be a terrifying experience. It's not merely the gain of a family member but also a tremendous loss—the loss of your sense of self as an individual in the world. Identical twins, especially, often complain of feeling like replicants or clones, a cluster of matching genes that are no longer unique. Twinship can undermine the very nature of the human self. For twins who have similar voices and mannerisms, it can be grating to hear somebody who speaks just like you (I, for one, flinch at the sound of my own voice) or to see someone who twists their hair in the same way.

"Part of my reluctance about having a twin is due to my steadfast belief that I'm my own invention," explained Paula Bernstein, one of a pair of identical twins, in a 2007 memoir, *Identical Strangers,* that she co-authored with her twin, Elyse Schein. The women, both adopted as infants to separate families, were reunited in their thirties. At one point Schein inquired, "If your family had raised me and mine had raised you, would I be you and would you be me?"

The same question hadn't occurred to Esther and Shuangjie. I asked them directly. Did Esther ever wonder what her life would have been if she'd remained in China, raised by her parents in Gaofeng village? Did

Shuangjie imagine herself as the twin who became an American? Were they ever envious of the experience of the other?

But when I asked them, they said no. They told me separately—they were confident in who they were.

AFTER A FEW days of talks mediated by the interpreter, Shuangjie and Esther decided they wanted to meet alone. The interpreter, who was exhausted and growing a little hoarse, was happy to help them download a translation app on Shuangjie's smartphone. With the phone in hand, they ducked into one of the hotel rooms. It would be an imperfect way to conduct a conversation, but the privacy was welcome.

They spent over an hour in the hotel room. Whatever they talked about, I could tell their relationship had become more intimate. When we went out later in the mall, they held hands on the escalator. Shuangjie was starting to get a cold, and Esther helped her fasten the complicated barrel-shaped buttons of her coat. She held an umbrella over Shuangjie's head to deflect the insistent rain. Each time the day wound down and Shuangjie had to head back to her dorm, there was a pall that fell over them, anticipating the time to say goodbye. Staying longer was impossible. Permanent separation felt unthinkable.

We discussed inviting Shuangjie to Texas. The planning made our imminent departure more bearable. We talked about cost and logistics. Who would come. Even the menu for the next reunion. "Shuangjie doesn't like hamburgers. I'm not sure what she'll eat," Esther remarked.

LANTERN FESTIVAL FALLS two weeks after New Year's Day and marks the end of the holiday period. Traditionally, the festival is celebrated with lanterns decorated with characters spelling out riddles that children are supposed to solve. Nowadays, it is mostly known for its big, showy displays of fireworks. Seasonal kiosks are set up along roadsides throughout the country, selling garishly packaged fireworks. Up-and-coming Chinese show off their new wealth with lavish displays in front of their homes, hoping that they will survive the holiday with all fingers, limbs, and eyes intact—accidents are rife, predictably. Chinese authorities have discouraged too many fireworks out of safety and environmental concerns, but the tradition persists. All cities of any size sponsor their own fireworks displays. The holiday is a riotous sound-and-light show. This would be the last full day of our trip, in effect the finale. I'd scheduled it that way thinking that the family would enjoy the spectacle and so that the trip could end with a big bang. The evening didn't go entirely according to plan.

We were packing that evening, since our flight was scheduled for early the next morning. Our rooms were in disarray, clothing strewn around the beds, when Shuangjie arrived at the hotel to meet us for the fireworks. By then, she was truly sick, her face flushed and her eyes glassy. We fussed around, making lemon ginger tea, trying to figure out if she had a fever or was suffering from exhaustion at the end of the reunion. We had intended to go out to watch the fireworks display over the Xiang River, less than half a mile to our west. But the night was so stormy that we looked for a viewing point from the upper floors of the hotel. The restaurant staff let us use an empty banquet room. We dimmed the lights as the show began. The windows faced due south, not exactly the right direction, so we had to press our faces against the cold glass and crane our heads to see anything. The fireworks looked like blurry splotches of color dancing through a curtain of rain.

Shuangjie and Esther huddled together on a ledge at the base of the window, resting their heads on each other's shoulders. They'd arranged their hair in the same style, again the French braids, and wore no makeup or jewelry, almost as though they were attending a funeral. Esther was dressed entirely in black. Shuangjie kept on a white fleecy coat, hugging herself for warmth. As the evening wore on, she looked increasingly miserable.

The hotel restaurant delivered food to the banquet room—noodles, pork with scallions, greens, dumplings, traditional New Year's dishes. It was supposed to be our festive final dinner, but the platters sat barely touched on the table. Shuangjie was too sick to eat; nobody else was in the mood. We could barely tell when the fireworks ended, the explosions muffled by the rain. Almost silently, we went back to our hotel rooms to collect the coats. The twins went back to the room for a last private conversation, enabled by technology. But it was time.

All of us—Marsha, Victoria and Esther (Sam had flown home two days earlier), the translator and I—wanted to say goodbye to Shuangjie. We took the elevator down to the mall underneath, now nearly deserted, and walked past the shops that sold the silly souvenirs. Shuangjie and Esther held hands as they descended the escalator. The rest of us kept a respectable distance, giving them space. At the bottom of the escalator, we discussed again the logistics of getting Shuangjie back to her dorm. We didn't have the van anymore, so we had ordered a DiDi *dache,* the Chinese equivalent of an Uber. I assumed somebody would be accompanying her at least to the entrance of her dormitory, as I'd done in the past. But this time she was insistent about going alone.

As we watched through the revolving door leading out to the street, waiting for the car to arrive, she told us, "I want to be brave like Esther." That was how they bonded—by making themselves alike.

Part Five

ROSETTA STONE

Tongue rolling.

IN THE POPULATION OF CHINESE ADOPTEES, RESEARCHERS HAVE so far examined twenty-two pairs of twins who were separated in those frenetic peak years of adoption, when it seemed as though babies were flying off the shelves. Chinese orphanages didn't have a consistent policy about keeping twins together, either because they didn't bother or because they didn't know. In some cases, twins were abandoned at different times or locations, leaving those who found them unaware. As of this writing, I don't know of another situation where one child remained in China with the birth parents and another was adopted by Americans. That makes Esther and Shuangjie unique, and especially intriguing at a time when so much intellectual energy is expended on the rivalry between China and the United States. Here you have two genetically identical human beings. Except that one is Chinese and one is American.

Meeting with them, I wondered to what extent their personalities and preferences reflected the most superficial of cultural differences. So what if one liked to do charcoal sketches, while the other practiced calligraphy?

Of more substance, was Shuangjie's reluctance to put herself forward distinctly Chinese? A proverb that originated in Japan and spread throughout Asia in varying permutations is that the nail that sticks out is hammered down. In China, one constantly hears people deflect compliments with the expression *Nali, nali,* a colloquial way of saying "It's not so." As for Esther, she was raised with the stereotypically American directive that she could be anything that she wanted to be. She radiated that can-do Texas confidence.

WAS THAT NATURE or nurture? I'm not the first to ponder these kinds of questions. International adoptees, and for that matter all immigrants, wonder what they would have become had they remained in their countries of birth. What if? Who would I be? Grace Newton, the adoptee blogger, now thirty and a PhD student at the University of Chicago, told me that she had become fixated on the randomness of her life: "I was born in this tiny blip of time when you think of the vastness of Chinese history. . . . I could have had an entirely different life in China."

Psychologists and geneticists have long looked to separated twins to try to disentangle the genetic and environmental influences that make people who they are. There exists an entire academic subspecialty of twin studies across the disciplines of psychology, biology, and behavioral genetics in universities and research institutes around the world. Many countries—Denmark, Norway, Sweden, the United Kingdom, Finland, Australia, and Sri Lanka among them—maintain national registries of twin birth for the purpose of future research. In the United States, twins and other multiple births can enroll voluntarily in registries maintained by universities. At the New York Public Library, where I was a visiting fellow, I typed the word "twins" into the online catalog and pulled up 9,374 listings. The International Society for Twin Studies publishes an academic journal, *Twin Research and Human Genetics*, through Cambridge University Press and holds regular academic conferences. The Gucci fashion house in 2022 invited sixty-eight pairs of identical twins to its "Twinsburg" show in Milan, where they strolled the runway hand in hand modeling the fashions of designer Alessandro Michele.

The actual Twinsburg is a town in Ohio that hosts an annual summer gathering of twins. Up to three thousand sets of twins descend on the town the first week of August, invariably trailed by geneticists, evolutionary biologists, psychiatrists, and psychologists hoping to study them.

Twins aren't merely a novelty or a cheap plot device. Serious scholars of human development love twins, all twins, but especially identical twins separated in infancy. Identical twins are not common to begin with. Those raised apart are the rarest of the rare. They provide a unique opportunity to untangle the genetic and environmental strands that shape a human being.

Thomas Bouchard, a psychologist and a pioneer of modern-day twin research, has called them the "Rosetta Stone" after the Egyptian stele that proved invaluable in deciphering ancient languages. For many scientists, identical twins are the key to solving the riddles of human development.

Bouchard started studying twins in 1979 after one of his graduate students at the University of Minnesota showed him a clipping from the *Minneapolis Star Tribune* about a pair who had been adopted separately and discovered each other at the age of thirty-nine. Both men were named James, worked in law enforcement, enjoyed woodworking as a hobby, and smoked Salem cigarettes. Strangely, they had both married women named Linda, divorced, and remarried women named Betty. Their sons and their pets had similar names.

The so-nicknamed "Jim twins" were recruited to be the first subjects in what became the Minnesota Center for Twin and Family Research. The researchers were so intrigued by them that they launched a worldwide hunt for other twins raised apart. Their search was enabled by the enduring fascination of the news media with stories of separation and reunion. ("The separated-twin story is a chestnut of American journalism—one that is guaranteed to gain national exposure, along with pets that have trekked across the country to find their masters," author Lawrence Wright wrote in *The New Yorker*.) Through newspaper stories and talk shows, researchers eventually located 137 pairs of twins raised apart, 81 of them identical.

Among the headliners were the "Nazi and Jew" twins—born in 1933, separated as babies when their parents divorced. One grew up in Germany and joined the Hitler Youth, while the other was raised Jewish and lived for a time on a kibbutz in Israel.

An extraordinary case emerged from Colombia, where two pairs of identical twins were mixed up in a Bogotá hospital. The four mismatched brothers grew up with the wrong twins—assuming they were fraternal, since they had no physical resemblance. They discovered one another at age twenty-five after a woman buying pork ribs mistook the butcher for her colleague at an engineering firm.

Most famous are the triplets featured in the 2018 documentary *Three Identical Strangers*. They were adopted in 1961 through a prominent Jewish agency, Louise Wise Services, which had separated the children as newborns in a secretive study of how genetically identical babies would develop in different environments. They discovered one another in 1981 when then-nineteen-year-old Bobby Shafran started at a community college in New York State. First setting foot on campus, he was startled when classmates kept slapping him on the back, girls coming up to kiss him, calling him "Eddy." In the evening, a student introduced him to an astonished Eddy Galland, who turned out to be his identical twin. After extensive media coverage, another college student, David Kellman, recognized himself as the third man. The triplegängers became minor celebrities—talk show guests, photographed by Annie Leibovitz, given cameo parts in a Madonna movie. But it wasn't all euphoria. The triplets went through episodes of depression, and one, Shafran, pleaded guilty to manslaughter as a teenager for his role in the death of a woman he helped to rob of her diamond rings. Galland committed suicide at the age of thirty-four.

In addition to the triplets, at least nine pairs of identical twins were unwitting participants in the Louise Wise Services study. These included Elyse Schein and Paula Bernstein, the twins referred to in the previous chapter. Researchers came regularly to the children's homes, subjecting them to a battery of tests assessing IQs, motor skills, developmental markers, and personality, trying to assess how they were shaped by their environments. The families were told that these were routine follow-up visits to make sure the children had adjusted to their adoptive homes. They were never informed they were twins (or triplets) or that they had been deliberately separated for the purpose of the experiment. Viola Bernard, the Columbia University psychiatrist who launched the study, insisted the children could best develop their individual identities if they were reared apart without knowing of the existence of a twin. But when the deception came to light in the 1980s, the twins complained they felt like "lab rats" and some threatened lawsuits. The study was never released. Peter Neubauer, an Austrian-born protégé of Anna Freud who took over the research after Bernard's death, died himself in 2008, leaving his papers to Yale University on the condition they be sealed until 2065.

The secret experiment by a Jewish agency was all the more shocking given the notorious abuses of twins during World War II by Josef Mengele, who hoped to use twin research to validate Nazi theories about racial differences. He experimented on an estimated three thousand twins, most of them Jewish, often infecting one with a disease, then killing both so that he could dissect their organs to analyze the effects of the disease. Only about 160 of the twins survived.

Episodes like these have left twin studies with an unsavory reputation. The founder of the discipline, Sir Francis Galton, a half cousin of Charles Darwin and the author of the 1875 paper "The History of Twins, as a Criterion of the Relative Powers of Nature and Nurture," was an unabashed racist who embraced the pseudoscience of eugenics.

He and his disciples used their research into the likeness of twins to assert that the well-educated elites excelled in life because of their innate superiority rather than the advantages of their upbringing. Those findings were used to justify the privileges of the upper classes.

One highly esteemed scholar, Sir Cyril Burt, was accused after his death in 1971 of having manipulated data to exaggerate the heritability of IQ.

With reunited twins, there is an inherent tendency to sensationalize: The twins often overemphasize their similarities and downplay their differences, perhaps innocently out of a surfeit of enthusiasm.

Twin studies have never entirely shaken off that whiff of racism. The Minnesota study, which was terminated in 2006, received financing from a charity associated with the right-wing Koch brothers and the Pioneer Fund, a foundation formed in 1937 to promote eugenics. In the 1980s, the University of Minnesota offered the excuse that "we could take bad money and do good things with it."

But the problem went far beyond funding. The intrinsic nature of twin research, emphasizing the determinative role of nature over nurture, goes against the belief that humans can rise above the circumstance of their birth. The debate runs along the fault lines of modern political discourse. Liberals push for more spending on early childhood education and affordable housing, hoping to lift up the underprivileged. Conservatives counter that the poor are in conditions of their own making and that intervention is of limited use. If human potential is conscribed from the moment of conception, if genes are thought to be destiny, there is less impetus to lavish spending on social-improvement projects.

"There is nothing I can think of in science that is more political than twin studies. These studies have been used to justify racism, classism, Nazism" is how the writer Lawrence Wright (also author of *Twins: And What They Tell Us About Who We Are*) put it in a documentary about twins. "So they are potent and explosive politically. Yet they are also really useful and very helpful if you look at them soberly." He has called twin studies "one of the principal sources of information about human heritability."

Scientists credit twin studies with breakthroughs in autism, once blamed on "refrigerator mothers" who raised their children without enough affection. The same research has established strong genetic links to alcoholism and obesity, as well as mental illnesses like schizophrenia and more commonplace neuroses, phobias, mannerisms, and tics, even nail biting.

In the Nordic countries, which maintain nationwide twin registries, scientists have used twins' health information to tease out the relative influence of genes on various cancers. Their research helped determine that skin, prostate, kidney, breast, and ovarian cancers are highly heritable, as opposed to lung cancer, for which cigarette smoking is the highest risk factor. For a study of vegan diets published in 2023, Stanford University recruited twenty-two pairs of identical twins, asking one to eat strictly vegan for eight weeks and the other to eat a healthy low-fat but mixed diet, determining afterward that eating vegan really did lead to great improvements in cardiovascular health. As the late David Lykken, one of the lead scientists in the Minnesota study, has said, "Almost any experiment one might think of doing with human subjects will be more interesting and yield more valuable results if one does it with twins."

In the name of science, twins have been poked and prodded, measured and interrogated. Scientists analyze their heights, weights, girths, and head circumferences. They administer pulmonary function tests and cardiograms. They quiz twins about their frailties and strengths, subject them to IQ tests, and have them fill out questionnaires on everything from religiosity to sexual and political preferences.

Scientists have also conducted experiments in which they put twins in separate rooms and asked them what the other was thinking or experiencing, trying to determine if there was any validity to the common belief that twins communicate telepathically. The answer was a resounding *no*. They couldn't. The CIA has reportedly conducted similar experiments with similar results.

The most prolific twin expert is Nancy Segal, a veteran of the Minnesota project who runs the Twin Studies Center at California State University, Fullerton. She has published nine books and numerous articles and is a vocal defender of her discipline. "Twin studies have respectability now. They are part of behavior genetics, which was formally recognized in 1980 as a legitimate psychological discipline," Segal told me. "But there are definitely critics out there who don't believe in genetics, despite the evidence. When you look at twins reared apart, twins reared together, adoptees, it all converges on the same conclusion—that genetics is more pervasive and affects more of our behaviors than we ever would have realized."

Still, as Segal likes to point out, identical twins are not truly identical. She prefers to use the scientific term "monozygotic"—"resulting from the division of a single fertilized egg." In the womb, they begin to distinguish themselves, competing for space and nutrition, and one tends to be dominant, sometimes doing harm to the other. Their sizes often vary considerably. It's not uncommon for one identical twin to be gay and the other straight.

A surprising finding of Segal's studies is that twins raised apart can be as much alike as twins raised together. In some cases, they are actually more alike, because those raised together will make a conscious effort to distinguish themselves from each other, avoiding whatever the other twin has selected. What researchers have also observed is that separated twins tend to become more alike as they age. That's because as adults, free from the parents who raised them, they can pick their clothing, curate their own environment, and select their own professions and interests, often reverting in later life to inherited tendencies, which are likely shared by their twin.

In my reporting on Esther and Shuangjie, I tried to restrain my journalistic curiosity, avoiding intrusive queries. Both are rather reserved people. I allowed them to take the lead in questioning each other. Together, they explored the discrepancy in their sizes, their allergies and nosebleeds, their similar tastes in fashion. If at some point in the future they decide to volunteer themselves for twin studies research, I'm sure their participation would be welcome.

ALTHOUGH SOCIAL MEDIA and commercial DNA testing have made it easier for long-lost twins to discover each other, identical twins raised apart remain scarce. Adding up all the studies she knew of from over the past century in the United States, the UK, and Asia, Segal counted just 852 people who were part of sets of identical multiple births that had been separated. But new pairs keep cropping up at a pace more rapid than could be imagined in the not-so-distant era.

The latest frontier in twin studies is international adoption. The South Korean adoptee pool has produced several documented cases, one quite famous case—the reunion between a young French student, Anaïs Bordier, and American actress Samantha Futerman, which was the subject of the 2015 documentary *Twinsters*.

China is proving exceptionally fertile ground for scholars. Segal has been studying Chinese adopted twins since 2001. For a paper published in 2021, she examined the twenty-two pairs of separated twins (fifteen of them identical and seven fraternal) as well as other twin adoptees raised together. As in previous studies, her examinations showed close correlations in IQ between the identical twins, whether raised apart or together: A follow-up paper in 2024 found that gaps early in life had started to disappear, as twins grew more alike with age.

With 160,000 Chinese children adopted abroad, there could be hundreds of adoptees who have an identical twin out there, and likely more than one thousand fraternal twins, although the adoptees and their families may not realize it. While they are less common, identical twins are more likely to discover each other through instances of mistaken identity.

In 2010, Sarah Heath, an adoptee from Nashville attending her freshman orientation at Georgetown University, was approached by another student, who told her she looked exactly like one of his high school friends. He snapped a photo and sent it to his friend, Celena Kopinski, who was unimpressed.

"Coming from a Caucasian male, this sounds a little bit racist" is how Kopinski would later describe her initial reaction to researchers. "Oh, you know, all Asians look alike."

But she was curious enough to reach out to Heath on Facebook. Once they connected and compared photos dating back to childhood, they were floored by the resemblance. They couldn't completely tell who was who in the photos.

When they finally arranged to meet in 2014, first over Skype and then in person, the encounters were much like Shuangjie and Esther's early interactions. "It was like a very long first date," Sarah Heath said. "We were asking the most ridiculous, basic questions, like 'So what's your favorite color?'"

Sarah had grown up in Nashville, the daughter of a single mother. Her twin, Celena Kopinski, was a New Yorker whose parents had lived in Japan. Both were raised as only children. They loved to eat and travel and read. They tended to share opinions on a range of subjects from politics to books—they're both fans of *The Lord of the Rings*. They differed considerably, though, in their attitudes toward China. Sarah studied Mandarin Chinese in college and lived in China for several months, volunteering. Her husband is Chinese American. Celena had less interest, although as a child, she traveled back to China with her parents and was enrolled briefly in Chinese lessons.

Other Chinese-born twins who have discovered each other are living farther apart—in Brisbane, Australia, and Bath, England. In Sacramento, California, and Fresvik, Norway. Except for one recent case, in which a Dutch adoptee located a twin inside China, they were geographically far apart but not all that different in upbringing.

They were all adoptees raised in affluent Western countries. Their parents were middle and upper middle class, well educated, somewhat older, and mostly Caucasian and in the United States, often devout Christians.

Of more value for research is when identical twins grow up in dramatically different cultures and circumstances, such as the case of Esther and Shuangjie. In her 2022 book *Somewhere Sisters: A Story of Adoption, Identity, and the Meaning of Family*, journalist Erika Hayasaki chronicled the evolving relationship between an adoptee growing up in Illinois and her identical twin sister left in Vietnam. The adoptee had been given up because her impoverished mother felt she couldn't afford to raise both children. The twins were reunited as thirteen-year-olds thanks to the persistence of both the adoptive mother and the Vietnamese family.

A more revealing case involves middle-aged South Korean twins separated for nearly half a century. One of the twins got lost as a toddler in 1974 in a crowded market and ended up adopted in the United States. The other was reared by her birth parents in South Korea. They discovered each other in 2020 through a Korean government–run program that helps adoptees locate their birth families.

In 2022, Nancy Segal published a study on this set of Korean twins that questioned the benefits of being adopted into a wealthier country. She found that the American adoptee had a more turbulent home life as both a child and an adult and suffered from poorer health than her identical twin in Korea. She was shorter and heavier. Both twins had diabetes and ovarian tumors, but the U.S. twin had had to undergo a complete removal of her ovaries as a young woman, which left her infertile. The American twin had had three concussions, one from a car accident, which she told researchers might have impaired her cognitive abilities. She tested with a lower IQ than the twin raised in South Korea with her parents. Although the birth family lived in a very poor neighborhood of Seoul, their household provided the Korean twin with a more "supportive and cohesive atmosphere where personal growth was encouraged."

The study of the Korean twins turned on its head some of the preconceptions about international adoption. With our sense of exceptionalism, Americans often assume that adoption into an American home and possession of U.S. citizenship confer incalculable advantages in life in terms of wealth, education, and opportunity.

*   *   *

OFTEN PEOPLE SPEAK of international adoptees as the "lucky children" and insist they must be "grateful" to have been transplanted to a wealthier country and given a "second chance" at life. Although well-intentioned, these comments can sound dismissive to adoptees. They ignore the trauma adoptees experienced of being ripped away from their birth mothers ("the primal wound," as psychologist Nancy Verrier called it in a book of the same name) and the challenges of fitting into an alien culture, usually with people of a different race.

Grace Newton, the blogger, recalled a conversation with a Chinese man who was seated next to her on a flight in China. Before long, her seatmate inquired about her Chinese appearance, and upon finding out she was an adoptee, he launched into the familiar spiel about how "lucky" she was: "I didn't tell him how unlucky it is to not know your first family, to not know your medical history, to not know who you are and to have to fly seven thousand miles to try to figure it out, to feel like a foreigner wherever you go. Adoption has given me great opportunity, but it has come at great cost," she wrote on her website, Red Thread Broken.

Nowadays, people are more attuned to the emotional cost of adoption, and if they are not, they can find powerful writing online by adoptees themselves. Red Thread Broken lists nearly one hundred other sites that publish adoptee writing—including essays by some adoptees who argue that international adoption is tantamount to "involuntary immigration" and should be abolished entirely.

But the assumption persists that international adoptees somehow hit the jackpot, the equivalent of winning the U.S. green card lottery. In both the United States and, even more so, China, I repeatedly hear about the good luck of the adoptees. An official in Guizhou Province, trying to justify his role in removing babies from their birth parents, told me, "The children are better off with their adoptive parents than their birth parents." The midwife said Esther was lucky to be in the United States and could send money to her birth family.

If Esther and Shuangjie didn't do it themselves, everybody else around them was inclined to compare and contrast. Who had gotten the better deal out of life?

It wasn't at all obvious to me. Although in a household of limited means, Esther grew up enjoying the creature comforts of a home with modern heating and plumbing, parents with an automobile, and uncensored access to the internet. But she had lost her adoptive father at the age of nine. And homeschooled, she had an insular lifestyle and, until our trip to China, relatively little chance to travel. College didn't appear to be on the horizon. At the time of our trip, she was still living at home with her mother and working part-time in a supermarket. And yet she had an entrepreneurial spirit that would serve her well in the future, as would soon become apparent.

Shuangjie was more fortunate than many other rural children, including her own sisters. She remained with devoted parents throughout her childhood. Her family had a large house, land, a reliable source of clean, fresh food. Already at eighteen Shuangjie had been launched into adulthood, headed down a secure career path as a teacher, self-supporting, albeit with a modest salary. Although she lived in a dormitory in an older neighborhood, she was in Changsha, a city that embodied the energy of rising China. At the time of our visit in 2019, I thought that Shuangjie might be in a more secure position, having grown up in her country of birth, a country that at the time felt flush with optimism.

As I was setting up our trip, *The New York Times* published an article suggesting that the fabled American dream was more robust in China.

"There are two 18-year-olds, one in China, the other in the United States. . . . You have to pick the one with the better chance at upward mobility," the November 18, 2018, article opened. "The answer today is startling: China has risen so quickly that your chances of improving your station in life there vastly exceed those in the United States." The authors based their conclusion on World Bank data showing that real incomes had fallen for the poorest Americans between 1980 and 2014, while they had risen some 200 percent for Chinese. Although China remained much poorer, it was on an upward trajectory, with people earning more than their parents and living longer than their parents. "Chinese have taken a commanding lead in that most intangible but valuable of economic indicators: optimism."

As it happens, this article was published two months after Shuangjie and Esther celebrated their eighteenth birthday. It could have been written about them.

It is hard to extrapolate about China and the United States based on the experiences of one pair of young women. They are at an age when their tastes and preferences still developing. Their lives are in a state of flux, as are the relative fortunes of their countries. At the time of our trip, China had wrapped up the year 2018 with its economy having expanded 6.7 percent, down from the vertiginous double-digit boom years but strong enough to remain on a trajectory to surpass the United States as the world's largest economy. The juggernaut looked unstoppable. That was the consensus of many of the world's economists. I too believed it, as did my American traveling companions. China was dressed to impress and had succeeded. Between the spotless airports, the graffiti-free subways, and the touchless menus, the future looked as clear as the new eight-lane highway that had whisked us into the countryside.

So much has changed since that trip. I wonder: Were we fooled? Or was it just that nobody could have predicted what would happen?

CHAPTER TWENTY-SEVEN

STEPPING BACKWARD

The Zeng family home.

When we flew home from China in February 2019, we couldn't have imagined how quickly everything would fall apart. Relations between nations, relations between families and loved ones, the supply chains that kept global commerce afloat. A previously unknown respiratory virus was mutating and replicating at a wet market in Wuhan, two hundred miles from Changsha, quietly at first, then explosively. By the next year, it would turn the world upside down.

During our final days in Hunan Province, we had started to plan a follow-up trip for Shuangjie to visit the United States. We were on a high, giddy with the success of a trip that had defied our expectations. Nobody had gotten seriously ill, lost, or detained. There were no false notes, no quarrels. We wanted to arrange another reunion, this time in the United States. Zanhua was keen to come, as was Yan, the second sister. Shuangjie had said her favorite subject in middle school was English, and we wondered if she could learn enough English to allow us to forgo an interpreter. It wouldn't be too expensive if the Chinese visitors spent most of their time with Esther's family in Texas. The last thing that Marsha had said to Shuangjie when they'd hugged goodbye in the Changsha hotel was "Don't worry. Esther's already planning the menu for your visit."

We didn't have a specific date, but the idea was coalescing. I went to see Esther and her family in Texas a few months after our trip to China. Over a meal of Chinese dumplings, expertly prepared from scratch by Esther in her mother's kitchen, we discussed inviting Shuangjie to the United States. I was heading to China the next Lunar New Year and promised to talk more to the Zeng family about logistics. Ahead of the trip, Esther mailed gifts that I was to bring to the family. She had packed a nice polo shirt for her father, red silk scarves for the women, fancy gift boxes of nuts for their New Year's table. I ate the nuts a year ago. Some of the clothing is still in my closet in New York.

MY FLIGHT WAS departing January 25, 2020, from New York's John F. Kennedy International Airport to Shanghai, where I planned to change planes for Changsha. Changsha is a little more than two hundred miles away from Wuhan, which two days earlier had been locked down by Chinese authorities to prevent the spread of this little-known atypical pneumonia. As far as I knew at the time, the virus hadn't spread elsewhere in China. The night before my flight, I attended a Lunar New Year party at the home of some friends. The journalists in attendance spoke with the bravado typical of our profession. ("You're a foreign correspondent. Don't worry about it. You've been to more dangerous places, right?") Chinese friends disagreed. "It would be fucking crazy to go to China right now" is, I believe, an exact quote from a Chinese-born friend at the party. I spent a sleepless night talking and texting with contacts inside China who told me the virus was spreading faster than the government had admitted. The next morning, with my suitcase packed and ready next to the door, and minutes before it was time to leave for the airport, I canceled my flight. I thought I'd reschedule in a few months.

Within days, Changsha was reporting its first cases of the virus. Everything rapidly deteriorated. On February 7, Li Wenliang, an ophthalmologist in Wuhan, succumbed at the age of thirty-four to the novel coronavirus in a Wuhan hospital. Li had been an early whistleblower who had been reprimanded merely for warning medical school classmates about the virus. His death plunged China into an undeniable crisis as millions of Chinese flooded the internet with outrage over his death and fear over their future. The Chinese government enacted ever-harsher measures to restrict freedom of movement and freedom of speech. Roadblocks were erected outside villages to keep out visitors who might be carrying the contagion. Lockdowns paralyzed major cities. Mandatory apps were installed on smartphones that tracked travel, contact history, and biometric data such as body temperature. A green health code was required to use public transit, enter a shopping mall, or eat in a restaurant. It was hard to distinguish whether these were measures intended to control the virus or expressions of discontent. The country was sealed tight. Almost all flights between China and the United States were canceled. Even Chinese citizens who had been working or studying abroad weren't permitted to return home. Visas were suspended. The few foreigners allowed to visit China were locked inside hotel rooms for up to three weeks of quarantine upon arrival.

As Covid-19 engulfed the world, diplomatic relations cratered. Some pundits had predicted that the United States and China would find common cause combating the new enemy presented by the virus. Instead, the respective leaders pointed fingers. The U.S. government accused China (rightfully) of obstructing investigators trying to determine whether the outbreak had originated among the live animals at the Wuhan market or leaked from a research laboratory. The Chinese government whipped up a wave of anti-U.S. hysteria, and Chinese diplomats peddled an implausible conspiracy theory that the virus was seeded by Americans competing in military games that had taken place in Wuhan in October. President Trump did his part to inflame the crisis with snarling references to the "China virus." His foot-in-the-mouth commerce secretary, Wilbur Ross, hailed the outbreak as an opportunity for the "return of jobs to North America." But what most infuriated the Chinese government was an editorial in *The Wall Street Journal* that called the country the "sick man of Asia," a term that evoked the humiliation of the nineteenth century, when dynastic China was overrun by colonial powers.

Nearly the entire U.S. press corps was expelled from China. Those who remained found it treacherous to go out reporting. They were assaulted and trolled online. Alice Su, a gifted reporter who had taken over my old position as *Los Angeles Times* bureau chief in Beijing, was grabbed by the throat and tossed in a lockup while reporting on a language-rights protest in the Chinese province of Inner Mongolia. Mobs surrounded and threatened foreign correspondents who were covering a relatively apolitical story, flooding in Henan Province, in 2021, accusing them of "slandering China."

When I'd lived in China before, the complaints I'd heard about unfair press coverage usually came from people in Beijing and Shanghai—who were the winners in their society by virtue of their privileged residency—not from those left behind in the back of beyond. Now it felt like the anti-American mood was trickling down into the most far-flung reaches of the Chinese countryside, where foreign journalists had once been greeted as champions of the poor. Any foreigner was suspect, an enemy or a spy.

ESTHER HAD STAYED in touch with Shuangjie for months after the trip, holding monthly video chats. Their contacts grew more intermittent. It might have been that the honeymoon had worn off. I'd read in adoption literature that a "time-out" was a normal stage after a reunion and in fact necessary in establishing an ongoing relationship. The translation apps were cumbersome. Or it might have been that everybody was so depressed by the pandemic that they'd sunk into isolation. I wondered too if the vitriol at the upper levels had curdled their relationship, perhaps in ways that the family was not even conscious of. Normally sensible people can be exposed to only so much propaganda—which, like secondhand smoke, is inadvertently ingested—before they begin to agree with it. Chinese friends living in the United States told me their conversations with relatives back home were increasingly contentious because of spats about Covid.

It was out of the question for me to go to China. I sent an occasional text message to the Zeng family, wishing them well. I was told by my Chinese friends that it would be unwise to ask them too many direct questions, even to make polite inquiries about their health and well-being during the Covid crisis.

China initially boasted of its success containing Covid, keeping schools, offices, and restaurants open while the United States struggled to find body bags for the dead. Xi Jinping used Covid to bolster his rhetoric about the rising East and declining West. He spoke too soon. China had spurned the modern mRNA vaccines in favor of its own domestic product, which proved ineffective, especially as the virus evolved. By late 2021, as the rest of the world reopened, China shut down.

Xi implemented a "zero-Covid policy" so unforgiving that millions of people were placed under siege. If a single positive Covid case was detected in an apartment complex, thousands of residents were confined to their homes, unable to buy food or medicine. Enforcers in hazmat suits beat back people who tried to escape. Apartment dwellers "walked" their dogs by lowering them from upper floors on harnesses to relieve themselves outdoors before reeling them back inside. People who tested positive were rounded up and confined to quarantine centers with prison-style cots, twenty-four-hour lighting, and overflowing toilets. Shanghai, China's largest city, with twenty-five million people, was almost completely locked down for two months.

By late 2022, people rebelled. After ten perished in a fire in Ürümqi, unable to escape their barricaded apartment building or admit firefighters, protests erupted around the country—the largest nationwide protests in decades. Finally, in December, the government threw in the towel. With almost no preparation, without stocking up on antivirals or offering boosters to the elderly, it abruptly lifted all restrictions. Epidemiologists estimate that 1.4 million Chinese died in the five weeks after the lockdown was lifted.

CHINA REOPENED FOR BUSINESS in 2023. Direct flights resumed. The foreign ministry started issuing visas again. But China is not back to normal, at least not to the normal that I knew. Gone is the vibrancy I remember from 2007 to 2014—the lively interactions between Chinese and expatriates, the packed calendar of art gallery openings, provocative theater, and poetry readings. Beijing once had two competing book festivals—one at an English-language bookstore, another at an upscale restaurant, both now shuttered.

In January 2023, Xi Jinping assumed a third five-year term as China's leader, after amending the constitution to abolish the term limits set in place expressly to prevent the emergence of another dictator. As feared, Xi has created a cult of personality along the lines of Mao Zedong. His photo is plastered throughout China. Bookstores feature multiple display tables stacked with books authored by Xi Jinping, on topics ranging from governance to poverty alleviation—nearly one hundred titles were available when I checked a Chinese online bookstore. Students are required to attend lectures in what is called "Xi Jinping Thought on Socialism with Chinese Characteristics for a New Era." In 2019, the prestigious Fudan University in Shanghai had to amend its charter promising "freedom of thought," replacing that phrase with a clause about following the guidance of the Communist Party. Other universities followed.

The very same social media platforms that exposed the abuses of Family Planning, which we thought were transforming China for the better, have been harnessed as tools to propagate state power. I had been naïvely awed during our trip in 2019 by China's tech-savvy use of QR codes, without fully appreciating how insidious they are as a method of surveillance. Many vendors in China no longer accept cash: It is difficult to rent a bicycle, buy a transit pass, order a car service, or have food delivered without apps like WeChat Pay. Recurring crackdowns have swept up many professionals, from lawyers to technology entrepreneurs to government ministers, arrested on charges ranging from corruption to separatism. International companies are pulling their executives out of mainland China as well as Hong Kong, which has largely lost its autonomy following the implementation of a new national security law.

CHINA IS NOT only retrenching—it is literally shrinking for the first time since the famine of Mao's Great Leap Forward in the 1950s and 1960s. For two years in a row, beginning in 2022, births have fallen below deaths, meaning the country is not repopulating itself. In 2023, the country recorded 9 million births and 11.1 million deaths.

A funny thing—that day in 2015 when China announced it was abolishing the one-child policy, share prices for companies that made strollers, diapers, and baby formula spiked on the Asian stock markets. Condom-manufacturing companies' shares slumped. Stock analysts predicted that the policy change would bring about the births of three to six million more babies each year. There was a modest baby bump immediately after. But within two years, the birth rate started sliding, and it has continued to do so since 2018. A panicked Chinese leadership has ordered an about-face. Now the Family Planning officers—the very same people who enforced the involuntary sterilizations and abortions— have been tasked with encouraging more births. One wonders if these hapless bureaucrats aren't suffering from whiplash from the abrupt change in their marching orders. In Beijing, a Family Planning association offers women rice cookers and water bottles to attend lectures about having more babies. Dozens of cities are offering incentive payments of up to $8,500 to families who have two or three children. Zanhua told me recently that families in her village can get incentives for having babies. "It was so nasty the way they punished people for having children before, and now they reward people," she said. Now an unabashed pronatalist, Xi Jinping was quoted in October 2023 telling the state news about the need to "actively cultivate a new culture of marriage and childbearing and strengthen guidance on young people's view on marriage, childbirth and family." The fixation on childbearing has raised fears that China might enact more coercive measures, as happened in the 1970s when incentives were not enough to adjust the birth rate to the leadership's liking. Already young married Chinese women have complained they are being pestered by government officials asking intrusive questions about their reproductive plans, including some who asked about the date of their last menstrual cycle.

A small birth spike was possible in 2024 because it was the Year of the Dragon, a fortuitous time to give birth. But demographers say that the declining birth rate will be almost impossible to reverse. The one-child policy, revoked a decade ago, is proving to have a long half-life. So many baby girls went missing in the 1980s and 1990s that there simply aren't enough women today of childbearing age. The latest UN World Population Prospects report released in 2024 estimated that China's population of 1.4 billion will fall to less than 800 million by the end of the century. Young Chinese, men and women, are showing an aversion to early marriage. They don't want to repeat the mistakes of their parents, who left them alone while they worked as migrants in the cities, hoping to build a better life for their children at the expense of a happy home life. The left-behind children don't have a model of a happy family life.

China formally pulled the plug on its international-adoption program in September 2024. It was no surprise. China didn't have enough babies for itself—let alone to send abroad. Adoptions from China had been steadily declining since the trafficking and baby-confiscation scandals of the mid-2000s. They were suspended entirely during the Covid lockdown. In 2023, only sixteen children were sent to the United States. Almost all the adoptees in recent years had special needs and were equal numbers male and female.

China's decision is in keeping with international trends disfavoring international adoption. A 2019 UN resolution on the rights of the child called for all countries to reduce their orphanage populations by placing children in foster homes or allowing them to be adopted in their country of origin. Recurrent scandals about coercion and corruption throughout the world led the Dutch government in May 2024 to block its nationals from adopting from foreign countries. Many U.S. adoption agencies have stopped international adoptions for some of the same reasons. "There is no need for international adoption right now," said Melody Zhang, the official with Children's Hope who had helped to set up the program in 1992. Chinese adoption, she said, came out of a "special time and special circumstances that produced children in need. It was not a normal situation." Robert Glover, the head of UK-based Care for Children, who advised the Chinese on reforming their social welfare system, says that the Chinese government approved 8,000 domestic adoptions in 2024 and placed another 102,000 children in temporary care with families.

"Every Chinese person felt bad seeing their children being exported to other countries," Glover told me.

As of this writing, the Chinese economy hasn't fully rebounded to its pre-Covid levels and the vital signs are not encouraging. Foreign investment is down. Consumer spending is sluggish. Decades of overbuilding have produced a glut of apartments, their values now plunging, wiping out the savings of China's fledgling middle class. Heavily indebted real estate developers have run out of money, leaving apartments unfinished and leaving buyers who already made down payments in the lurch. The same pundits who predicted China would soon overtake the United States are now warning that the country's growth may have peaked already and at best will plateau in the coming years.

This is bewildering to people who came of age in the late twentieth century. After decades of vertiginous rises in personal income, living standards, and quality of life, many Chinese assumed these would continue in perpetuity. Or at least over the course of their lifetime. Or maybe they did not fully appreciate that what goes up can come down. Pessimism about the future has led to an upsurge in emigration. Intellectuals, academics, and artists have been decamping for Japan in the past few years. An unprecedented stream of Chinese migrants has been trying to enter the United States through the southern border. In 2023, more than thirty-seven thousand were picked up by immigration authorities illegally crossing from Mexico, having already made the long and expensive journey to Ecuador, which doesn't require a visa for Chinese nationals.

Among social media–obsessed young Chinese, a once-obscure academic term became a buzzword a few years back to sum up the current mood: *neijuan*, made up of the characters for "inside" and "curling." It suggests endless striving and competing, moving in circles without advancement. It is sometimes translated as "involution"—the opposite of evolution. Another buzzword is *tangping*, or "lying flat," embraced by young Chinese who are shunning marriage and work, rejecting the endless striving of life in China. Essays about the mood of the nation in 2023 have alternately used the terms "stagnation" and "malaise."

THIS IS A snapshot of China at a point in time, late 2024. Caveats are in order: China has reinvented itself time and time again, licking its wounds and rebuilding after far worse disasters—the famine of Mao's Great Leap Forward, the Cultural Revolution, the antidemocracy crackdowns of 1989. A global financial crisis came and went in 2008, barely denting the Chinese economy even though its exports took a hit.

As for the present, my sense is that the brunt of the downturn is affecting the middle and upper classes, along with the highly educated recent graduates bristling with ambition that is not satisfied by the current job market.

Back in Gaofeng village, the Zeng family doesn't appear to be suffering, perhaps because they don't have as much to lose. They are not heavily invested in urban real estate. They have their nearly two acres of farmland, the ancestral rice paddies, and their ever-expanding brick house. The lower-level jobs to which they aspire remain accessible. The only member of the family not working is the oldest sister, Ping, who had a third child—no penalties this time. But they cycle through various jobs, their lives in a constant state of churn. Zanhua left her restaurant job in southern China during the Covid lockdowns and returned to Hunan to be closer to her elderly mother, who had taken ill and has since died. Although Zanhua was close to fifty, the retirement age for women, factories are less choosy these days. She easily landed a job in a factory closer to home in Hunan Province making cellphone cases. But she quit, confident she would get another job with better pay than her salary of roughly four hundred dollars monthly. Her son, she told me proudly, is earning double that as a mechanic. Yan, the second sister, left her job as a barista and is now working as a hairdresser.

Shuangjie's kindergarten had to close during the Covid lockdown, and the financial losses forced it permanently out of business. For a time, she was stuck alone in the city, unable to return home to the village because of the lockdowns. She found another job at a government-run kindergarten. The work was more stable, but the hours longer. She switched again to a position tutoring calligraphy to primary school students, easier to handle than kindergarteners. She's been living with her sister, Yan, in a small city a few hours north in Hubei Province. She's taking driving lessons. During the 2019 reunion, she was adamant that she didn't want to follow the example of her sisters, marrying young and getting tied down with children. She has been true to her word as of this writing. Zanhua told me she approved. "My daughter should have her freedom."

I'm in more contact with Esther and her family. I worried about her in 2020, when she and her sister continued to work cash registers in the supermarket, wearing masks for which they were sometimes criticized. They were largely unscathed by the wave of anti-Asian sentiment sweeping the country, although they once encountered a customer in the grocery store wearing a face mask that read "Thanks China." They slipped away to avoid confrontation.

Then, somewhat surprisingly given the prolonged pandemic, Esther's career as a wedding photographer took off. She began shooting weddings close to home in Texas and quickly attracted new clients around the country from her Instagram account and website. She works often in Seattle and New York. She shoots primarily on film, often in black-and-white, and has developed a whimsical, romantic brand that has kept her in demand in a highly competitive business. She also does fashion shoots, runs a blog, and is sufficiently adept at social media that she advises other photographers. She's done well enough to take vacations in Hawaii with her sister Victoria, who is now in college studying accounting. She has shed the tentativeness of her teenage years, plunging headlong into adulthood. She cut her hair to just below shoulder length, bought a car.

Esther was also the first of the twins to marry. In 2022 she was wed to a man she met through mutual friends, in a small civil ceremony attended by their close family. Mindful of her promise to introduce her husband to her birth family, she did so with a video call since it wasn't feasible to visit in person.

During the last two Lunar New Year holidays in 2024 and 2025, I joined video chats with Esther and her Chinese family. Zeng Youdong and Zanhua spoke from the dining room where we'd sat around the old wooden table, and I could see recent modernizations—a dropped ceiling with recessed lighting, modern IKEA-style shelves on the walls. Although this big house is fully occupied only during the holiday, the Zengs make the most of it. I could hear the grandchildren—the Zengs now have four—squealing over a video game. I imagined the Zengs were congratulating themselves for having flouted the one-child policy. Shuangjie perched over her parents' shoulders. She looked the same as ever, the bangs, the round cheeks, no older, but she sounded radiant and happy, as she spoke about her life with her sister. The estrangement of those Covid years felt like it was receding.

Esther told me once, when I asked her why she'd decided to go to China to see her birth family, "I couldn't imagine going through life without meeting them." I imagine too that the reunion helped her move forward, allowing her to put behind her the losses of her past. Up to now, she shows few visible scars from the violent abduction she doesn't remember, although she has recurring nightmares of being chased, possibly related to her forcible removal from her family. She seems to have less anguish about her identity as an adoptee than many others I've met. Maybe because she was raised by family members until she was nearly two, or because she knows she wasn't abandoned. Having an older adoptee sister helped. Or perhaps it is that she inherited the stoicism of her parents. Esther hasn't gained (or regained) the ability to speak Chinese, but she considers herself Chinese. She retains the Hunan habit of eating numbingly spicy food. At times, when she refers in conversation to "my mother," I have to inquire: Which one? Although our trip was largely motivated by Esther's desire to meet her identical twin, it is the relationship with Zanhua that has blossomed over the years. Esther and Zanhua text regularly. Given the language barrier and Zanhua's imperfect literacy, the mother-daughter bond is largely nonverbal, conveyed through exchanges of photos and emojis. Zanhua loves seeing photos of Esther at work as a photographer. She seems to feel vicarious pleasure that her daughter is enjoying a career that she could never experience as a rural daughter of 1960s China.

As for the twins, I think about Nancy Segal's observation that separated identical twins grow more similar as they age. I wonder if their cultural differences will prove merely skin-deep, peeling away over time and revealing a core inner sameness. Like Esther, Shuangjie is both artistic and entrepreneurial. She told me before that her ambition is to start her own kindergarten, admittedly a much more capital-intensive ambition than becoming a self-employed photographer that might not be achievable in today's China. Xi Jinping has cracked down on private education on the grounds that it promotes social inequality.

When and if Esther and Shuangjie will meet again I cannot say. The political climate in China, as well as in the United States, following the return of Donald Trump to the presidency, still discourages travel between the countries. There is no tidy ending to their story, no ending at all, really, because so much can happen in a lifetime. Both of their lives are cluttered with the complications of young adulthood. Perhaps their one reunion was enough emotion to process for the time being. Maybe Shuangjie won't be ready to go to the United States for some years yet. As for Esther, when I asked if she planned to go back to China, she responded, "Yes, of course. But first I want to go to Italy."

CHAPTER TWENTY-EIGHT

SEARCHING

Zhou Changqi and wife, behind him, and new baby.

IN THE FIFTEEN YEARS SINCE I FIRST STARTED REPORTING about Chinese adoptees, the world has shrunk. Social media and communication technology, facial recognition, and DNA testing have erased the thousands of miles that once separated international adoptees from their birth families. Back in 2009, it felt like there was as much chance of locating a Chinese adoptee's birth parents as of finding a grain of sand in a desert. They were so far away in a country unimaginably big, with its population of 1.4 billion. Distant and unknowable. There were no original birth certificates to be unearthed. Most of these children entered the world secretly, born in the privacy of family homes or, in the case of the twins, in a bamboo grove deep in the mountains. If there were records, they'd vanished. Their histories were scrubbed clean of any identifying documentation. There was a finality to these adoptions unlike almost any others in the world. The orphanages often didn't know the origins of the children sent out for adoption. Adoptees were told that searching would only lead them to heartbreak. "I calculated that because China was the most populous country in the world, I could spend my entire life searching and come up empty—devastatingly, gut-wrenchingly empty," wrote a young woman in 2023 on an adoption site.

That illusion has been punctured in recent years. The techniques I used in 2009 to trace the Zeng family's missing twin from the mountains of Hunan Province to Texas are now in common use and have been enhanced by technology. Like it or not—and many don't—social media and the easy availability of autosomal DNA testing have compressed this vast world into a village. It has never been easier for people across the globe to find one another and to communicate. Not unlike the way homicide detectives are using commercial genetic testing to crack cold murder cases, adoptees are locating their birth families in the most distant reaches of the world.

As of this writing, I know of several hundred adoptees who have identified their birth families in China. Their numbers are rising at an exponential pace as more adoptees and birth families realize that it is indeed possible. The coronavirus shutdown in 2020 delayed in-person meetings, but many adoptees are in contact with family members through WeChat and other social media.

For at least two decades now, adoptive families with sufficient resources and nerve have been playing private eye in China, searching for birth families. There used to be a standard plan of attack. The family would fly to China, hire a Chinese guide, and head to the location where the child was reported to have been abandoned. They'd be using the information gleaned from the child's orphanage files and "finding ads" purchased from the Stuys. If they were lucky, they would be able to get a police report with more detail about who found the child. They would tack up notices, translated into Chinese, at the location and on the wall of a nearby market or bus station, hand out flyers, and try to get the local newspaper to write a story.

Sometimes it worked. In 2009, fourteen-year-old Haley Butler of

Nashville traveled with her mother and other adoptees to a small town in Anhui Province, where she had been abandoned at the age of six months. She'd written up a poster, translated into Chinese, which she tacked to walls.

> My name is Haley. I was adopted in 1995. I now live in America. I enjoy singing and playing the violin and hanging out with my friends. I have a good life, but I would like to find my biological family.

While Haley was still putting up the posters, a woman tapped her on the shoulder and said excitedly that Haley resembled the daughters of a cousin. A flurry of phone calls ensued. By that evening, Haley was taking selfies with her birth father in her hotel lobby while siblings and cousins looked on in amazement. DNA testing later confirmed the relationship.

But these success stories were the exception. More often than not, the searches drew a blank because the families were looking in the wrong place. So many had been trafficked from their birthplaces to orphanages that had covered up evidence of buying babies. There was a paper trail, but it led to a dead end because it was mostly fabricated.

"The families would get very grumpy, very impatient," said a Chinese guide who worked with Brian Stuy's outfit helping adoptive families search. "The percentage who found their birth families this way is very small. That's because the orphanages made up the finding locations."

BRIAN STUY IS no doubt the granddaddy of searching. He and his wife, Longlan, have been doing it longer and more successfully than anybody else to date. As of early 2025, they had matched 240 adoptees with birth parents. They've also found siblings and cousins inside China, as well as in the U.S. adoption community.

I talked frequently with Stuy when I was based in Beijing, and since returning to the United States, I've met several times with him and Longlan. Stuy is now in his sixties, his formerly blond hair fading to silver. He's an outdoorsy type, a hiker and climber, but with the sardonic personality of a gadfly. He has unearthed some inconvenient truths about child trafficking that were not welcomed by parents who preferred believing they were rescuing babies. Stuy is "taking off the halo of the white savior" is how my friend the journalist Peter Goodman put it.

"I can't seem to keep my mouth shut," Stuy admitted one of the first times we spoke.

In the mid-2000s, the Stuys started an advisory service to help families search. They'd connect them with a Chinese guide, and, like private detectives, they would collect clues and interrogate possible witnesses around the listed finding locations, which they assumed to be accurate. It was old-fashioned shoe-leather investigating, but Stuy had become increasingly skeptical of the information given adoptive families. There was his own anecdotal experience—discovering that the women who'd supposedly found his infant daughter in 1998 had been instructed to tell him a fabricated story.

Over time, Stuy started conducting more methodical analyses of adoption patterns. He'd look at clusters of babies found in the same week, which suggested a wholesale delivery from a trafficker like the Duans or a Family Planning campaign to confiscate babies. Working together with Longlan, he compiled a list of more than a dozen orphanages suspected of buying babies. Most were in Hunan Province, but also Jiangxi, Guangxi, Guangdong, and Chongqing—a wide swath of southern China that produced most of the adopted babies. The Stuys offer adoptive families what they call "orphanage reliability analysis"— an assessment of the veracity of the information they were given. Brian Stuy suspected that up to 90 percent of the information that adoptive families received about their Chinese children was erroneous, if not entirely fabricated.

After a few years struggling to make matches, the Stuys came to the obvious conclusion: The future belonged to science. In 2013, they started a new service, DNAConnect. He and Longlan still traipsed through China, visiting finding locations and tracking down witnesses. But they also carried plastic vials in their backpacks for collecting DNA. When they encountered Chinese parents who wanted to find lost children, they'd pull out the kits and try to convince the parents to give genetic samples. Once those samples were tested, they would transfer the data files to a larger company that compiles information from multiple testing services. They are currently using GEDmatch. (This California company earned some notoriety in 2018 when its data was used by police to catch Joseph James DeAngelo, a prolific murderer known as the Golden State Killer.)

Often the Stuys would test an adoptee's possible birth parent, who proved to be unrelated but who would match another adoptee. Stuy realized it was a waste of money and effort to launch a search for a single client instead of pooling the information they collected. "By fishing with a net rather than a hook, we will reap far more success as a community than if each of us fishes individually," Stuy explained.

As of this writing, the Stuys have collected DNA profiles of 1,300 birth families seeking children. (Stuy says the numbers would be larger, except that some birth families still remain unaware of international adoption.) They regularly submit these profiles on behalf of the Chinese families to commercial testing services, which Stuy believes contain profiles of at least 25,000 adoptees.

The results are pouring in quickly. In 2023, DNAConnect matched twenty-nine adoptees with their birth parents: in 2024, the number soared to sixty-one, including a boy. Another nonprofit, the Nanchang Project, also uses genetic testing to locate birth families. Unlike the Stuys, they rely primarily on a DNA registry that was set up in 2009 by the Chinese National Police to combat child trafficking. They've made seven matches as of this writing, and their numbers are also growing. "The largest percentage of Chinese adoptees are entering adulthood, or are adults, and there is just a lot more interest in finding their roots," said Erin Valentino, an adoptive mother who co-founded the project in 2018 and now shares management with adoptees.

*   *   *

IN THE PAST, almost all searching was driven by the adoptive families, initially the parents, more recently the adoptees. Now, to the dismay of some adoptive families, Chinese are initiating the searches. Not just birth parents but often older siblings.

The most proactive are the families who had children confiscated or stolen. One of those birth parents is especially close to my heart. Zhou Changqi (mentioned in chapter 9) is the Hunan father whose six-month-old daughter vanished after his wife ran away from a hotel where the government was holding her to be sterilized. When I first spoke to Zhou, it was 2009—seven years after the girl was taken—and his determination to recover his daughter was undiminished. Although poor and functionally illiterate, he was clever and persistent. He'd found a women's federation to help him file a lawsuit. It was dismissed on the grounds that he hadn't registered the birth. He didn't give up. By then a single parent—he and his wife split up after the incident—he traveled from the village to Changsha to Beijing with his young son in tow, submitting petitions, imploring government officials and journalists for help. Zhou used to telephone my office almost weekly to inquire what I'd learned about his daughter. Zhou spoke at a rapid clip in a high-pitched dialect that the Chinese staff in our office struggled to understand, but we listened anyway because his case was so gut-wrenching.

After I located Esther, the Zengs' missing twin, I thought I might be able to help Zhou. I tried. But Zhou's daughter was close in age to other adoptees, giving her fewer identifiable features. I never forgot about Zhou, and was still thinking of him in 2019 when I traveled to China with Esther.

Again it was DNA that came to the rescue. Zhou Changqi had been one of the first Chinese parents to submit a sample to Brian and Longlan Stuy, back in 2013 when they were just starting with genetic testing.

In the autumn of 2022, word came in from Indiana. Zhou's daughter had been found.

Mia Griffin, a twenty-one-year-old college student, had purchased a

23andMe testing kit. It was an impulse buy. She was taking advantage of a $123 sale on Amazon, curious to find out whether she had a genetic predisposition to breast or ovarian cancer. There was a box to check if she was also interested in looking for relatives, and she thought, *Well, why not?*

"I'd never really wanted to find my birth parents because, well, I couldn't handle rejection twice," Griffin told me. But when her results came in, she noticed a tab that led her to a family tree. At the top was an unfamiliar name, "Zhou Chang Qi." The genetic relationship was listed: Father.

Griffin thought it might be a mistake, but she clicked anyway on a button that asked if she wanted to connect.

Again, why not? It turned out to be Brian Stuy, who explained that he had submitted a DNA sample as the agent for Zhou, who did not speak English or own a computer. At first suspecting a scam, she researched his website. Reassured, she gave him her email address.

"Does this mean he has been searching for me?"

"He has been. Desperately," Stuy wrote back.

Griffin would later describe her reaction as akin to a car crash. She was in a state of shock. Time stood still.

With Stuy's help, Griffin set up a WeChat account to connect with other family members. She soon received a message request, this one from another Chinese name she did not recognize.

"Hi. Are you my cousin?" Mia asked him.

"No. I'm your brother."

It was Zhou Jiahai, the boy who'd spent much of his childhood accompanying his father in the futile search for a sister he'd been too young to remember. He spoke enough English to explain to Mia everything that had happened—the itinerant life, the futile search, the poverty, the disappearance of their mother, who has remarried and refuses all contact with her first family. Their father, now in his mid-sixties, is in poor health, physically and emotionally. Hardly a fairy-tale ending. But Mia told me she was gratified by her discoveries. "It makes me proud, honestly, because I'm also a person who has a hard time accepting the status quo if there's something unjust happening, and to learn that my birth father was the same way makes me happy."

PROBABLY THE BIGGEST impediment to searching is that not everybody wants to be found. There are adoptees who prefer not to know anything about their birth families and want nothing at all to do with China. Within the same family, adoptees may feel differently. Although Esther's sister enthusiastically joined our trip and sponged up impressive amounts of the language in less than two weeks, she was adamant about not wanting to research her own past. "You've got to be careful what doors you open," Victoria told me recently. "You have to ask yourself, What is the need I'm trying to fulfill? For me, I don't have that need. I'm not going to go seeking trouble in my life." Other adoptees wholeheartedly embrace a return to China. They learn the language and revert to Chinese names. It would be misleading to generalize. Like any other community, Chinese adoptees have wildly disparate, often contradictory views about China, about their birth families, their adoptive families, and the merits of international adoption. There are some who have told me they feel incredibly lucky to have been adopted to the United States; others are processing wounds from growing up in an alien culture. Many applauded when China in September 2024 announced it was ending international adoption, believing it is wrong to rip children away from their culture and heritage. They can express these emotions more powerfully in their own words, so I have provided links to adoptee writings and memoirs in the endnotes.

I'm not an adoptee myself, nor a therapist, and I can only start to imagine how terrifying it must be to meet a birth parent who could disrupt your sense of identity and belonging to a new family and environment. Or, as Mia Griffin said, to open yourself up to another rejection. In my experience, I have on several occasions had adoptees ask for my help and then pull back. With valid reason, many adoptees fear they will not be able to meet the emotional and perhaps financial expectations of a birth family. They worry that they might be perceived as disloyal to their adoptive families—or that most dreaded insult for an adoptee, "ungrateful." Many are still seething over being abandoned. "I have more rage than I can contain at times," wrote one adoptee anonymously in an essay posted in 2015 on the site Lost Daughters. "The wounds of being separated, left, relinquished, abandoned—whatever you want to call it—from the very ones who were supposed to hold onto me no matter what are just so deep and irrevocable and consuming that they crush me at times."

For all its wonders, genetic testing can be an unwelcome intrusion in people's lives. With an estimated thirty million genetic profiles in databases, lives are more often than ever disrupted by unwelcome findings of extramarital affairs and illegitimate children. Many adoptees, like Mia Griffin, discover birth families inadvertently by submitting their DNA samples out of health concerns. "The adoptee has been told so many times, 'We'll never be able to find your birth family. China is too big. Don't even think about it,'" said Stuy. "Then when it happens, it is like a lightning bolt." Although 23andMe and other popular sites promise users confidentiality, as well as the right to opt out of notifications about relatives, Stuy allows, "Anytime you put your DNA out there, there is a chance of somebody finding something you didn't want." Privacy can be elusive. One adoptive mother, Jennifer Doering, told me bluntly that anonymity was one of the attractions of adopting from China. "We didn't want to be here in America with somebody coming forward and saying, 'That's my child,' 'That's my grandchild.'" But when they ordered their daughter's finding ad from Brian Stuy, he also sent a photo with her foster mother holding not one but two girls who looked exactly the same and who had similar names, although their birth dates were five days apart. Doering managed to track down the other family. The girls took DNA tests, which proved they were indeed identical twins and also ended up leading them to a second cousin living in the United States. That in turn revealed the identity of the birth parents. "Once you see something like that, you can't unsee it. That's a problem, like opening a Pandora's box," Doering said.

THE MATCHES BETWEEN adoptees and birth parents bear some resemblance to dating. The timing is key. "It's like landing two planes on a runway. They have to be perfect," said Brian Stuy. "Sometimes the birth parents are all gung ho, and the adoptee is unsure if she is ready."

Adoptive parents factor in as well. Stuy recalls one case where he located a confiscated child, but the adoptive father in the United States was frightened the birth family would file a lawsuit. In another instance, when a birth sister in China located her younger sister through genetic testing, the adoptive father blocked contact. "'Her birth family left her at the side of the road to die. They are dead to us,'" Stuy said the father told him. "'Don't contact us again.'"

Conversely, I happen to have encountered many adoptive parents who are keener than their children to chase down birth families. One father who fell down a rabbit hole searching was Wesley O. Hagood, a business consultant from the Washington, D.C., area, who in 2021 published a how-to manual titled *Searching for Your Chinese Birth Family*. His story is a rollicking cautionary tale of misadventures that is most instructive in what not to do.

In 2007, when his then-four-year-old daughter, Mia, started asking the inevitable questions, Hagood recalls he was "tired of providing my well-worn 'non-answers' to all of her questions."

"I will do whatever I can to help you find your birth parents," he told her. A dogged researcher who had once written a book about presidential sex scandals, Hagood pursued this mission with a vengeance. In 2010, he went to China, tried to visit the orphanage where Mia had lived as a baby, distributed flyers, and produced a video called "Mia's Dream" to post on Chinese social media. He printed English vocabulary flash cards for middle school students that included a plea for information. He was interviewed by a local journalist at a famous tea shop in Xinyi City, the town where his daughter had reportedly been abandoned, but the story was censored and ran in the newspaper under the forgettable headline "Foreigner Visits Xinyi to Drink Tea."

On the next trip to China, Hagood discovered paperwork that listed the name of his daughter's finder as *Luo Si,* a common name for both men and women, but he quickly fixated on one suspect—a man who was superintendent of Xinyi's school system. When this Luo Si refused to talk to him, he developed a new theory—that Luo Si was Mia's biological father. Stalking him online, he discovered that Luo Si often drank tea at public school meetings. He convinced a reluctant researcher to steal the man's teacup and to send it to the United States for DNA testing. The report came back negative.

By then, Hagood was going over the edge. "I was obsessed," he admitted. "I just wasn't going to give up." He attended a hacker convention, hoping to hire somebody who could get into the orphanage's computer system to learn more. It was fortunate for his sanity and legal standing that nobody took him up on the offer.

In the end, it proved simpler than he would have imagined. In 2015, his then-thirteen-year-old daughter did a DNA test with 23andMe. She matched with three cousins, one a fellow adoptee, and two young Chinese men studying at U.S. universities. The Chinese students both had family from Xinyi City, but the genetic markers weren't clear enough to determine how exactly they might be related to Mia or to each other. But they were able to narrow down the possibilities through a process known as triangulation, where genetic researchers look for common ancestors. Eventually, they uploaded Mia's information into 23Mofang, a Chinese DNA service. This time she matched a first cousin. That cousin told her she had an aunt and uncle who had placed a younger daughter up for adoption the very same year that Mia was born. That quickly led her to her birth parents.

CHINA IS NOT the only country where adoptees are digging around for their roots. Genetic testing has spurred a new wave of searching in situations where it would have been deemed impossible a decade ago. New nonprofits crop up regularly to enable searching in countries like Cambodia and Ethiopia that have sent out children for adoption. Middle-aged Italian Americans are returning to look for birth mothers who were coerced by the Catholic Church into relinquishing their babies. In South Korea, the government maintains an extensive database to enable searches by its twenty thousand adoptees—still the largest international adoptee population in the world. In 2023, South Korea's Truth and Reconciliation Commission, set up to probe human rights abuses dating back to the early twentieth century, opened an investigation into allegations that children's files were manipulated to facilitate lucrative overseas adoptions.

But that's South Korea, a democracy. In China, looking for a missing child is an implicit criticism of what was the signature policy of the Communist Party. The government, while welcoming adoptee tourism and even allowing adoptees to use the police database, discourages pointed questions about exactly how and why they were adopted. And parents who admit to having abandoned babies could in theory be charged criminally, since it was technically against the law (although I know of few prosecutions).

The obstacles are psychological as well as legal. In many families, the relinquishment of a child remains secret. There is the shame of being so heartless as to surrender your own child, or the shame over being so poor and powerless that your child was taken away, as happened to the Zengs.

However parents were separated from their children, the pain is real. Birth parents often left their children with notes they could use to trace them later or dates and times of birth, crucial information in traditional Chinese fortune-telling. "I collected the notes. But I couldn't read, so I threw them out," admitted Chen Zhijin, the Duan family matriarch, who used to pick up abandoned children.

In one well-documented case, an impoverished young couple whose baby was born secretly on a houseboat in 1995 left a note saying she should meet them in ten or twenty years on the first day of the Qixi Festival, a holiday that is China's equivalent of Valentine's Day. Although in this case the note was given to the adoptive parents, they were reluctant to tell their daughter until she reached adulthood. The birth parents went to the bridge in 2005 and returned every year thereafter, hoping. Reporters got wind of the story. It finally happened in 2018, when their then-twenty-two-year-old daughter, Kati Pohler, a violinist from Michigan, showed up on the bridge for a reunion that had been arranged as part of a documentary.

Another revealing story comes from Jenna Cook, who as a twenty-year-old Yale undergraduate in 2012 received a fellowship to document the search for her birth parents in Wuhan. Whether it was her earnest smile or her Ivy League credentials, hundreds of people contacted her wondering if she was their daughter.

Cook met with fifty families who could have plausibly been her parents, given the time and place she was found. They explained how they'd left their babies with distinctive clothing, sometimes embroidered with a message, with the hope she would grow up and know how to find them. One family wrote the daughter's date of birth on cigarette paper because they didn't have anything else.

These parents threw their arms around her. They bowed and begged forgiveness.

"I'm so sorry. Do you forgive me?" parents would sob, Cook later wrote of her trip in an article in *Foreign Policy*.

"I forgive you. I forgive you," Cook would reply, as though answering on behalf of another birth daughter the family might never meet.

Cook never did find her own birth parents. Instead, she found a "nationwide pain, forged over decades, with which the country is still reckoning."

To this day, everything relating to the one-child policy remains *mingan*, "sensitive" in Chinese political parlance, as it evokes the unspeakable blunders of the still-ruling Communist Party. Like the Great Leap Forward, which led to forty million deaths from starvation, or the Cultural Revolution, which killed millions more and led to the annihilation of years' worth of learning and culture, these are episodes of very recent

Chinese history that are willfully submerged. There is an enforced culture of forgetting in China, so much so that author Louisa Lim has described it as "The People's Republic of Amnesia," the title of her book about the 1989 crackdown on prodemocracy demonstrators at Tiananmen Square. "China is scarred by loss and violence on a staggering scale," writes another author, Tania Branigan, in a recent book about the Cultural Revolution, *Red Memory*. She describes the country as a "crime scene" where all that is left are "chalk marks and onlookers keeping their distance."

Some Chinese scholars, most emphatically demographer Wang Feng, now at the University of California, Irvine, ranks the one-child policy as the Communist Party's biggest mistake, even worse than the previous debacles. Enduring for more than thirty-five years, the policy shattered marriages, led to the deaths of countless children and the suicides of parents, and left China with a population expected to continue declining into the next century. It was all-encompassing, leaving almost everybody a victim or a perpetrator or both.

I can't think of anybody I met in China who wasn't touched by the one-child policy. Most of my younger Chinese friends are only children, their futures clouded with worry about their parents, the entire burden of the family upon their shoulders. I encountered so many farmers worried sick about their future without surviving offspring—those whose children were killed in the 2008 Sichuan earthquake, for instance, and those who had to abandon them due to birth limits. I wonder what happened to the little girl I met in Shandong Province whose mother died after a forced abortion, trying to give birth to a son. Is she burdened with regret for not being the boy her mother wanted?

There are the boys too: The sons who carry the knowledge that they owe their lives to the sacrifice of their older sisters. And the millions of bachelors—as many as twenty million, by the estimates of demographers—who can't find wives.

Then there are those who were complicit in the abusive system and who suffer nightmares of contrition over what they did. The doctors who felt compelled to inject formaldehyde into the crowning heads of induced full-term babies. The midwives who had to perform late-term abortions. The Family Planning officers who chased pregnant women down the street, who coerced their neighbors into forced sterilizations. Those very same people who wrested babies from the arms of parents and grandparents—or in the case of Fangfang, from an aunt.

Outside of China, you have up to 160,000 Chinese adoptees in the United States, Canada, Europe, and Australia living under new identities, citizens of their adopted countries but tethered by blood to another family and country they struggle to comprehend. Living in this in-between space between worlds.

Knowing China, I would not expect anything like a Truth and Reconciliation Commission. It's not in the nature of the Chinese Communist Party to dwell on mistakes. If Chinese people were allowed to talk openly about what happened and to set up a centralized DNA bank, as exists in South Korea, I believe most of the Chinese adoptees would be able to learn their origins.

That is, if the adoptees and their Chinese families so desire.

Acknowledgments

During the seven years when I was based in Beijing, many Chinese families welcomed me into their homes and shared their stories. At times, they opened up at their own peril and almost always they were dredging up painful memories. I especially thank the Zeng family for their hospitality and patience, understanding why it took a decade before their missing daughter could return to China. I don't think any of the other Shaoyang parents have physically reunited with their children, but I hope they can at least learn what happened and understand why it is so difficult for these children to reengage. I am especially grateful to Yang Libing, whose persistence enabled this story to see the light of day. And to Yuan Chaoren, the scribe who drafted the petition and navigated me through various twists in the story.

Often the "scoops" of foreign correspondents in China result from the work of Chinese journalists and researchers. Although he wasn't able to publish until 2011, Pang Jiaoming was way ahead of me and especially generous in sharing materials he had unearthed. Some of the quotes I use come from his book *The Orphans of Shao*. I also received help from Deng Fei, an investigative reporter who was based in Beijing, and others who might better be left nameless here.

Brian and Longlan Stuy informed my reporting at every step of the way. Their passion and insight are reflected in their many contributions in these pages.

In the Beijing bureau of the *Los Angeles Times,* Nicole Liu was not so much an interpreter as my reporting partner from 2009 through the completion of this book. Tommy Yang provided invaluable research, hunting down sources and obscure petitions on the Chinese internet. Wang Yuan reported and interpreted in the latter stages of the project and contributed deft analyses of Chinese cultural nuances that I had missed. Violet Law provided additional translation and research in Hong Kong. Wang Ai helped me decipher reams of handwritten Chinese police notes. Liu Hongbin took excellent photographs of the family reunion in 2019.

In the American press, Peter Goodman of *The Washington Post*, I believe, was the first to report on the trafficking of babies for adoption. The media and adoption community in the Netherlands took the lead in reporting on the role of family planning in Shaoyang with a report in 2008 aired as part of a *Netwerk* television series on corruption in foreign adoption. I thank producers and especially Igor Nuijten for passing on their contacts.

In the United States, I am so grateful to Esther and her family members. Although we came from very different backgrounds and encountered adoption from opposite perspectives, we became fast friends. They were excellent traveling companions and I hope will be part of my life for years to come. I understand that the reporting and publication of this book exposed their lives to unaccustomed scrutiny. That was a considerable sacrifice for which I am grateful. I hope readers will respect a modicum of their privacy and give them their space.

Mei Fong's book *One Child* was always nearby while writing. Mei also contributed ideas and steered me to other resources.

Special thanks to Nanfu Wang and Jialing Zhang, the extremely talented co-directors of the incredible documentary *One Child Nation*. They helped me reconnect with the Zeng family in 2017. Their film was a revelation to anybody involved with international adoption.

My uncle David Schmerler served as an early reader and an excellent editor of countless first drafts. My friend Margaret Scott read and consulted from the inception of this project to the very end. She and her husband, Ben Rauch, and their daughter, Isabel Rauch, were an inspiration from the outset. Friends and fellow authors Lijia Zhang and Gabrielle Glaser were also early readers, and their writings are cited in my own.

My longtime friend the filmmaker Julie Talen taught me more about the art of storytelling than anybody else in my life.

The *Los Angeles Times* gave me the incredible opportunity of a posting in China and the freedom to stray from the daily grind. I thank editors Scott Kraft and Marjorie Miller, who sent me to China, and Norman Pearlstine, who supported me during his too-brief reign at the newspaper. Editors Bruce Wallace, Mark Porubcansky, Mitchell Landsberg, and Kim Murphy had a hand in this project. Steve Padilla deftly edited the 2019 version of the family's return to

China, and his tweaks are reflected in this book. I had very talented colleagues in China—Mark Magnier, Julie Makinen, Ching-Ching Ni, David Pierson, and Megan Stack as well as Alice Su, who joined the bureau after I left but whose writing informed my own work. Tracy Wilkinson, now of the Washington bureau, who brought me into the *Los Angeles Times* and who has been a friend since we met years ago under fire at Sarajevo's Holiday Inn. And the wonderful Simon Li, who first hired me. To Patrick Soon-Shiong—may he please keep the *Los Angeles Times* afloat. Although the newspaper, like many, is a shadow of its former self, its foreign correspondents individually are some of the best in the world as they have to compete single-handedly against staffs up to ten times larger. Along with my two previous books, about North Korea and Tibet, this book should help to show why we need more journalists out there reporting on the world. We need multiple voices. In an age of disinformation, we can't relegate all coverage to one or two big players.

The China gang: There is a moveable conversation about China that floats between New York and Beijing and Washington. Each of these people in some way contributed their wisdom to my reporting: Hannah Beech, Sarabeth Berman, Melissa Chan, Larry Fay, Sheila Fay, Anna Fifield, Ed Gargan, Lindsey Hilsum, Ian Johnson, Stephanie Kleine-Ahlbrandt, Elizabeth Knup, Arthur Kroeber, Brook Larmer, Jen-Lin Liu, Karen Ma, Jane Macartney, Alexa Olesen, Evan Osnos, Philip Pan, Jane Perlez, Sarah Shaeffer, Didi Tatlow, Tini Tran. And especially Gady Epstein, who was the driving force behind many of our gatherings, and a sharp commentator on China. My first mentor when it came to China was my longtime friend Lena Sun, former Beijing bureau chief for *The Washington Post*. Ed Wong and I were writing our books at the same time and exchanged advice and commiseration. Shannon Wu provided invaluable advice at a critical juncture.

Many of my friends are writers and journalists themselves, and all of them committed readers. They listened to me prattle on about this project for many years and offered input: Anna Boorstin, Molly Fowler, Robin Golden, Madeleine Grant, Lee Hockstader, Terri Jentz, Harold Jordan, Ruth Marcus, Veronica McFall, Barbara Milrod, Nomi Morris, Steve Newhouse, Jocelyn Noveck, Miriam Rozen, Tim Weiner, Laura Wides-Muñoz. Eden Mullon and Nicholas Demick were, as always, supporters and companions.

Being a self-employed writer is a solitary existence; my Sunday morning video chats with high school friends Catherine Peterson and Bethany Mott have been the underpinning of my life since we began during the 2020 lockdown.

A shout-out to libraries: The New York Public Library is essential to writers like myself unaffiliated with a university or media outlet, working out of overcrowded New York bedrooms. This book was enabled by the library's Cullman Fellowship, funded by the Janice B. and Milford D. Gerton / Arts and Letters Foundation. Thanks to Cullman director Salvadore Scibona, Lauren Goldenberg and Paul Delaverdac, as well as the other fellows in the class of 2021–2022. The library gave me a desperately needed workplace and access to research during the Covid lockdown when everything else was shut tight. Unable to return to China that year, I hunkered down with books and journals in the Cullman Center and drafted the beginning of the book, which I completed in the library's Allen Room. I also want to thank Princeton University, which hosted me as a teaching fellow in 2022, offering financial support, a workplace, and the companionship of fellow professors Razia Iqbal and Deb Amos, program director Joseph Stephens, and old friends Gary Bass and Jeff Nunokawa. Not to speak of Princeton students, who, as I found teaching in 2006–2007, offered fresh insights from a younger generation. Special thanks to Kajal Schiller.

My agent and friend, Flip Brophy, shepherded my transition from daily newspaper reporter to author. She took me on (thanks to the urging of the late Jim Dwyer) at a time I was ready to give up. It wouldn't have happened without her. At Sterling Lord Literistic, Jessica Friedman and Szilvia Molnar were always there for me.

I am eternally grateful to Julie Grau, who was my first book editor and who shaped me into a book writer. At Random House, I had the good fortune to work with Molly Turpin, an excellent editor who stepped in late in the process. I appreciate Marie Pantojan's encouragement and guidance shaping this project. Andrew Ward supported all of us through challenging times and listened sympathetically to my various quibbles. As always, I rely on the superb editor Bella Lacey at *Granta*.

Many people involved with adoption had input into my reporting. They include adoptive parents Moya Smith, Wendy Mailman, Deborah Talen, Cathy Wagner, Laurie Brown, and Jennifer Doering, and agency officials Mary House and Melody Zhang. And the many adoptees to whom this book is dedicated.

Notes

These notes are intended to serve multiple purposes. Most obvious is to disclose the sources of my information. Rather than slow down the flow of a book written in the style of narrative nonfiction, I haven't used the journalistic convention of attributing all facts and quotes within the text. I also wanted to provide additional context for readers who want to further explore aspects of Chinese culture and adoption issues that I've given only cursory treatment in this book. I've made an effort to list resources that readers can find with relatively little effort and expense. I don't always include page numbers, because many of these resources were accessed in ebook format or online. Similarly, with websites, I don't always list exact links, because they are subject to change. The exception is for links to articles that might otherwise be difficult for readers to access on their own.

CHAPTER ONE: BORN IN THE BAMBOO

This account of life in Gaofeng village is based on four visits between 2009 and 2019. I interviewed most members of the immediate family, as well as Li Guihua, the midwife who delivered the twins. A 2020 trip to the village had to be canceled because of the Covid pandemic, but I conducted subsequent interviews by WeChat. Zanhua's village was originally called Shanghuang, "on the yellow," but it was later merged with Gaofeng.

A recent book that informed my thinking about Chinese village life is Karoline Kan's *Under Red Skies: Three Generations of Life, Loss, and Hope in China* (Legacy Lit, 2019).

Leslie Chang's *Factory Girls: From Village to City in a Changing China* (Random House, 2009) offers great insight into the young women who left their villages to work in the cities. Zanhua didn't work in a factory in her teens, but her experience of escaping to earn money is similar.

The twentieth-century Chinese history is drawn from multiple sources: About Mao Zedong, Hunan's most famous son, there are several excellent biographies: Alexander V. Pantsov and Steven I. Levine, *Mao: The Real Story* (Simon & Schuster, 2013); Philip Short, *Mao: The Man Who Made China* (Bloomsbury Academic, 2023); Jonathan Spence, *Mao: A Life* (Penguin Books, 2006).

On the post-Mao years, when the twins' parents were coming of age, see Frank Dikötter's *China After Mao: The Rise of a Superpower* (Bloomsbury, 2022).

During my visits to the villages, I became fascinated with the terraced rice paddies. They are truly among the wonders of the world, dating back several millennia and maintained by successive generations. One of the few articles I found about terraced farming was by anthropologist Francesca Bray, "Rice, Technology, and History: The Case of China," *Education About Asia*, Winter 2004.

CHAPTER TWO: COMEUPPANCE

In writing about the one-child system, I'm heavily indebted to Mei Fong's wonderful *One Child: The Story of China's Most Radical Experiment* (Mariner Books, 2016). I quote from her analysis about the mathematical manipulation used to boost per-capita income by reducing births (p. 48).

For the history of China's ever-changing attitudes toward population growth, I relied on the essay "Population Control and State Coercion," by Yanzhong Huang and Dali L. Yang, published in *Holding China Together: Diversity and National Integration in the Post-Deng Era* (Cambridge University Press, 2009), and Susan Greenhalgh's *Just One Child: Science and Policy in Deng's China* (University of California Press, 2008). The estimate of the number of people involved in Family Planning comes from Huang and Yang.

The account of the "period police" comes from Lijia Zhang's *"Socialism Is Great!": A Worker's Memoir of the New China* (Anchor Books, 2009).

The abuses committed by Family Planning officials are cited in a petition later filed by villagers.

He Yafu's estimates of the funds raised in fines or "social maintenance fees" were cited in "The Brutal Truth," *Economist*, June 23, 2012.

On how the national tax reform starved local government of revenue, I turned to a report published by the Rhodium Group, an economic research firm. "Tax Reform, Impact on Local Government," by Daniel H. Rosen Group, July 11, 2014.

On the intellectual underpinnings of population control, Paul R. Ehrlich's *The Population Bomb* (Ballantine Books, 1968) was a hugely influential bestseller. (His wife, Anne Howland Ehrlich, is listed as co-author on some editions.) The Chinese counterpart was *Population System and Control*, by Song Jian and Yu Jingyuan (English edition, Springer-Verlag, 1988). The quote from Guan Zhong is found on p. 236.

The dizzying rules in Hunan Province that governed how many children a family was allowed were supplied to me by Pang Jiaoming, an investigative reporter and the author of *The Orphans of Shao: A True Account of the Blood and Tears of the One-Child Policy in China* (Women's Rights in China, 2014). The account of the forced vasectomy of the childless man is from his book. Pang was very generous in sharing original research material he obtained, and his work is quoted frequently in this book.

The quote from the doctor who admitted to injecting formaldehyde into the heads of babies in the birth canal came from a 1985 series by Michael Weisskopf of *The Washington Post*. It was one of the first major investigations into Family Planning abuses and was considered so sensitive that the newspaper withheld publication until Weisskopf, wrapping up a four-year tour as Beijing correspondent, had left China.

And from John Aird, who was a scholar at the conservative American Enterprise Institute, see *Slaughter of the Innocents: Coercive Birth Control in China* (AEI Press, 1990).

The family-planning slogans quoted throughout come from a variety of sources. Some were seen by me and colleagues. Others were included in a paper by Guoyan Wang, "Wall Slogans: The Communication of China's Family Planning Policy in Rural Areas," *Rural History*, April 2018. The slogan including "kill, kill, kill" was cited in Ma Jian's "China's Barbaric One-Child Policy," *Guardian*, May 6, 2013.

The savagery of the massacres that took place in Hunan Province during the Cultural Revolution is documented in Tan Hecheng's *The Killing Wing:*

A Chinese County's Descent into Madness During the Cultural Revolution, translated by Stacy Mosher (Oxford University Press, 2017). It makes for sobering reading.

CHAPTER THREE: SUBTERFUGE

So much has been written about the discrimination against females in Asia, I can't possibly list all the titles. Here are a few:

D. E. Mungello, *Drowning Girls in China: Female Infanticide Since 1650* (Rowman & Littlefield, 2008). The book contains quotes from writings of Christian missionaries who provided some of the first Western accounts of the practice. The quote comparing baby girls to unwanted kittens comes from Adele Fielde's 1884 memoir, *Pagoda Shadows: Studies from Life in China* (p. 85). Another reference is Julie Jimmerson, "Female Infanticide in China: An Examination of Cultural and Legal Norms," *Pacific Basin Law Journal* 8, no. 1 (1990).

The British Chinese writer whose pen name is Xinran has written extensively on the situation of women in China. Here I quote from *Message from an Unknown Chinese Mother: Stories of Loss and Love* (Simon & Schuster, 2012).

The 2019 Oscar-short-listed *One Child Nation* contains heart-wrenching, candid interviews with filmmaker Nanfu Wang's family members and neighbors who were involved in abandoning infant girls.

The late Kay Ann Johnson, an adoptive mother and the author of *China's Hidden Children: Abandonment, Adoption, and the Human Costs of the One-Child Policy* (University of Chicago Press, 2017), took a contrarian view on Chinese attitudes toward girls. She believed that most Chinese who abandoned girls did so only under extreme duress. She also found it was relatively rare for Chinese families to abandon firstborn girls and that most abandoned girls had older sisters. The quote about the policymakers in Beijing having pensions comes from this book (p. 16). Johnson made similar arguments in an earlier book, *Wanting a Daughter, Needing a Son: Abandonment, Adoption, and Orphanage Care in China* (Yeong & Yeong, 2004).

Scholars John James Kennedy and Yaojiang Shi expanded on Johnson's work in *Lost and Found: The "Missing Girls" in Rural China* (Oxford University Press, 2019). They found that many families employed ruses like that used to hide the twins in order to keep their daughters.

There are no accurate statistics on infanticide resulting from the one-child policy, but demographers have estimated based on census data. Judith Banister, *China: Recent Trends in Health and Mortality* (U.S. Bureau of the Census, 1986), found a sharp rise in reported infant mortality from a low of forty per thousand live births in 1977–1978 to sixty-one per thousand births in 1981–1982, after the policy was implemented. Banister noted that the increased mortality affected both males and females and took place in all parts of China, rural and urban, and across all education levels.

To understand the importance of *hukou* and the plight of unregistered children, see Shen Yang's *More Than One Child: Memoirs of an Illegal Daughter*, translated by Nicky Harman (Balestier Press, 2021), a compelling first-person account of what it was like to be "born a crime."

The story of the father, Liu Chunsan, throwing his daughter into a well was also in this series. "One Couple, One Child," *Washington Post*, January 7, 1985.

For another perspective on child abandonment, the late Yale historian John Boswell wrote persuasively about the practice in Europe in *The Kindness of Strangers: The Abandonment of Children in Western Europe from Late Antiquity to the Renaissance* (University of Chicago Press, 1998).

CHAPTER FOUR: THE BABY SNATCHERS

The bang-bang men of Chongqing have inspired many profiles, one by my former colleague, Henry Chu, that ran in the *Los Angeles Times*, "A Chinese City's Porters Carry the Weight of History," November 10, 2012. Evan Osnos wrote a lovely piece on Chongqing for the *Chicago Tribune*, "An Odyssey into the Heart of China," September 13, 2007.

On "left-behind children": The figure of sixty-one million Chinese children whose parents migrated to urban areas comes from UNICEF. The agency estimated that 22 percent of Chinese children were raised with both parents living away from home.

On child kidnapping, I used information from Charles Custer's "China's Missing Children," *Foreign Policy*, October 10, 2011. That article contained a very apt observation by criminologist Pi Yijun about how easy it is to steal a child. I often was dismayed to see very young children playing unsuper-vised. One night while I was eating dinner in a small town in Hunan Prov-ince with my colleague Nicole, we spotted through the front window a toddler wandering from the sidewalk into a busy street. We rushed out to bring her back inside, where her mother was cooking our noodles, and watched her for the duration of the meal. While in China, I wrote frequently about human trafficking. One piece dealt with teenagers and mentally dis-abled adults being kidnapped to work in brick factories: "China's Disabled Exploited as Slaves," *Los Angeles Times*, February 26, 2011.

CHAPTER FIVE: A PETITION SIGNED IN BLOOD

The account of babies confiscated by Family Planning in Shaoyang comes primarily from the text of the petition. I interviewed Yang Libing's family at some length in 2009 and met briefly with some of the other families. I spoke frequently with "Old Yuan," Yuan Chaoren, and had a long interview with him in 2017. Additional details about the cases came from Pang Jiaoming's book *Orphans of Shao*. Pang was familiar with the various personalities at the Family Planning office.

On petitioning, interested readers can find many articles about the persis-tence of this archaic practice. I would recommend a report by Human Rights Watch, "'We Could Disappear at Any Time': Retaliation and Abuses Against Chinese Petitioners," December 2005. The report contains a useful primer on the history of petitioning and is available at HRW.org. I visited the peti-tion village several times while based in Beijing and wrote about a crackdown by police in the run-up to the 2008 Summer Olympics: "Silences for Now on the Streets of Beijing," *Los Angeles Times*, August 5, 2008.

CHAPTER SIX: THE SCANDAL

On the criminal case, I've heard and read many varying accounts of how the arrests went down, and even eyewitness accounts have a *Rashomon*-like com-plexity. I'm using mostly my own firsthand reporting. In January 2010, I was one of the first foreign journalists to interview Duan family members who had been released from prison ("A Family in China Made Babies Their Busi-ness," *Los Angeles Times*, January 24, 2010). I met them in their home in

Changning. Their lawyer had obtained a wealth of police notes and documents from orphanages, and I photographed as many of them as I was able.

Some of the first detailed accounts of the case in English were published by Research-China.org, the site run by adoptive parents Brian and Longlan Stuy. Their site has a wealth of information about child trafficking and adoption and is frequently cited in this book.

Longlan Stuy also copied some of the Duan legal documents and shared them with me. These included logs showing how much the orphanages paid for babies, transcripts of interviews with orphanage officials, and handwritten police notes. During my interview, Duan Yueneng said that his gang had trafficked "several thousand" babies. In a later interview for the documentary *One Child Nation*, he put the number at ten thousand.

On the origins of the Chinese name for the United States, see John Pomfret's *The Beautiful Country and the Middle Kingdom: America and China, 1776 to the Present* (Henry Holt, 2016).

Interview with Melody Zhang, September 9, 2009.

The quote from Guo Sijin is cited by Karen Miller-Loessi and Zeynep Kilic in "A Unique Diaspora? The Case of Adopted Girls from the People's Republic of China," *Diaspora: A Journal of Transnational Studies*, University of Toronto Press, Fall 2001.

The full name of the international agreement covering adoption is the Hague Convention on Protection of Children and Co-operation in Respect of Intercountry Adoption. The U.S. State Department's website has a useful explanation on the history and implementation of the law: "Understanding the Hague Convention," https://travel.state.gov/content/travel/en/Intercountry-Adoption/Adoption-Process/understanding-the-hague-convention.html.

In the early years of adoption, the Chinese babies sent overseas were overwhelmingly female. After the mid-2000s, when more special-needs children were adopted, the numbers tilted more heavily male.

Ellen Goodman's syndicated column about her adopted daughter ran in various news outlets in July 2004. Bruce Porter's *New York Times Magazine* story ran on April 11, 1993.

The estimate of 100,000 to 160,000 abandoned babies per year was cited by Kay Johnson, Huang Banghan, and Wang Liyao in "Infant Abandonment and Adoption in China," *Population and Development Review*, September 1988.

The example of the orphanage director buying a Mercedes was cited in "Open Secret: Cash and Coercion in China's International Adoption Program," by Brian H. Stuy (with foreword by David Smolin), *Cumberland Law Review*, 2014.

China experimented at times with setting up baby hatches so children could be safely abandoned, but the programs were not successful. The babies left were almost all sick or disabled and hospitals couldn't cope. In one case, a father who left a severely ill newborn—he claimed, with the hope she could be saved by authorities—was later arrested for the crime of child abandonment, which carries a penalty of up to five years in prison. The Chinese magazine *Caixin* reported on problems in the baby hatches. Wang Jing, "Baby Hatch Programs Struggle to Cope with Number of Infants with Birth Defects," January 9, 2015.

Leslie K. Wang is an American sociologist who volunteered at Chinese social welfare institutes. Her excellent book *Outsourced Child: Orphanage Care and Adoption in Globalizing China* (Stanford University Press, 2016) has the best up-close reporting of the situation inside the orphanages, and their inability to cope with disabled children, particularly boys, who were less favored for adoption.

Anthropologist Toby Volkman has written that adoption from China offered Americans a "less fraught space in which to deal with race than stories about transracial black-white adoption in the U.S." "Embodying Chinese Culture: Transnational Adoption in the United States," *Social Text*, 2003.

The most thorough study I found on abductions is "Where Have All the Children Gone? An Empirical Study of Child Abandonment and Abduction in China," by Xiaojia Bao, Sebastian Galiani, and Kai Li, a working paper published by the National Bureau of Economic Research, November 2019, revised in April 2020.

The Dongyuan kidnapping was described in a story by Peter Goodman, I think the first American journalist to examine the origins of the Chinese adoptees. "Stealing Babies for Adoption: With U.S. Couples Eager to Adopt, Some Infants Are Abducted and Sold in China," *Washington Post*, March 12, 2006. It was Peter who suggested to me that I further investigate this issue.

The Chongqing teahouse case was reported in Chinese social media and picked up on September 24, 2008, by the Chinese website baobeihuijia.com ("babycomehome.com"), which had been set up for families searching for missing children. I read about it on Brian Stuy's Research-China.org blog: "Do Orphanages Really Want to Find Birth Parents?," June 25, 2008.

The quote from Chen Ming, the orphanage director who served prison time, is from an interview I conducted along with *Los Angeles Times* staff in 2009. The quote from Wang Huachun is from notes of an interview conducted with him by the Hengyang police. The police notes were obtained by the lawyer for the Duan family and shared with me by the Stuys.

CHAPTER SEVEN: CREATING ORPHANS

The information about Jiang Dewei came from the website of the Standing Committee of the Shaoyand People's Congress. https://www.hnsyrd.gov .cn/. The page has since been removed.

The unpublished Longhui County investigative report of March 12, 2006, was given to me by Pang Jiaoming.

The "finding ads" for the babies were discovered by Longlan Stuy of Research-China.org.

CHAPTER EIGHT: MY STORY

The White Swan Hotel: On the scene among adoptive parents in Guangzhou, see Finn-Olaf Jones, "The Happiest Hotel on Earth," *Forbes*, February 25, 2011. Also see David Barboza's "A Chinese Hotel, Full of Proud American Parents," *New York Times*, March 31, 2003.

Reporting in the countryside, I was accompanied by Chinese colleagues on these assignments. They did not receive bylines because of the government's limitations on Chinese nationals reporting for the foreign press. At times, they wanted to remain anonymous for their own protection. But these stories could not have been produced without them.

In *Assignment China: An Oral History of American Journalists in the People's Republic* (Columbia University Press, 2023), longtime China correspondent Mike Chinoy captured the window of openness for journalists around the time of the Beijing Summer Olympics. I was among the journalists interviewed for the book. The taxi driver in Henan Province mentioned here was only one of many Chinese who took great personal risks to help us report. In this case, he managed to help us lose a tail by pulling into a taxi parking lot at the bus station where there were hundreds of identical-looking cars. He arranged for us to duck down and slip into another taxi driven by a friend in order to escape. He didn't want to be paid, but I slipped money between the seats for him as I sneaked out and escaped into the other car.

The description of foreign correspondents in China comes from Alec Ash, *The Mountains Are High: A Year of Escape and Discovery in Rural China* (Scribe UK, 2024).

The Association for Asian Studies has a useful primer online about how Chinese social media at least initially empowered challenges to one-party rule: "China's Weibo: Political and Social Implications?," published in *Education About Asia* 18, no. 2 (Fall 2013), https://www.asianstudies.org/publications/eaa/archives/chinas-weibo-political-and-social-implications/. An excellent book about the promise and betrayal of internet freedom is *Consent of the Networked: The Worldwide Struggle for Internet Freedom*, by Rebecca MacKinnon (Basic Books, 2013).

Brian Stuy's description of his meeting with the "finder" of his daughter comes from an essay on his blog, "It Is Time for the Adoption Community to Take Searching Seriously," which appeared on Research-China.org on January 4, 2021.

CHAPTER NINE: HUNAN PROVINCE

The *South China Morning Post* story ran on March 21, 2006. Here is a link that might still be working: https://www.scmp.com/article/541264/united-grief-farmers-lament-loss-children-stolen-officials.

The Dutch television report aired on *Netwerk* on March 14, 2008. It was one of the first media investigations of child trafficking in China and international adoption. The *Netwerk* journalists were very generous in sharing contacts when I visited Hunan Province the following year. The *Netwerk* report (which unfortunately is not available online) prompted the 2009 resignation of Ina Hut, the director of the Netherlands' largest adoption agency. She complained that the Dutch government had refused to investigate for fear of endangering trade relations with China. When I interviewed Hut in 2009, she told me, "In the beginning, I think, adoption from China was a very good thing because there were so many abandoned girls. But then it became a supply-and-demand-driven market and a lot of people at the local level were making too much money."

CHAPTER TEN: MUG SHOTS

The story, "Stolen Chinese Babies Supply Adoption Demand," September 20, 2009, and the sidebar about the twins, "A Young Girl Pines for Her Twin," are still available on the *Los Angeles Times* website.

The Adopt the World website is no longer on the internet.

The father who threw his daughter down the well was Liu Chunsan of Shandong Province. Michael Weisskopf of *The Washington Post* wrote about it in his 1985 series. Marsha believes she read the story in *Reader's Digest,* although I was never able to find it.

Caixin's Hu Shuli was the subject of a profile in *The New Yorker* by Evan Osnos: "The Forbidden Zone," July 13, 2009. *Caixin*'s 2011 article is still online as of this writing: https://magazine.caixin.com/2011/cw449/. *Caixin*'s article received much more attention than mine, prompting a new investigation and editorial in the state media's *Global Times* (https://www .globaltimes.cn/content/653697.shtml) and more coverage in the foreign press.

CHAPTER ELEVEN: THE POPULATION BUST

Demographer Wang Feng was quoted by Sui-Lee Wee, "China Risks Getting Old Before It Gets Rich," Reuters, April 27, 2011.

The authoritative book on Chinese women after the one-child policy is Leta Hong Fincher's masterful *Leftover Women: The Resurgence of Gender Inequality in China* (Zed Books, 2016). The quote from *People's Daily* about unmarried men engaging in crime is from her book. Hong Fincher refers to a cartoon of a woman in heavy eyeglasses, indicating a high level of education, standing unhappily next to a birthday cake with "27" in ominously melting candles.

The story about the families trying to have "replacement babies" after the 2008 Sichuan earthquake ran under the headline "And Baby Makes Three" in the *Los Angeles Times,* May 3, 2009.

Mei Fong's *One Child* provided the information about the experiments in allowing control groups more than one child.

Chen Guangcheng's account of his life is *The Barefoot Lawyer: A Blind Man's Fight for Justice and Freedom in China* (Picador, 2016).

The headline "China vs. the Batman" appeared in *The Washington Post* on December 19, 2011, on a column by Alexandra Petri.

The English translation of Mo Yan's *Frog* (by Howard Goldblatt, Viking) wasn't released until 2015, so it can't be said that the Nobel Prize was awarded for that book as much as for earlier novels like *Red Sorghum* and *The Garlic Ballads.*

The story about the woman who died during a forced abortion ran on June 15, 2012, in the *Los Angeles Times* under the headline "China One-Child Policy Leads to Forced Abortions, Mothers' Deaths."

On Xi Jinping, I recommend the podcast *The Prince,* a ten-part series produced by *The Economist.*

My "obituary" for the one-child policy, "Judging China's One-Child Policy," ran on *The New Yorker*'s website on October 30, 2015. I also did an interview with Mei Fong for the magazine, which ran November 2, 2015.

CHAPTER TWELVE: MARSHA'S STORY

The University of Oregon maintains a very useful Adoption History Project, which can be accessed online at https://pages.uoregon.edu/adoption/studies/index.html and has fuller accounts about Pearl Buck and the Holts and links to other articles and books about adoption.

Korea remains the largest source of the international adoptee population in the United States and Europe. During the five years I was based in Seoul, I often ran into adoptees. See "Chasing Glimpses of the Past," *Los Angeles Times,* August 28, 2004. In recent years, there have been allegations that records of Korean children were falsified in order to make them more adoptable.

The quote from the Vietnamese mother is from Michael Knight, "Vietnam 'Orphans' Face New Battle," *New York Times,* September 26, 1976.

Gabrielle Glaser's *American Baby: A Mother, a Child, and the Shadow History of Adoption* (Viking, 2021) is a heartbreaking story of an American mother forced to give up her son during the "baby scoop era." The book contains a wealth of information about the scramble for adoptable babies and the laws that prevented birth parents and adoptees from finding each other. The figures about the decline of adoptable U.S. babies are taken from this book. A 2010 study by the Center for American Progress found that abortion numbers have also declined, suggesting that it is the viability of single motherhood rather than abortion that has led to the drop in available babies for domestic adoption.

The National Council for Adoption published a report in 2022 with updated figures, although the numbers were depressed by the Covid pandemic. The domestic adoption figures do not include children adopted by stepparents or out of foster care. See https://adoptioncouncil.org/research/adoption-by-the-numbers.

The Human Rights Watch Report is "Death by Default: A Policy of Fatal Neglect in China's State Orphanages," January 1996, available at HRW.org.

CHAPTER THIRTEEN: ADOPT THE WORLD

Kathryn Joyce is the expert on the role of evangelical Christians and adoption and author of *The Child Catchers: Rescue, Trafficking, and the New Gospel of Adoption* (Public Affairs, 2013).

The story about the families with large numbers of adoptees comes from her book. Rick Warren's quote come from a *Mother Jones* articles by Joyce: "Orphan Fever: The Evangelical Movement's Adoption Obsession," May/June 2013. The quotes from *Above Rubies* are cited in Joyce's writings as well as on the website aboverubies.org.

More information about the "orphan summit" is available on the home page of the Christian Alliance for Orphans, cafo.org.

CHAPTER FOURTEEN: ESTHER'S STORY

This chapter is based on my interviews with Marsha, Esther, and Victoria. Victoria remembered the restaurant serving pigs' feet at a McDonald's, but I couldn't find any evidence of pigs' feet on the McDonald's China menu.

CHAPTER FIFTEEN: THE GO-BETWEEN

Florence Fisher, who died at the age of ninety-five in 2022, was one of the early advocates for adoptee rights. Although dated, her memoir, *The Search for Anna Fisher* (A. Fields, 1973), makes for powerful reading about an adult who struggled for decades to discover her identity and to help others do the same. Gabrielle Glaser's 2021 *American Baby,* which I've cited above, deals with similar issues in an updated context.

The Adoptee Rights Law Center (adopteerightslaw.com) and Adoptees United (adopteesunited.org) both follow legislation related to the rights of adoptees, including the evolving state laws regarding access to original birth certificates.

The quote about the anonymity of Chinese adoption is from Chinese Children Adoption International, a Colorado-based adoption agency. It comes from Brian Stuy's previously cited article in the *Cumberland Law Review*. Stuy wrote that he found it on the agency's website in 2014. It has since been removed.

CHAPTER SIXTEEN: VIRTUAL REUNION

The three Mao biographies cited above have fuller descriptions of Changsha in the early twentieth century.

I learned more about the insulting girls' names from the online publication Sixth Tone: Fresh Voices from Today's China. See Fang Qian, "Don't Call Me 'Zhaodi,'" January 5, 2021. Fang was originally named *Zhaodi*, "seeking younger brother," and battled the Chinese bureaucracy to get her name changed.

CHAPTER SEVENTEEN: THE AMERICAN DAUGHTER

Li Guihua denied any involvement in forced abortions. But certainly, other midwives were compelled to do the bidding of Family Planning offices. The documentary *One Child Nation* contains a moving and candid interview with a midwife regretting the many babies she aborted against the wishes of their parents.

The filmmakers had been in the village shortly before my visit in 2017 and had some unpleasant encounters with security, which made me cautious about my own movements.

CHAPTER EIGHTEEN: TEXAS

The DNA testing was conducted through ARCpoint Labs. The zygosity test is designed to determine whether twins are identical or fraternal. The lab used a database of unrelated Asian individuals. Twins are less common in

Asian populations, and identical twins are born with relatively higher frequency. Researchers suspect that later childbearing and fertility treatments result in more fraternal twin births in Western countries. A useful article explaining this is available on the website of the National Library of Medicine: Jeroen Smits and Christiaan Monden, "Twinning Across the Developing World," September 28, 2011.

CHAPTER NINETEEN: CHINA BOUND

On the crackdown on unregistered churches, see Alice Su, "For China's Underground Churches, This Was No Easy Christmas," *Los Angeles Times,* December 25, 2019; and Ian Johnson, "Chinese Police Detain Prominent Pastor and Over 100 Protestants," *New York Times,* December 10, 2018. Johnson is the authority on religion in modern-day China, and those who are interested might turn to his book *The Souls of China: The Return of Religion After Mao* (Pantheon, 2017).

Hunan Province was known for its resistance to Western missionaries and has relatively few Christians, barely more than 1 percent. Estimates of the percentage of Christians in the Chinese population range from 2 to 6 percent.

CHAPTER TWENTY: HOMECOMING

On the lack of central heating in southern China, see Julie Makinen, "For Central Heat, China Has a North-South Divide at Qin-Huai Line," *Los Angeles Times,* November 15, 2014.

The very emotional and complicated reunion I covered previously was of a teenage boy, Christian Norris: Barbara Demick, "Adopted Teen Finds Answers, Mystery in China," *Los Angeles Times,* August 30, 2009.

CHAPTER TWENTY-ONE: MEMBERS OF THE FAMILY

Chinese terms for family members are complicated. There are eight different words for "cousin" and seven for "aunt," depending on how exactly they are related. For a useful primer, see https://blog.tutorabcchinese.com/chinese -learning-tips/family-tree-relatives-in-chinese.

In 2011, for what was supposed to be a light holiday feature, a colleague and I accompanied a migrant worker returning to his village. The worker and his wife fought the entire holiday, a reflection of the tensions in a marriage in which the couple lived apart most of the year. Megan K. Stack and Barbara Demick, "China's Annual Long March," *Los Angeles Times*, February 20, 2011.

CHAPTER TWENTY-THREE: SHAOYANG

The blog post about the finding location was "Identity and the 'Origin Story,'" published on Research-China.org on September 6, 2023. The author of this essay, which I quote from twice, prefers to remain anonymous.

Olivia Wolf, a young woman adopted from the Shaoyang orphanage in 1995, was able to visit the orphanage with her parents in 2017. She wrote several blog posts about the experience of visiting Shaoyang and the orphanage. She was told as well that the children at that time all had special needs and would be difficult to place for adoption. Wolf's writings can be found on asamnews.com and immigrantstory.org.

On the city of Shaoyang, I found a book written by Antoinette Farnham Stepanek, *A Town Called Shaoyang: Witnessing Dynastic Changes in China* (Gold Hill Publications, 1992), about life in Shaoyang during the late 1940s. A more recent take on Shaoyang is Nick Holdstock's *Chasing the Chinese Dream: Stories from Modern China* (I. B. Tauris, 2018). His book is the source of the observation that Shaoyang is famous only for murders and clementines.

The quote from the orphanage director about paying for babies was cited in the Stuy article in the *Cumberland Law Review*.

CHAPTER TWENTY-FOUR: ESCAPE FROM THE VILLAGE

Grace Newton has written eloquently about the discomfort of touring China as an adoptee, slipping into crowds unrecognized and yet not belonging, being constantly asked to explain herself. Her writings are available on redthreadbroken.com.

CHAPTER TWENTY-FIVE: TWIN TALK

Aatish Taseer's article is "Why We're Living in an Age of Twins," *New York Times Style Magazine*, February 12, 2024.

Elyse Schein and Paula Bernstein, *Identical Strangers: A Memoir of Twins Separated and Reunited* (Random House, 2007). Elyse and Paula were among the twins deliberately separated by their adoption agency as part of an experiment into nature versus nurture.

CHAPTER TWENTY-SIX: ROSETTA STONE

As of this writing, I know of only one confirmed case of identical twins split between China and the United States. In the Netherlands, adoptee Paula Vrolijk discovered a Chinese twin sister in 2023. The International Society for Twin Studies lists upcoming conferences and links to its journal on its website, twinstudies.org.

Nancy L. Segal is a prolific writer about twins. A veteran of the Minnesota studies, she now runs the Twin Studies Center at California State University, Fullerton. Her books are cited frequently in this chapter. Thomas Bouchard writes about keeping a reproduction of the Rosetta Stone in the foreword to Nancy L. Segal's *Entwined Lives: Twins and What They Tell Us About Human Behavior* (Plume, 2000). Segal's study of Chinese separated twins, as well as her paper about the South Korean adoptee, can be viewed on her website, drnancysegaltwins.org.

The Rosetta Stone contains a decree written in two languages, Ancient Greek and Ancient Egyptian, and in three different scripts.

David Lykken's quote is from his article "Research with Twins: The Concept of Emergenesis," *Psychophysiology* 19, no. 4 (July 1982).

The Stanford study, M. J. Landry et al., "Cardiometabolic Effects of Omnivorous vs Vegan Diets in Identical Twins: A Randomized Clinical Trial," is available on the JAMA open-access medical journal network. There was also an article about it in *The Washington Post*: Kyle Melnick, "Scientists Studied Twins' Diets. Those Who Ate Vegan Saw Fast Results," December 6, 2023.

Science writer Lawrence Wright is the author of *Twins: And What They Tell Us About Who We Are* (Trade Paper Press, 1999). *The New Yorker* quote is from his article "Double Mystery," July 30, 1995. He was also quoted in the 2017 documentary *The Twinning Reaction*, by filmmaker Lori Shinseki.

The most celebrated separated twins have garnered so much publicity that there are too many articles to enumerate here. Their cases are described in detail in the Nancy Segal and Lawrence Wright books listed above. Segal also wrote a book about the Louise Wise adoption agency scandal: *Deliberately Divided: Inside the Controversial Study of Twins and Triplets Adopted Apart* (Rowman & Littlefield, 2021). An in-depth article about the Colombian twins is "The Mixed-Up Brothers of Bogotá," by Susan Dominus, *New York Times Magazine*, July 19, 2015.

Sarah Heath and Celena Kopinski tell their story in detail in a lengthy and fascinating audio interview by Jena Heath (no relation) posted on http:// ourchinastories.com/collections/show/18 and at https://texashistory.unt .edu/ark:/67531/metapth1256324/. Celena Kopinski's quotes are from that interview. I also interviewed Sarah Heath in 2022.

The article comparing the prospects for two eighteen-year-olds, one Chinese and one American, is "How China Became a Superpower," by Javier C. Hernandez and Quoctrung Bui, *New York Times*, November 18, 2018.

CHAPTER TWENTY-SEVEN: STEPPING BACKWARD

China's handling of Covid received ample coverage. On hostility toward the media, the Committee to Protect Journalists released a report on September 11, 2020: "Chinese Authorities Detain, Assault Los Angeles Times Bureau Chief, Force Her Out of Region." My colleague Alice Su was also targeted covering flooding the following year, as detailed in Li Yuan, "After the Floods, China Found a Target for Its Pain: Foreign Media," *New York Times*, August 8, 2021.

On the process of reuniting, Origins Canada is a nonprofit advising people separated from family members by adoption. Its article on the stages of reunion was very insightful. I wish all of us had read it before the trip. It describes the journey from fantasy to first meeting to honeymoon . . . then an inevitable "time-out" and adjustments before deciding on the nature of the ongoing relationship. See https://www.originscanada.org/services/ adoption-reunion/stages-of-reunion/. The guidance on this page is largely based on the work of psychologist Marlou Russell.

China experts at a 2022 panel assessed U.S.-China relations to be at their lowest level since the 1970s. See https://washdiplomat.com/us-china -relations-at-their-worst-in-years-wilson-center-scholars-warn/.

After China lifted Covid restrictions in late 2022, many longtime China experts returned and assessed the mood of the nation in unflattering terms. See Ian Johnson, "Xi's Age of Stagnation," *Foreign Affairs*, September/October 2023; Evan Osnos, "China's Age of Malaise," *New Yorker*, October 23, 2023; and Howard French, "China Is Closing In on Itself," *Foreign Policy*, August 30, 2023.

On the stock market's giddy expectations of a baby boom, see "Condom Shares Fall After China Abandons One-Child Policy," Associated Press, October 30, 2015.

And on what actually happened—the population bust—and Family Planning officials giving out rice cookers and water bottles to encourage births, see Liyan Qi, "Enforcers of China's One-Child Policy Are Now Cajoling People to Have Three," *Wall Street Journal*, June 5, 2023.

On the intrusiveness of birth-planning officials, see Vivian Wang, "So, Are You Pregnant Yet? China's In-Your-Face Push for More Babies," *New York Times*, October 8, 2024.

Figures on international adoption to the United States are released each year when the State Department files its Annual Report on Intercountry Adoption.

Esther traveled with me to Italy in October 2024 after this manuscript was completed.

CHAPTER TWENTY-EIGHT: SEARCHING

The quote about the futility of searching is from the same anonymous adoptee I quoted in chapter 23. Her writing appeared on Research-China.org on September 6, 2023.

I wrote about Haley Butler's case in 2009 with a colleague: Martha Groves and Barbara Demick, "Adoptive Families' Quests to Trace Chinese Roots Often Meet Dead Ends," *Los Angeles Times*, December 28, 2009.

Butler's meeting with her birth family is shown in the 2011 documentary *Somewhere Between*, directed by Linda Goldstein Knowlton.

Another excellent documentary is *Found* (2021), about three teenage adoptees who discover through DNA testing that they are distantly related and travel together to China to look for their birth parents.

On Brian and Longlan Stuy, this account is based on many interviews with them and writings on their own website.

In 2022 I interviewed the Chinese searcher, on the condition that her name not be used.

Jennifer Doering's daughter, Audrey Doering, and her identical twin, Gracie Rainsberry, were reunited on a broadcast of *Good Morning America*.

A useful how-to guide with a very entertaining backstory is Wesley O. Hagood's *Searching for Your Chinese Birth Family* (Heritage Books, 2021).

South Korean adoptees have demanded an investigation into allegations of fraud in the adoption process. See Choe Sang-Hun, "World's Largest 'Baby Exporter' Confronts Its Painful Past," *New York Times*, September 17, 2023.

Although South Korea has done more than China to facilitate searches, birth parents are often reluctant to acknowledge their children because of the stronger social stigmas against premarital sex and divorce. When I reported in 2004 on Korean adoptees, an official from the Holt adoption agency told me, "If the mother was unmarried at the time, in about half the cases they'll deny being the birth mother and say you've contacted the wrong person."

The blog Harlow's Monkey (harlows-monkey.com) offers the perspective of an adult Korean adoptee and has excellent links to memoirs, essays, and anthologies.

Redthreadbroken.com (mentioned earlier) compiles writing by adoptees from China and elsewhere. The name refers to a Chinese proverb saying that people destined to meet are connected by an invisible red thread. It was often cited to justify adoptions.

Nanchangproject.com also has a blog of adoptee writings. They are expected to be compiled shortly into a book.

On Italian adoptees, Maria Laurino's *The Price of Children: Stolen Lives in a Land Without Choice* (Open Road Integrated Media, 2024) is a moving account of the Vatican's role in stripping unwed mothers of their parental rights so that their children could be sent to the United States.

A wonderful piece by Jenna Cook is "A 'Lost' Daughter of China Speaks, and All of China Listens," *Foreign Policy*, March 30, 2016.

On China's enforced forgetfulness, see *The People's Republic of Amnesia*, by Louisa Lim (Oxford University Press, 2015), and *Red Memory: The Afterlives of China's Cultural Revolution*, by Tania Branigan (W. W. Norton, 2023).

Index

Photograph Credits

All photographs not listed below are courtesy of the author.

About the Author

BARBARA DEMICK is the author of *Eat the Buddha: Life and Death in a Tibetan Town*, named one of the best books of the year by *The New York Times; Nothing to Envy: Ordinary Lives in North Korea*, which was a finalist for the National Book Award and the National Book Critics Circle Award and the winner of the Samuel Johnson Prize in the United Kingdom; and *Logavina Street: Life and Death in a Sarajevo Neighborhood*. Her books have been translated into more than twenty-five languages. She is a former foreign correspondent who covered Eastern Europe, the Middle East, and Asia, most recently as China bureau chief for the *Los Angeles Times*. She has been a fellow at the Council on Foreign Relations, the New York Public Library, and Princeton University.

About the Type

This book was set in Fournier, a typeface named for Pierre-Simon Fournier (1712–68), the youngest son of a French printing family. He started out engraving woodblocks and large capitals, then moved on to fonts of type. In 1736 he began his own foundry and made several important contributions in the field of type design; he is said to have cut 147 alphabets of his own creation. Fournier is probably best remembered as the designer of St. Augustine Ordinaire, a face that served as the model for the Monotype Corporation's Fournier, which was released in 1925.